THE

DISEASE

CONCEPT OF

ALCOHOLISM

by

E. M. JELLINEK

Martino Publishing
Mansfield Centre, CT
2010

Martino Publishing
P.O. Box 373,
Mansfield Centre, CT 06250 USA

www.martinopublishing.com

ISBN 1-57898-936-1

Cover design by T. Matarazzo

Printed in the United States of America On 100% Acid-Free Paper

THE

DISEASE

CONCEPT OF

ALCOHOLISM

by

E. M. JELLINEK

Alcohol Research Documentation, Inc.
P. O. Box 969
Piscataway, N.J • 08855-0969

Library of Congress Catalog Card Number: 60–9206

56789 CCCC 432198

TO

PROFESSOR JORGE MARDONES R.

IN FRIENDSHIP

Contents

Preface

The subject of this study represents not more than a small section of the problems of alcohol—a very small section indeed.

Readers are often under the impression that the choice of a subject by a scientific writer is an indication of the supreme importance which he attaches to the matter in question. Furthermore, many readers are inclined to believe that the author regards his chosen topic as the core of the problem. In order to avoid any misunderstanding on this score, I wish to state that the question of the disease nature of "alcoholism" is a part issue, but as such a fairly important one. I have undertaken this study at the request of The Christopher D. Smithers Foundation; the idea appealed to me as an opportunity for an attempt to analyze opinions and attitudes concerning this question.

It goes against my grain to use the expression disease concept—the proper wording would be disease conception. But the publisher's objection that conception sounds awkward must be admitted. The misuse of concept for conception has become so well established in American writing and conversation that it has become a quasi-correct use. Strictly speaking, alcoholism is a concept; so is disease. But that alcoholism is a disease is a viewpoint and thus a conception. Nevertheless I have bowed to the prevalent usage of concept, especially for the title of this book. Indeed, alcoholism itself is only a part issue—but this book is limited to the disease concept issue.

The opinions expressed in this book are those of the author and do not necessarily reflect the attitudes or opinions of the Christopher D. Smithers Foundation.

I

The "New Approach"

AROUND 1940 the phrase "new approach to alcoholism" was coined, and since then this phrase has been heard again and again, every time that the Yale Center of Alcohol Studies, the National Council on Alcoholism, Alcoholics Anonymous, or individual students of the problem make an utterance to the effect that "alcoholism is a disease."

Renewed approach would be the more correct expression. The alleged statements by St. John the Damascene, and the enactments of an "early Spanish king" on the disease nature of inebriety, are not invoked here as evidence, as they turn out to refer to intoxication rather than alcoholism. Nor would I regard the famous writings of the late 18th and early 19th centuries, those of the American Surgeon General Dr. Benjamin Rush and the British physician Dr. Thomas Trotter, as the start of a new era in the views on "inebriety" as an illness. These two physicians were forerunners of a movement and undoubtedly had an influence on later students of the problem but their ideas on inebriety as an illness did not bear fruit until 60 or 70 years later. Their descriptions of the bodily effects of alcohol did, however, become a source for the armory of the temperance organizations and stimulated research. Between the times of these two students of inebriety and the creation of an organization to propagate the illness conception of inebriety some physicians in the 1830's, notably Dr. Samuel Woodward, the first superintendent of the Worcester State Hospital, and Dr. Eli Todd of Hartford, as well as the Connecticut Medical Society, suggested special institutions for inebriates. These suggestions did not explicitly view inebriety as an illness but the demand for special institutions reveals a recognition that this deviant behavior could be classed neither with criminal behavior nor with the mental disorders. In the same decade the French social investigator Dr. A.

Fregier (quoted by Baer, 1878) expressed his ideas against the penal attitude toward inebriates.

While the Washingtonian Home at Boston was first opened in 1841, it was soon closed because of lack of funds and did not re-open until 1857. Between that date and the year 1874 at least 11 nonprofit hospitals and homes for inebriates came into existence in the United States of America. Among these institutions were the New York State Inebriate Asylum, the project of Dr. Joseph E. Turner in Binghamton, which opened in 1868 (although its origins date back to 1854), and the New York City Asylum, opened in 1869, operated by the Police Department and the Board of Charities of New York City. The latter institution may be regarded as the forerunner of the present-day Bridge House. The superintendents of these early special institutions—on the basis of their experiences—soon gave voice to the slogan that "intemperance is a disease."

I.2. The Early Propaganda

In 1872 the managers of the various hospitals and homes for inebriates founded a society for the study of inebriety which merged in 1904 with the Medical Temperance Society, variously changed its name and ultimately became known by the somewhat grandiloquent title of The American Medical Association for the Study of Inebriety and Narcotics. For the sake of simplicity it will be referred to here as the Society. "The idea was to formulate some working basis, from which these great truths [inebriety as a disease] could be made practical," as one of the cofounders, Dr. T. D. Crothers, said.

In 1876 the above named organization began to publish a periodical, *The Journal of Inebriety*. Later, after Professor Freud's visit at Clark University, the Journal described itself on the masthead as "The first and only journal devoted to spirit and drug neurosis."

The *Journal of Inebriety* existed (although precariously) for about 38 years and in the course of that period published roughly 700 papers of which at least 100 were entirely or partly devoted to the idea that inebriety is a disease. "The policy of the *Journal of Inebriety* from the beginning has been to keep prominent the fact that inebriety is a neurosis and psychosis and that alcohol is both an exciting and contributing cause as well as a symptom of conditions which existed before" (Crothers, 1912).

The Society, its ideas and its Journal went through many tribulations and had very little success. The relatively long life of this publication may be attributed to the financial backing of a few devotees. Crothers (1911) wrote:

"The first issue of 5,000 copies was received with some opposition and very little commendation. A few journals spoke well of it. Most of the medical press was content to make a mere notice of it. At the end of the first year a small number of subscribers appeared, and an interest was manifested by librarians for copies, and occasionally a review appeared. . . .

"The second and third years were marked by stronger papers and an improvement in the tone and scientific presentation of the work, showing that its growth was appreciated and in many ways recognized. Both the Society and Journal received very sharp criticism from several prominent religious papers, which denounced the work as materialistic and an effort to excuse crime and dignify vice.

"This sentiment was shared by physicians and various criticisms of great severity were published. A prominent Boston clergyman and educator, and the editor of a leading New York religious paper, seemed to out-do all the others and to seek every opportunity to condemn the Journal and the idea that inebriates were diseased.

"A Brooklyn clergyman on one occasion offered prayers in his church that these infidel efforts to dignify vice might be neutralized and pointed out with great emphasis, the evidence of Satan in the promotion of these efforts.

"In the medical world, one of the most prominent alienists of that time, condemned the efforts with much bitterness. Later he was joined by an English physician [Doctor Bucknell?] of much eminence. Curiously enough, the very harshness of their condemnation, and their dogmatic statements, that inebriates are always vicious and cannot be diseased, drew attention to the subject, and literally raised up a host of friends, who would not have been attracted otherwise. . . .

"The *Journal of Inebriety* went on serenely without noticing the adverse criticisms and bitter condemnations which were poured out on the Society, the Journal and its editor."

The nature of the early controversy around the illness conception of inebriety is exemplified in Appendix A. This type of polemic has flourished for many years and has not died out entirely even today although it is clad in more modern terms.

Apart from the *Journal of Inebriety* other medical and scientific periodicals in the United States and abroad published papers on the disease nature of inebriety in the second half of the 19th century. [For a selected list of the more important papers see Appendix C, which has been culled chiefly from Abderhalden (1904).]

Furthermore, in 1892 the *British Journal of Inebriety* was launched.
It is now in its 68th year (although not issued in some of those
years) and has been renamed the *British Journal of Addiction*.
This periodical, right from its beginnings, was on a much higher
scientific level than its older American sister. While the British
Journal published papers on alcoholism as an illness, it did not make
a cult of this idea and concentrated much more on the exploration
of the physiopathological effects and the metabolism of alcohol.

The virulent criticism directed at the American Society and its
Journal ebbed off toward the turn of the century, and it received
some small recognition. The proceedings of one of the meetings of
the Society were published as a Senate Document through the kind
intervention of a friendly Senator, but this document remained a
cryptic publication. The Society and its Journal did not make a
dent with the public at large and not even with their own profession. They disappeared before prohibition got started. After the
repeal of the 18th Amendment physicians and other scientists again
took up the study of inebriety which, by then, was called alcoholism[1] but the old movement was forgotten by all except the older
temperance workers. The work of the "Founding Fathers" was
swallowed up in a collective blackout. When the idea of "alcoholism" as an illness was revived it was hailed as "the new approach."

One may ask what were the reasons for the lack of success of
40 years of earnest labor, especially in view of the fact that the new
"new approach" achieved remarkable success in the first 10 years
of its existence and in its second decade spread nationwide.

The elements of the failure of the earlier activities were various,
and one may make some reasonable conjectures as to their nature.
First we may ask why the medical profession failed to respond.

From the start there was the chaos in the management of the
public and charitable institutions for inebriates. The accusations
and recriminations directed against the Binghamton hospital and its
first superintendent, Dr. Joseph Turner, spread also to the other
institutions. The superintendents of most of those institutions were
engaged in confused thinking and in even more confused procedures. In addition many commercial quack undertakings emerged
against which the *Journal of Inebriety* battled, but without success.

[1] The expression alcoholism had been used fairly consistently long before that in
Europe. In America, too, this term was used around the turn of the century but
the preferred term was inebriety.

All this was, of course, not conducive to the acceptance of the idea of inebriety as a disease by the medical profession at large. Nor was it helpful that the founders of the Society and of its Journal were the managers of the controversial public and charitable institutions.

The medical profession, moreover, did not take to the idealization of inebriates and it may be pointed out that even at the present time the propagandization of the illness conception of "alcoholism" is encumbered with too much sentimentalism. True, as far as the broad lay public is concerned some emotional appeal is necessary, but the "alcoholic" would become a more acceptable human being without a halo hovering over his head.

For wide medical acceptance the formulations of the illness conception—if they deserve that name—were much too vague. The proponents of the idea did distinguish between common drunkenness and inebriety and attached the illness conception to the latter only. But the distinction was not properly outlined and the formulations were not even first approaches to definitions. Here are a few examples of this vagueness, all of them by the pen of one of the more sophisticated students of the problem, Dr. I. H. Neff (1910):

"Drunkenness is a condition resulting from alcoholism and inebriety is an expression of alcoholism. . . .

"It has always seemed to me that much of the misunderstanding about inebriety can be traced to our misconception of the word 'inebriate.' An inebriate is an habitual drinker. All cases of drunkenness are not cases of inebriety, but all confirmed or habitual drinkers are properly classed as inebriates. . . .

"I have before contended that inebriety is a condition of nervous weakness on which is engrafted a habit. This conception of the condition seems to me to qualify the assertion that inebriety is a disease. While calling it a 'disease' we do not by accepting such a definition imply that the inebriate is irresponsible."

The vagueness of the conception must have struck the proponents themselves and they felt that they could not make out a strong enough case. This is reflected in such statements as that ". . . the social and judicial problems would seem to outweigh the immediate medical considerations."

There was much too little prestige attached to the *Journal of Inebriety* as it did not live up to the standards of American medical and psychiatric periodicals of its times; not even in the first 14 years of the present century which were the terminal years of the Journal's existence. The disease conception was pushed with great vigor but with little clinical penetration. It seemed sufficient to designate inebriety as an "alcohol neurosis" without so much as giving a description of it.

While American workers had made some important contributions to the physiopathology and experimental psychology of alcohol before 1920, the psychiatric exploration and description of alcohol addiction was far below the level of the work of such Frenchmen as Lancereaux, Mignot and Esquirol, the German psychiatrists Bonhoeffer, Gaupp, Heilbronner and Graeter, and the eminent British physician Dr. Norman Kerr; nor did it come near the much earlier descriptions of Thomas Trotter and Magnus Huss.

The sum total of the factors discussed above did not create favorable conditions for the medical profession's acceptance of the ideas propagated by the Society.

The temperance and prohibition movements regarded the Society as inimical to temperance goals. In fact, however, the Society and its Journal were rather close to the temperance views on alcohol although not to its ideas about "alcoholism." Perusal of the Journal reveals that its contributors were by no means averse to the idea of total abstinence, nor did they seem to have been seriously opposed to prohibition. Furthermore the papers published in the Journal were in agreement with temperance views on the role of alcohol in the causation of mental disorders, germ damage, crime and the widest variety of diseases. The language of these papers did not differ particularly from the mode of expression used by the proponents of the temperance movement. In the views of the latter, however, the idea of inebriety as a disease weakened the basis of the temperance ideology and thus the efforts of the Society had to be rejected in toto.

On the other hand, that part of the public which was not influenced by the temperance movement saw in the goals of the Society only a somewhat different version of the old-line temperance groups. This fact explains to some extent why the illness conception of inebriety or "alcoholism" did not make headway with the general public, except only an insignificant proportion of it.

Other factors which have been mentioned before in explaining the lack of response of the medical profession, such as the extreme vagueness of the conception, the exaggerated sentimentalism, and so forth, also prejudiced public acceptance.

The foremost reason for the unresponsiveness of the American public was perhaps the fact that the movement of the Society was directed entirely by a small group of physicians specialized (without any particular know-how) in the treatment of inebriates, rather than by a mixed group of scientists and representatives of American community life.

After the cessation of the Society and its Journal came some 6 years of growth of dry territories and 12 years of national prohibition. In those 18 years the interest of American scientists in the problems of alcohol waned, and in the last 12 years even the temperance workers relaxed, as their crusade had attained its goal. Americans were interested in the problems of bootlegging but not in the problem of alcoholism. This relatively long period of disinterest sufficed to relegate the efforts of the proponents of the illness conception to oblivion, but somehow the idea that "alcoholism" is an illness was still hovering in order to be "rediscovered."

I.3. New Light on Old Ideas

The repeal of the 18th Amendment reawakened the interest of research workers in "alcoholism." No one was so deluded as to imagine that repeal would solve the problem. Research workers got ready to face the developments. But this alerting was far from being the only factor in renewed research. A great incentive came from the increasing knowledge of the avitaminoses and their role in the diseases of chronic alcoholism, so called. The rise of this new phase in the science of nutrition coincided with enactment of the 21st Amendment.

The early metabolic studies on alcohol centered around the question whether or not alcohol was a food, a question which arose out of the wet–dry controversy. Toward the end of the last century industrial management gave a new impetus to certain researches relating the effects of alcohol to fatigue and efficiency. The sharp rise of motorized road traffic and the contribution of alcohol intoxication to traffic accidents next gave a new incentive to metabolic studies in Europe as well as in America. Such studies had been in progress for some time but in the 1930's they became increasingly important. Police magistrates needed biochemical and psychological tests of alcohol intoxication and they needed interpretation of test results.

The tests and their interpretation required a much greater knowledge of the metabolism of alcohol than had existed theretofore. While many of the metabolic investigations were prompted by practical police problems, the investigations soon stimulated more research which went far beyond the "practical" questions.

The nutritional deficiency aspects of the "chronic alcoholic diseases" and the refined metabolic studies are just two among many factors which induced outstanding physicians and other scientists to engage in alcohol research. They had refrained from it on account of the emotional and political loading of the question. Such American scientific notables as Chittenden, Miles, Benedict and Carpenter had given time to alcohol studies but beginning in the early 1930's more and more eminent men of medicine and science appeared among the contributors to the alcohol literature. That literature, which had been dominated by German, English and French investigators, became now predominantly American.

And as nutritionists, biochemists and physiologists had entered on the "peripheral" aspects of "alcoholism," psychiatrists and psychologists of great repute engaged in clinical researches on "alcoholism" itself.

While the work of the old Society and its slogan, "inebriety is a disease," was practically forgotten in America, it remained alive in Europe, although not prominently, and it floated back to America to be developed and elaborated here by psychiatrists. This psychiatric work gave a new impetus to physiopathologists for turning from the study of peripheral problems to research on the etiology of "alcoholism." This trend gave rise to vigorous polemics between psychiatrists on the one side and physiopathologists and pharmacologists on the other side, but the controversy brought and continues to bring clarification, even though at times it engenders some confusion.

The conception of alcoholism as a disease became not only a working hypothesis in research and in the clinical treatment of some varieties of alcoholism but also the central point of certain community activities related to the problems of alcohol. The "renewed" idea found its way not only into professional circles but far into public opinion, until now in America one may speak of a majority acceptance of the illness conception of "alcoholism."

That the so-called "new approach" has penetrated public opinion rapidly may be ascribed to a number of organizations devoted to research or education or rehabilitation or all three. The greatest roles were played in this process by the "Yale group;" the Research Council on Problems of Alcohol (now defunct); the National Council on Alcoholism (formerly National Committee for Education on Alcoholism) and its local affiliates; the Committee on Alcoholism of the American Medical Association; the state government agencies in charge of "alcoholism programs;" and last but not least, that large group of men and women who would not like to be called an organization, namely the fellowship of Alcoholics Anonymous.

In the early 1930's at the old Laboratory of Applied Physiology (now the Laboratory of Applied Biodynamics) at Yale University, Dr. Howard W. Haggard, dynamic scholar and scientist of great vision, started certain experiments on alcohol metabolism which by 1940 had developed into a highly systematized coordinated research, and which branched out far beyond its original projects. Apart from a generation of research workers trained at the Laboratory, representatives of the medical, biological and social sciences and of law were attracted to the Laboratory. There were founded the *Quarterly Journal of Studies on Alcohol*, the Section of Studies on Alcohol (now known as the Yale Center of Alcohol Studies), the Yale Summer School of Alcohol Studies, the Classified Abstract Archive of the Alcohol Literature, and the Yale Plan Clinic.

The illness conception of alcoholism was not a central idea of the activities of the Yale group except in its Summer School, and even there it was developed against a background of the widest span. The Summer School was devised originally for interested educated laymen rather than for any specific profession. The students of that School came from all walks of life, many of them were in strategic positions, and they carried the knowledge gained at the School back to their communities. Thus the School did reach a fairly wide public and it made its impact with the prestige of a great university. The School became one of the factors in the spread of the illness conception of alcoholism.

The Yale group realized that in America a voluntary organization of citizens has much greater power in changing attitudes toward such matters as alcoholism than any group of specialists. When Mrs. Marty Mann presented her ideas on a voluntary lay organization devoted to education on alcoholism, the Section of Studies on Alcohol was ready to sponsor such an organization. That sponsorship extended for several years, after which the affiliation ended and the National Committee for Education on Alcoholism continued on its own and developed its program, becoming the National Council on Alcoholism. This lay organization and its local affiliates achieved the widest spread of the idea that "alcoholism" is an illness. It must be pointed out, however, that in the long run the lay group could not have maintained its influence without the support of professional circles. In this matter the work of the American Medical Association's Committee on Alcoholism (a subgroup of its Commission on Mental Health) was a decisive factor.

One of the greatest roles in bringing the illness conception to the widest reaches of public opinion was played by the fellowship of Alcoholics Anonymous. Here again recognition by the medical profession was an indispensable factor.

All these activities and achievements led state governments to recognize the varieties of alcoholism as public health problems and to establish programs of their own. This of course added to the prestige of the illness conception of alcoholism and gave a further impetus to its public acceptance.

But the spread of the idea would not have been possible if in the past 20 years there had been no significant clarification of the illness conception, although the multiplicity of hypotheses may confuse the public. To some extent the differences in the hypotheses denote the fact that there is not one alcoholism but a whole variety. It must be admitted, however, that some of the old vagueness still adheres to the newer conceptions and that if this is not overcome the gains of the illness conception may be lost again. The process of clarification will be examined later but at this point one important aspect may be mentioned which has been concisely summarized by Hargreaves (1952):

". . . From the work the clinician has already done and the knowledge of the natural history of alcoholism which it has provided, one surprising conclusion must be drawn—namely, that what the physician in the past has seen and regarded as the disorder of alcoholism was, in fact, its end result, complicated by the long-term effects both physical and mental of a heavy intake of alcohol over many years. It was analogous to the end result of a cancer of the breast with secondary growths in the brain, the spine and the liver."

There have been many proposals of working hypotheses and some valuable critical analyses of those hypotheses, e.g., the thoughtful studies of Wexberg (1950, 1951a). In addition there have been some theories which are regarded as illuminating the etiology of alcoholism but these are in reality heuristic principles for the *role* of disease in the struggle for survival some of which have been applied to alcoholism. Such are the idea of the adaptation syndrome to stress and various ventures into existentialist psychiatry. In human biology teleology is hard to avoid, and it is not avoided successfully even by those who vigorously remonstrate against it. On the other hand, teleology is not etiology but it hits the phenomenon at an entirely different level.

After 20 years of the so-called "new approach" it seems in order to analyze what the present status of the illness conception of alcoholism is in America. This task is not as simple as it may seem. One might say that all that is required is to state the criteria of "alcoholism" and to see whether or not they are in conformity with the definition of disease. But then one finds difficulties arising out of the fact that alcoholism has too many definitions and disease has practically none.

Medical dictionaries[2,3] give the following definition: "Disease, an illness, a sickness." And that is about all. In the "Queries and Minor Notes" of the *Journal of the American Medical Association* (1957a), in answer to an inquiry concerning the grounds for "considering alcoholism as a medical illness," the following definition was given: "A disease is defined as follows: In general, any deviation from a state of health; an illness or sickness; more specifically, a definite marked process having a characteristic train of symptoms. It may affect the whole body or any of its parts, and its etiology, pathology, and prognosis may be known or unknown."

This is a private definition which adds to the dictionary definition only the marked process having a train of symptoms. The answer is much longer than the part quoted here but it does not constitute any significant elaboration of the words cited above.

As some students of the problems of alcohol propose to call "alcoholism" an illness rather than a disease, it is of interest to note that the two terms are given as synonyms, not as shadings or degrees of a phenomenon. Nevertheless, from a semantic standpoint, the choice of the word illness may be more felicitous. For the nonmedical man, the word disease conjures up a vision of blood,

---

[2] The American Illustrated Medical Dictionary, 4th ed. 1938.
[3] Gould's Medical Dictionary, 5th ed. 1945.

rashes, emaciation, and generally a horrifying appearance. That is not the case with the word illness, which in everyday language denotes something less frightening. In connection with alcoholism the term illness is more acceptable to the public than disease, of which they think rather in terms of the infectious diseases.

Pointing out this lack of definition of disease by no means involves a reproach. The splendid progress of medicine shows that that branch of the sciences can function extremely well without such a definition. Physicians know what belongs in their realm.

It comes to this, that *a disease is what the medical profession recognizes as such.* The fact that they are not able to explain the nature of a condition does not constitute proof that it is not an illness. There are many instances in the history of medicine of diseases whose nature was unknown for many years. The nature of some is still unknown, but they are nevertheless unquestionably medical problems.

As will be seen later, the analysis shows that the medical profession has officially accepted alcoholism as an illness, and through this fact alone alcoholism becomes an illness, whether a part of the lay public likes it or not, and even if a minority of the medical profession is disinclined to accept the idea.

Of course, acceptance does not equal validity and one may inquire into this latter point, particularly into the matter of the facts and ideas that are in back of the illness conception, that is, into the nature or natures of some species of alcoholism.

The difficulty in this instance is that the proponents of the still somewhat vague illness conception operate with many concepts which either are not defined or are frequently used in a variety of connotations. Such, for instance, are the concepts of tolerance, craving, habituation, sensitivity, compulsion, "habit forming drug," withdrawal symptoms, "loss of control," and so forth. And there remain of course the definitions of alcoholism and the alcoholic, as well as of the term problem drinker, which are used in a variety of meanings. These concepts will be defined or discussed in various sections of Chapter III.

In the meantime it seems desirable to clarify to some extent the ideas of cultural, social and economic factors in the problems of alcoholism as they tend to complicate the question of the illness conception. For this purpose an excursion must be made into other parts of the world.

II

Social, Cultural and Economic Factors

II.1. General Considerations

THE etiquette of the American alcoholism literature demands that the psychiatrist should acknowledge that physiopathological, cultural and social elements have a role in the genesis of alcoholism. On the other hand, the physiopathologist is required to admit the existence of social, cultural, and possibly some individual psychological factors. With few exceptions, however, after having made the prescribed bow, specialists proceed to formulate their etiological theories exclusively in the terms of their respective disciplines. Sociologists and anthropologists, too, go their way and give a casual nod to psychology and physiopathology. Thus, the idea that presents itself to an omnivorous reader of the alcohol literature is usually that "alcoholism" is either an economic, a psychological, a physiological or a sociological problem to the exclusion of the other aspects. Such is the impression even after the perusal of a book in which representatives of the various branches of science collaborate.

As the majority of the students of alcoholism, including the sociologists, mention alcoholism as an illness or the symptom of an illness, one may be somewhat confused as to whether it is a personality disorder, a physical illness, or—figuratively speaking—a disease of economic life, of social structure or of culture.

As there is much emphasis in the scientific literature on the conception of alcoholism as an illness, and as the nature of the illness has so much bearing on treatment and prevention, it seems useful to attempt an assessment of various factors, at least sketchily.

A problem—whether in the field of medicine, sociology or economics—when viewed from a broad angle may be difficult or even impossible to delineate with any degree of wide acceptability, owing to its variation both from one national culture to another and among the subcultures of a given nation. However, the source of variation may be artificial in the sense that the "variation" arises out of inadequate definitions, or out of a lack of any serious attempt to find a sufficiently broad and meaningful category under which all of the variations may be gathered satisfactorily.

The variations in the nature of the problem may exist in reality, in appearance only, or in both. They may be so strongly marked that the assignment of the problem to a given field such as medicine, sociology or economics is meaningless. Of course, the question may be not whether the problem is medical, sociological or economic, but whether it exists in all of those three categories, in which case the question resolves itself to an assessment of contributions. If difficulties of delineation and, particularly, of definition originate from intrinsic differences between basic aspects of the problem one may query whether it is not some entirely unimportant common factor which led to the use of a collective term in the absence of a "collection." If there is no "collection" behind the collective term, the problem designated by that term is fictitious and thus not an object for solution.

On the other hand, some common element may be sufficiently relevant and potent to hold an apparently heterogeneous "collection" together. In that case every component of the "collection" will benefit from the recognition of the element which brings it into some "family of problems."

Furthermore, if a certain problem exists in many cultures, manifesting itself in different ways—yet without irreconcilable differences—the differences as well as the common elements must be considered in order to arrive at some conclusions applicable to a variety of cultures.

Alcoholism is a problem that is complicated by real as well as artificial differences. The latter stem from insufficient definition, terminological chaos and several other factors which will be considered at later junctures. It would seem that these differences could be profitably discussed in the light of international experience.

My experience comes to some extent from the informal give-and-take in the discussions of the World Health Organization's expert committees in the course of the formulation of their published reports concerning alcohol and alcoholism; to a much greater extent from the discussions in larger international seminars on alcoholism; from visits to many countries where it was possible to hear the opinions of numerous students of alcoholism and to see in action various facilities for the care and rehabilitation of "alcoholics;" and from personal contacts with alcoholics in those countries.

The most enlightening of these sources is the seminar, particularly the observation of the progress of discussion. In the beginning, conflicts arising from local experiences and local traditions concerning theoretical views about alcoholism seem to be so great as to preclude any generalization. Nevertheless, the seminar does not end in chaos for there develops a gradual understanding of the sources of difference as well as an inclination to revise one's ideas about the nature of the problem in one's own country. Parenthetically it may be said that these seminars, in spite of the limited number of participants, have important repercussions, as they lead to local seminars in which the experience of the international seminar forms the main subject of discussion. These statements are not intended to imply that all differences are "ironed out," particularly as many of the differences are not factitious but factual.

An analysis of this international experience suggests that an understanding could be reached much more readily if the term alcoholism were extended beyond the conception which is current in America and some Anglo-Saxon countries.

The greater part of the newer literature on alcoholism is of American and British origin. In these two nations the steady "problem drinkers" and the "true alcohol addicts" are so much in the foreground and engage the interest of the student of alcoholism to such a degree that the terms "alcoholic" and "alcoholism" are applied only to these drinkers and the problem is seen entirely in terms of their drinking. In the Nordic countries psychiatrists have an outlook approaching the British and American attitude. However, in the Nordic countries—with the exception of Denmark— the management of the problem is dominated by social workers and general practitioners and the psychiatric viewpoint has not as yet had a strong impact on the medical profession in general or on the lay public.

International experience leads to the conclusion that in many countries more serious problems of national magnitude arise from other types of drinkers than from those who are termed "alcoholics" in America. The latter do, of course, exist in every country where alcoholic beverages are consumed, but they may form a small group or, even if they are fairly numerous, the problems arising from them may be overshadowed by the problems which other types of drinking present.

To give a few examples: In Finland the sale of alcoholic beverages has been restricted to the urban areas. Men who work in isolated rural camps come to cities only once in 3 or 4 weeks; on those occasions they may have two or three drinks and, without any signs of acute intoxication, draw their knives and cause serious bodily harm and fatalities. These are "explosive drinkers." While Americans would not call this alcoholism, we must admit that this constitutes a most serious problem and we cannot deny the Finns the right to refer to it as alcoholism. The harm done by these "explosive drinkers" overshadows the problem created by the relatively small group of true alcohol addicts.

In connection with this "explosive drinker" it may be noted that Finnish culture demands maximum control from the individual. This is particularly so in the work situation, where cooperation and absence of conflict is essential in order to create new industrial sources of wealth to comply with international economic obligations.

In Spain the incidence of alcohol addiction is low on a world-wide comparative scale, although according to Viñes (1957) it is considerably higher than the Spaniards would like to think. On the other hand, marked damage may arise through violence and impairment of the family budget occasioned by "fiesta drinking" and weekend bouts which are not individual in nature but involve drinking in large groups, constituting a folkway. Similar conditions are predominant in Portugal, Brazil and Argentina. In Holland, where the rate of alcohol addiction is at the top of the low range of world-wide alcoholism rates, damage from occasional excess is somewhat greater in magnitude than that caused by true alcohol addiction. In Italy as well, where the alcohol addiction rate is now at the low tail end of the middle range, there is a somewhat greater problem from damage through occasional excess.[1]

In practically all countries where damage through occasional excessive drinking is great, or where it predominates over that caused by alcohol addiction, there is a tendency to include the occasional excess, particularly the quasi-institutionalized weekend excess, in the category of alcoholism.

In France, which after a lull during the second World War and

---

[1] A comparative table of the "alcoholism rates" and the magnitude of other alcohol problems will be presented in a separate publication at a later date.

the first 2 postwar years has again developed an outstandingly large alcohol problem, the nature of "alcoholism" is rather different.

There is a condition referred to by French students of alcohol problems as "alcoolisation." A large number of drinkers who are neither psychologically nor physically dependent upon alcohol have such a large daily consumption that their life span is shortened. Ledermann's masterly statistical studies have given the evidence for this statement. Damage through occasional excess, in relation to that from various types of alcohol addiction, is comparatively low. The predominant variety of alcohol addiction is one that is rarely recognized in America and the Anglo-Saxon countries, although its occurrence there would not seem to be a rarity but rather a minority phenomenon. On the other hand, the variety of alcoholism predominant in America and other Anglo-Saxon countries is in the minority in France and only recently has its existence found some recognition in that country. The major variety of alcohol addiction in France is one in which individual psychological factors play a minor role while the more decisive factors are habits related to social attitudes toward the use of alcoholic beverages, attitudes which are to some extent contingent upon economic elements. These social and economic factors are conducive to a drinking pattern which in the absence of overt signs of intoxication leads to a physical dependence upon alcohol without causing "loss of control," but which makes it "impossible" to abstain even for a day. This drinking pattern, which will be described at a later juncture, is not unique to France. It is predominant in Chile where it creates a very large problem, and it is seen in such viticultural countries as Italy, Spain, Portugal and Argentina, too, although its incidence in those countries is greatly limited by attitudes which favor a different drinking pattern.

Some American sociologists have proposed to explain the differences in alcoholism rates of different countries through social or sociocultural factors. Notably Ullman (1958) has broached this subject, with highly appropriate terms of reference but with inadequate material. Many students of alcohol problems have unfortunately placed too much reliance on the table of "alcoholism rates" in a number of countries as published in the first report of the Alcoholism Subcommittee of the World Health Organization (1951). The subcommittee published the data of that table "for what they may be worth," in order to stimulate research on the proper and useful constants of estimation. At a glance it is evident from the table that the rates are not quite comparable; for example, for one country they pertain to the year 1942, for another to the year 1948, and so forth. Furthermore for some countries, notably Italy and France, the alcoholism rates were given for war years during which not only was the supply of alcohol greatly limited but also control measures tended to decrease the alcoholism rates. Most important, however, the rates were vague approximations based, in the instance of some countries, on assumptions for which the foundations were inadequate. I am well qualified to make this statement as I was responsible for the table.

The rank orders of the countries should not be determined on the basis of data pertaining to different years or to war years for some countries, or on necessarily vague approximations. Methods for making more adequate assumptions of estimation constants for various countries have been developed since the the publication of that table.

To some extent Ullman's too broad generalization that neither the frequency nor the amount of drinking have much to do with variation in the magnitude of alcoholism may be attributed to the available data. It is true that frequency and extent are not the only factors, but they are factors of some importance when viewed in conjunction with drinking patterns and social attitudes toward drinking and intoxication. Ullman feels that more is known about drinking customs in the case of "primitive people," but ". . . particularly in civilized societies, we know something about the prevalence of alcoholism but have no adequate accounts of the drinking customs. . . ." For Italy there exists the excellent "Doxa" report (Luzzatto-Fegiz, 1952); for France there is the highly interesting opinion survey of Bastide (1954); for Sweden there is the report of the 1944 Temperance Commission (Sweden, 1952); and for Finland there have been increasingly useful descriptions beginning with Kuusi's survey of 1948.

I am now in the process of analyzing a survey of drinking customs and attitudes in seven European countries and one South American country which was carried out on behalf of the World Health Organization.

The variation in the magnitude of various alcohol problems in different nations must be viewed in the light of national customs and attitudes as revealed in such surveys, particularly in relation to drinking patterns which result from social attitudes and economic factors. Only a few illustrations and suggestions in this area can be given in the present study. Social and economic factors not only greatly influence the drinking patterns and the magnitude of the alcohol problems, but also leave their stamp on the process of alcoholism and even on some aspects of its clinical picture. They do not, however, change physiology as one sociologist or sociologically oriented psychologist would make it appear in a hypothesis which is nearer to Yoga than to sociology.

The economic and social factors and their influence on drinking patterns will be cursorily reviewed in the next few pages. This discussion may seem to lead far away from the subject of alcoholism as an illness, but some assessment of the role of socioeconomic factors in the etiology of excess and ultimately of alcoholism should not be neglected, and this can more easily be seen from foreign data. Even so the following treatment of these aspects remains on a superficial level—sketchy even for a sketch.

II.2. Economic Elements

The "economic origin" of alcoholism is an idea that is frequently expounded in European countries and in some of the South American wine-growing countries. This conception is in gross contrast to the psychiatric, psychopathological and physiopathological theories on etiology current in the Anglo-Saxon countries. While it cannot be taken at face value, the idea of the "economic origin" has some features that cannot be overlooked without detriment to a clear understanding of the problems of alcohol. These features may be much more prominent in one country than in another, but they are not entirely missing in any nation that uses alcoholic beverages. The economic factors must be studied precisely where they are glaring if they are to achieve recognition in those countries where they play a less obtrusive role.

By "economic origin" one may mean the economic condition of the individual, general economic depression of the country, or pressure from a national economy in which the production and distribution of alcoholic beverages play such vital roles that they give an incentive to large individual consumption.

The first two factors named above have played important roles in the past; they now are heard of less and less, but they have

not disappeared entirely. There was in the past much mention of
the slum dweller who was driven to "pubs," bars or saloons in order
to obtain relief from his dreary home. This was, and is, also referred
to as alcoholism of environmental origin. Housing conditions in
France at present, especially in the larger cities, are of such a low
order that large families or even two smaller families are pressed
into small spaces. Réquet (1955) says that these conditions have
led to promiscuity and even incest. Many contemporary French
writers on alcoholism have pointed out the escape from the dreary
home to the more pleasant tavern. Bresard (1958), in a study of
housing in relation to alcohol consumption, found a definite relation between daily wine intake and the number of rooms occupied
by families. Another factor belonging in the category of "economic
origin" is the type of economic insecurity that was particularly
prominent in the course of the industrial revolution.

In both instances a psychological readiness for escape into alcohol intoxication must be assumed, as only a minority of the persons
suffering under such economic conditions succumb to excessive
drinking, namely, persons with small resistance to these adversi-
ties and few resources to cope with them. One must concede, however, that the economic or environmental factors play a prominent
role in such cases.

In some countries, or rather some districts of certain countries,
the population is so poor, or there exists such a food shortage,
that the inhabitants derive a large proportion of their calories from
cheap wine. In the district of Minho, Portugal, a laborer's wages
amount to 23 escudos per day; a pound of meat costs 11 escudos
and the same price is paid for a pound of the cheapest fish, but
a quart of wine costs only 2 escudos (Portugal, 1956). According
to a nutritional survey by the Portuguese Ministry of the Interior,
Department of Health, the daily fare of the population of that district consists of a thin potato soup containing a little bread and a
few shreds of fish. The average daily intake of protein from animal
sources is 6 grams per day. The survey mentions daily consumption
of wine without stating the amount, and of course, no reference is
made to the incidence of alcoholism, but the enormous incidence of
death from cirrhosis of the liver indicates the role that alcohol must
play in the calorie economy. One may speak here of "nutritional
alcoholism," which undoubtedly plays havoc with all aspects of
metabolism, but on account of lack of information it is not possible

to determine the prevalence of true alcohol addiction. In this case one may speak of an "economic origin" with justification, but these instances are rather limited and play a small role in the picture of the problems of alcohol on a world-wide scale.

The price of alcoholic beverages has, of course, some effect on consumption in any country. The magnitude of the effect varies with the degree of prosperity of a nation and apart from that factor depends also upon a people's tendency toward thrift. Furthermore, it is not the absolute price of wine but the relation to the prices of other commodities that determines its consumption. An example of this relationship may be seen in Table 1.

In Switzerland the Federal Alcohol Administration fixed the prices of distilled spirits at a high level in order to discourage its consumption in favor of lighter beverages. The same result was aimed at in Denmark through an exorbitant price differential. In both of those countries the distilled spirits consumption dropped in the beginning, but when the price of foods and other consumer goods rose, the consumption of distilled spirits showed an upward trend.

When the French speak of the "economic origin" of alcoholism, they mean that viticultural interests and the related industrial and trade interests are the decisive factors in the genesis of alcoholism. This thesis requires more thorough analysis than can be afforded in the frame of the present study but a few essential points may be touched upon.

In France viticulture constitutes a highly important part of the country's agricultural wealth. There were recently approximately 3½ million orchard and wine growers who had distilling privileges;

TABLE 1.—*Per Capita Consumption (15 Years and Over) of Wine in Italy Compared to the Average Retail Price of One Liter of Wine as a Percentage of the Average Retail Price of One Kilogram of Pasta and One Kilogram of Bread**

Period	Cost of Wine as Per Cent of Cost of Bread	Cost of Wine as Per Cent of Cost of Pasta	Wine Consumption Rate of Population 15 Years and Over (liters)
1936–40	116	80	118
1941–45	245	162	98
1946–50	129	83	109
1951–52	99	66	122

* Computed from prices cited in the Annuario Statistico Italiano, 1953.

their number is being somewhat decreased (Ledermann, 1956).
All told, 8 million voters (approximately one-third of the electorate)
are partly or entirely dependent upon the production, processing
and distribution of alcoholic beverages (mainly wine), and to this
number must be added family members of voting age.

The interests of these groups contribute toward a general acceptance of large individual consumption. There exists an identification
of the general population with these interests which they recognize
as a national one. (In America there is no identification of the
nation with the particular alcohol interests.)

These interests demand a large number of outlets for alcoholic
beverages. In France there is about 1 outlet for every 97 inhabitants. The consequent ubiquitousness of alcoholic beverages may
be a factor in the magnitude of consumption but its role cannot be
assessed in quantitative terms at present.

In sharp contrast to France, some other large wine-growing countries where viticulture is a great national resource, such as Italy,
Spain and Argentina, have alcohol problems at the lower range-end
of the distribution.

In Italy the area under viticulture represents 10 per cent of the
arable land and is somewhat larger than in France. Two million
people (10 per cent of the "active population") earn their living
entirely or partly through the production and sale of wine. Nevertheless the rate of alcoholism in Italy is about 5 times less than in
France. In spite of all economic interests the number of inhabitants
per outlet is about 3 times as great as in France (and is progressively being restricted toward a limit of 400 inhabitants per outlet)
and the per capita consumption of total absolute alcohol is half
that of the French. The pattern of drinking in Italy also differs
greatly from the French pattern. In Italy drinking is restricted almost entirely to meals and distilled spirits play an insignificant role.
In France, on the other hand, while distilled spirits beverages contribute only 14 per cent toward the total absolute alcohol consumption, their per capita consumption rate is, nevertheless, larger than
in countries where they are the predominant source of alcohol (e.g.,
Finland, Sweden, Norway) or where they contribute from 30 to 40
per cent of all absolute alcohol consumed (e.g., the United States
and Canada).

These facts indicate that economic elements alone cannot account
for the extremely high alcoholism rate in France; there must be

some differentiating factors between France and other large wine-growing countries with marked vested interests. These differentiating factors must be sought in cultural patterns as well as in collective and individual psychological elements.

Nevertheless the economic factors play an important role. The true economic problem in France in relation to alcoholism is that, because of pressures of vested interests, it is extremely difficult to establish legal and educational controls or even to launch a nation-wide campaign for the public care of alcoholics. The slightest mention of anything of this nature provokes vigorous antagonism not only from the vested interests but also from the majority of the population. In Chile similar conditions obtain but the resistance to control campaigns is not quite so obtrusive as in France. Since in Spain, Portugal and Argentina, with their great viticultural interests, the problems of alcohol are relatively small, the clash of control and vested interests or public attitude does not arise, but it may be safely assumed that in case of the emergence of a large alcohol problem and an attempt to control it, the same difficulties would be encountered in these countries too.

The economic factor (in the sense of agricultural and industrial interests) is thus more marked in the management than in the origin of alcoholism. While etiologically one cannot assign to these economic factors a dominance over the psychological and cultural elements, the contribution of the first named is still considerable.

Large vested interests have their effects on public opinion and acceptance. There are definite interactions between the two: where there is a certain readiness to accept large individual consumption the pressure from vested interests may reinforce the public attitude to a high degree; or on the other hand the public attitude may greatly facilitate the assumption of power on the part of the vested interests. This is a complex question that merits thorough sociological and economic analysis and cannot be ignored by the student of alcoholism. In many countries scientific investigations of alcoholism have deliberately kept aloof from this aspect of the problem and have given the impression that these matters are not within the field of the scientist but belong to quasi-political wrangling. It is understandable that the scientist is reluctant to enter a field which may easily involve him in "partisanship," but on the other hand it is hardly objective to deny the relevance and scientific nature of these facts. They are facts of the social sciences and can be dealt with on the same level of objectivity that exists in physiological, psychological and psychiatric research.

It is of great practical importance to show the economic and social factors in their proper perspective. If public health authorities are led to believe that the problems of alcohol are entirely economic and social problems, they will not see the cogency of incorporating the control of alcoholism and the rehabilitation of alcoholics into their program of activities. On the other hand, if it can be shown that socioeconomic factors are only one contributing element to the etiology of the problems of alcohol they will not shy away from it, as socioeconomic factors are to some extent elements of most health problems with which they have to deal.

Coping with the economic factors is, of course, not within the sphere of public health authorities, but they can show other competent authorities how these factors interfere with the control of the health problem and engage their cooperation. As an example of socioeconomic factors which public health authorities meet in their work but cannot regulate directly, the case of undesirable features of drug advertising may be cited. In the United States the Food and Drug Administration, in whose sphere matters of drug advertising belong, has been surely guided by public health interests. As far as alcoholic beverages are concerned the restraining influence on advertising rests with the Alcohol and Tobacco Tax Division of the Treasury Department. That agency has probably been influenced by the temperance movement—which is pressing for elimination of alcoholic-beverage advertising—rather than by public health authorities. In spite of all the criticism which still may be leveled against that category of advertising in the United States, it is far less objectionable than in most European countries where it is permissible to extol the nutritional and medicinal properties of such beverages.

As advertising aims at influencing public attitudes, and as the latter play an important role in the genesis and control of the problems of alcohol, advertising cannot be ignored by the scientific student of these problems.

As has been said before, the economic aspects of the problem in the United States require a good deal more than just the mention that they exist—and that is usually as far as the scientific students of the problems of alcohol will go—but on the other hand they cannot be given the weight which is assigned to them in such countries as France or Chile. We must repeat that, while in Italy and Spain the economic interests are comparable to those in France, the problems of alcohol are not among the major problems of public health. One may add that in Sweden, where the economic pressure does not seem to exist, as the government monopoly is devised to eliminate the element of profit, the problems of alcohol are much greater than in any other European country except France, where the *relative* incidence of alcoholism exceeds that in Sweden by approximately 100 per cent.

II.3. Drinking Patterns and Social Attitudes

Abundance and ubiquitousness of wine and other alcoholic beverages, identification of the nation with vested alcohol interests, and pride in the national product combined with a belief in the utility of wine, bring about a high degree of general acceptance of large individual consumption.

Bastide's (1954) excellently devised and executed survey—carried out on behalf of the Institut National d'Etudes Démographiques—showed that in 1953, 88 per cent of the male and 72 per cent of the female interviewees (80 per cent for both sexes) in France held the opinion that wine was "good for one's health."

Seventy-eight per cent of the men and 62 per cent of the women (70 per cent for both sexes) said that wine was nourishing. When the interviewees were asked whether wine was indispensable, useful, useless, etc., the replies were distributed as shown in Table 2.

It is thus not surprising that in this survey the answers by men to the question what amount a working man could drink every day "without any inconvenience" averaged 1.8 liters (slightly under 2 quarts), i.e., 180 cc. (6 oz.) of absolute alcohol, and the answers by women averaged 1.4 liters (average for the opinion of both

TABLE 2.—*French Opinions on Usefulness of Wine*[*]

	Both Sexes, %	Men, %	Women, %
Indispensable	25	32	18
Useful	63	58	67
Useless	9	8	10
Noxious	1	1	2
No Response	2	1	3
Totals	*100*	*100*	*100*

* From Bastide (1954).

sexes, 1.6 liters). A daily intake of 2 liters by a working man was acceptable to 30 per cent of the men and 22 per cent of the women. A daily average of 2½ liters was found acceptable by 5 per cent of the men and of 3 liters or more by 13 per cent of the men. Thus the acceptance of amounts from 2 liters upward by men reached 48 per cent (by women, 29 per cent).

In a society where such attitudes prevail it is quite understandable that drinkers with minor vulnerabilities should develop diseases of "chronic alcoholism," and that in the course of many years of such drinking a certain proportion of these "inveterate drinkers" may develop true addiction in the physical sense yet, because of their particular patterns, without conspicuous display of drunkenness.

A French drinker at the high range-end of the distribution—particularly in the viticultural areas—may distribute a total of 3 liters of wine per day as follows: 200 cc. at 7 A.M. with his breakfast, and after that hourly amounts of about 100 cc. from 8 A.M. through 12 noon. At his meal between 1 and 2 P.M. he may consume 600 cc., to be followed by hourly amounts of 100 cc. until 6 P.M. At the evening meal, between 7 and 8 P.M., he may drink ¾ to 1 liter and at 9 and 10 P.M. perhaps 150 cc. each time. Allowing for all factors which may reduce the amount of alcohol to be oxidized, and particularly for slower absorption of the larger amounts during meal hours, it may be said that a drinker of average weight will hardly exceed a concentration of alcohol in the blood of 0.02 per cent between morning and noon and that his highest after the evening meal will hardly be over 0.12 per cent. The latter concentration, although fairly high, would not cause visible symptoms in a well-accustomed drinker. On the other hand, the organism of this drinker will hardly ever be entirely free of alcohol, although the blood alcohol concentration will be at levels of "sobriety" during a large part of the day. In a man of well above average weight or with an alcohol oxidation rate well above the average of 0.1 g. per kg. per hr. (rates of 0.15 g. per kg. per hour have been quite frequently observed), a similar time-distribution of 3 liters of wine would produce even lower alcohol concentrations, but not without nearly constant presence of alcohol in the organism.

The almost constant presence of alcohol in the organism can hardly be conceived of as not interfering with its normal functioning; and the likelihood of acquiring an increase in tissue tolerance which may lead to even larger consumption and ultimately to physical dependence, i.e., addiction in the strict pharmacological sense, must be considered.

This is not to imply that Frenchmen never get drunk. Intoxication is no rarity in France, but a large proportion of French drinkers may incur some damage characteristic of "chronic alcoholism," or develop addiction without their having ever shown intoxication except on certain celebrations. Psychiatrists in such predominantly wine drinking countries as France, Switzerland, and Italy, have frequently seen the withdrawal syndrome, including delirium tremens, in men who have rarely been intoxicated. And diseases of "chronic alcoholism" have been seen in men who by their past history did not appear to be "addictive drinkers" or even steady excessive "relief drinkers" without addictive features, and whose "chronic alcoholic" complications came as a surprise to everybody. This type of drinker is frequently called "inveterate drinker" in France. Later we shall assign another label to him.

With the exception of the younger psychiatrists, French students of alcoholism attribute this type of drinking entirely to "habit" and social attitudes which are greatly influenced by economic factors. In many countries all but a few psychiatrists believe that alcoholism becomes a psychiatric problem only after the excessive drinker develops an alcoholic mental disorder. In the origin of the "habit," they see no psychological or psychiatric involvements. Nothing can provoke greater dissent on the part of French physicians and others interested in alcoholism than the contention that pre-alcoholic maladjustments lead to the heavy use of alcoholic beverages. Suggestions of pre-alcoholic neurotic character or other marked psychological deviations (let alone the term psychopathy with its many different meanings) meet with strong rejection.

This antagonism to the "Anglo-Saxon" etiological ideas, which is not limited to the French alone, is to some extent justified in relation to certain types of steady excessive drinkers in wine-growing countries, but it cannot be accepted at face value for all of their alcoholics.

The presence of psychological factors in the Frenchman's drinking is borne out by some ideas that are prevalent in France about the properties of wine. In many small restaurants there is on the back of the menu a page with cartoons and slogans, three of which read as follows: "The wines of France create gaiety;" "The wines of France create optimism;" "The wines of France give self-assurance." This leaflet evidently reflects popular ideas about wine. And if optimism and self-assurance are to be derived from wine there can hardly be any denial of psychological factors in the Frenchman's drinking. The accent on creating optimism and self-assurance would indicate that these traits may often be deficient in excessive drinkers. Moreover, this deficiency, and its remedy through wine, suggest a certain psychological vulnerability, although it could hardly be called an abnormality.

Furthermore, despite the wide acceptance of high alcohol intake in France, only 7 per cent of male users consume 3 liters of wine or more per day and even users of 2 liters of wine per day are in the minority.

One may suspect, therefore, a differentiating factor between these heavy drinkers and the majority of wine consumers who drink much less. The "habit" and the social acceptance of heavy drinking are facilitating factors, but cannot account for the entire phenomenon.

The fact remains that the majority of French alcohol addicts do not display pre-alcoholic neurotic or other gross psychological vulnerabilities, but rather minor psychological vulnerabilities. (A minority of French addicts do show pre-alcoholic neuroticism, as pointed out by the younger psychiatrists and described by some of the French novelists.) In contrast, America and other Anglo-Saxon countries show a preponderance of neuroticism among their alcohol addicts while a minority have only minor vulnerabilities. This predominance of low vulnerability on the one side and high vulnerability on the other side poses a challenging question.

As mentioned before, the French show an extraordinarily high general social acceptance of large daily individual consumption (6 oz. of absolute alcohol). In America, Sweden, Denmark, Holland, England and other Anglo-Saxon countries, a good one-third of the adult population rejects the use of alcoholic beverages in any quantity, and the remaining two-thirds would—on the average—not approve of more than the equivalent of 2 to 3 oz. of absolute alcohol per day.

I should like to submit the following working hypothesis:

In societies which have a low degree of acceptance of large daily amounts of alcohol, mainly those will be exposed to the

risk of addiction who on account of high psychological vulner-
ability have an inducement to go against the social standards.
But in societies which have an extremely high degree of accept-
ance of large daily alcohol consumption, the presence of any
small vulnerability, whether psychological or physical, will suf-
fice for exposure to the risk of addiction.[2]

What has been said here about the French drinking pattern,
economic factors and acceptance of large intake (at least by the
male population) applies to Chile too and with similar consequences in the magnitude of the problem. In other wine countries,
however, the pattern is modified and the attitudes toward drinking
and drunkenness are different.

In Italy, which has the second highest wine consumption of the
world, the per capita consumption is just about half of that in
France and distilled spirits consumption plays a negligible role.
Privileged home distillers do not exist at all. The Italian wine
drinker does not spread a large quantity over 16 hours of the day
but drinks only with his noon and evening meals. One liter per day
is the maximum accepted amount and anything above that amount
is regarded as gross excess (Luzzatto-Fegiz, 1952). Not more than
17 per cent of the adult male population drink outside of meals
and most of these infrequently, on special occasions only.

The incidence of alcohol addiction is less than one-fifth of that
in France. This fact is accounted for by the much lower consumption rate; by the distribution of 1/3 to 1 liter over two meals; and,
as Lolli, Serianni et al. (1952) have pointed out, by the fact that
in these meals slowly soluble carbohydrates predominate which re-
tard the absorption of alcohol, averting gross fluctuations of blood
sugar and lowering the toxicity of alcohol. In addition there are many
other factors which contribute to the difference between the ex-
tents of the French and Italian alcohol problems. Among these
factors are attitudes toward drinking and drunkenness.

In Italy there is no social pressure for drinking; the polite refusal
of a drink meets with indifference while in France it arouses at
least ridicule, more often suspicion and quite frequently contempt.
Even in the Italian restaurants and taverns the consumption of

[2] These ideas have been presented by me in the periodical *World Health* (Jellinek,
1957) and in some unpublished lectures of which parts have been quoted or para-
phrased by some writers, e.g., Keller (1958).

wine is not regarded as an obligation of the guest. In a French restaurant the guest who does not order wine is met with a contemptuous lifting of the waiter's eyebrows; verbal disapproval may even be expressed. The Italian regards the total abstainer with indifference as long as he is not motivated by stinginess. The French abstainer does not have such an easy time. In France drinking is a must, in Italy it is a matter of choice.

Even more important is the Italian contempt for alcohol intoxication and the severe and consistent social sanctions against it which are lacking in France. In Italy a slight intoxication is regarded as something "piggish," like the consequences of overeating, something that the person in question deserved for his gluttony. Anything beyond slight intoxication is taken as a serious infringement of social expectations and is not condoned even on gay occasions, such as birthdays, New Years or national holidays. A reputation for getting drunk at parties or weekends would suffice to cause parents to refuse consent for marriage with their daughter, and the girls too would be disinclined to marry such a man. Advancement in employment would likewise be jeopardized by such behavior. In view of such severe, consistent social punishment, the "alcoholic way out" is greatly limited. The type of "inveterate drinker" described in the case of France does occur in selected Italian occupational groups, among farmhands for instance, but even there a much greater psychological vulnerability is required than in France.

These differences in attitudes account to a considerable extent for national differences in the magnitude of alcohol problems. But how do the differential attitudes arise? This question should be a challenge to thoughtful students of social and cultural structures.

In viticultural Argentina, where there is a large population of Italian extraction, the Italian and Spanish cultural patterns prevail and their attitudes and sanctions put the brakes on drunkenness and alcoholism. In Chile, on the other hand, also a viticultural country, the French, Irish, Lithuanian and Yugoslavian cultural influences are more pronounced; the attitudes and sanctions against drunken behavior are as weak as in France; and Chile ranks among the countries with the largest alcoholism problems.

The drinking pattern can determine the course of the alcoholic process, in the sense that such a pattern as described for France can lead to a constant presence of alcohol in the organism with little manifestation of overt intoxication, and result in a species of addiction in which there is no "loss of control" but instead an inability to "go on the water wagon," i.e., to abstain. On the other hand in the Anglo-Saxon countries there is—as the majority rule—no distribution of alcohol over the entire day but rather a shocklike impact of strongly intoxicating amounts toward evening. This pattern can produce "loss of control" but leaves the ability to "go on the water wagon," i.e., to abstain for shorter or longer periods, practically intact.

The drinking patterns are to a large extent ascribable to the beverages which contain the alcohol—i.e., wine (in some countries beer) for continual distribution, and distilled spirits for "concentrated" consumption over short periods with a shocklike intoxication. The drinking patterns are to a considerable extent governed by social attitudes. In the Anglo-Saxon countries there is a definite understanding about the "where and when" of drinking, while in France and Chile there is not. Thus to some extent the drinking pattern is influenced by social factors, and in turn influences the alcoholic process. While social factors, therefore, indirectly affect the alcoholic process, it cannot be said that they change the physiology of alcohol, or that various nations have a physiology of their own.

Certain social factors, however, may modify the clinical picture of alcohol addiction in its psychological aspects. As the vast majority of Frenchmen approve of a daily intake of approximately 2 liters of wine it is quite understandable that French alcohol addicts feel no guilt about their drinking and thus lack many symptoms which are related to that guilt. It is interesting to note that in Chile, where male society has a high degree of acceptance of large alcohol intake, comparable to that in France, but the great majority of women are opposed to it, alcoholics show no guilt feeling about drinking toward their fathers, brothers, sons and the male sex in general but do show marked guilt feeling toward their mothers, wives, daughters and the female sex in general. On the other hand, in America and other predominantly Anglo-Saxon countries the guilt about drinking felt toward both sexes is highly characteristic of the alcohol addict.

The addict of the "inveterate" type does not go through those difficulties with himself, his family and others; he does not experience those tribulations to which the Anglo-Saxon majority type of alcohol addict is subjected.

I would suggest that the difficulty in establishing Alcoholics Anonymous groups in Latin countries is largely due to the differences in the experiences of their alcohol addicts from those in the Anglo-Saxon countries. The ideology of Alcoholics Anonymous does not find an echo in the experiences of the French "inveterate" addicts who in that country form the majority of alcoholics. That French majority type is in America a minority type, and it may be that at least some of the alcoholics who drop out of Alcoholics Anonymous here belong to that type.

After this sketchy review of social and economic factors and their effects it may be easier to arrive at a tentative definition of alcoholism and some of its species.

III

Formulations of the Disease Nature
of Alcoholism

*Peril lurks in definitions, so runs an
ancient maxim of law.*

—BENJAMIN N. CARDOZO

III.1. Notes on Terminology

B EFORE entering on the discussion of the various conceptions of "alcoholism" as a disease, it may be in order to give
some enumeration of terms and to comment upon them.

First, explanations of the term alcoholism and of other terms
denoting its various species will be presented without any intention
of suggesting their acceptance. They are stated for the purpose of
making it clear what is meant by certain terms in the present study.
It is not intended here to go into a critique of current definitions.

III.1.1. Nature of Definitions

If one goes over the article on definition in Eisler's (1910) *Wör-
terbuch der philosophischen Begriffe*,[1] one must conclude that there
are more definitions of definition than there are "definitions" of
alcoholism. This may be a consolation for students of alcoholism
who complain about the plethora and conflict of definitions or so-
called definitions in their field. On the other hand it should impress
them that definition is nothing sacred and unalterable. One cannot
question whether definitions are right or wrong, unless they go
against the rules of the defining process, but one may debate their
utility. No attempt will be made here to go into a critique of the

---

[1] In spite of this date, this dictionary is by no means obsolete; as a matter of
fact it offers the widest range of documentation concerning statements on definition
from Socrates to Ernst Mach. While some more modern dictionaries may mention
more recent philosophers than Mach, they do not offer anything near the wealth
of documentation given by Eisler and they indulge in personal opinions which Eisler
avoids in his article of roughly 2,200 words.

numerous "definitions" which various students of alcoholism have submitted.

In spite of the fact that philosophers have defined definition in many ways, there are rules of the "game" which can be deduced from common elements in all definitions of this concept. First, it appears that there are two main kinds of definitions, namely, nominal and formal. And there are "admissible" but incomplete definitions, such as "delimitations" and operational definitions. The nominal definition formulates the concept in more familiar words than the original technical term or adds a few words which, however, do not reveal the character of the phenomenon. An example of a nominal definition of alcoholism (although not in more familiar words but rather a slight expansion of the term) could be that it denotes the internal use of ethyl alcohol either pure and simple or as contained in alcoholic beverages. Such a definition was actually proposed by Elster in the *Handwörterbuch der Staatswissenschaften* (cited by Levy, 1951). The utility of this statement is rather slight.

A formal definition dissects the concept and by this means shows its nature and its essential characteristics. From all that is said by philosophers on this subject, a formal definition should not go into classification, it should not be negative, it should not enumerate the characteristics which are not involved, it should not be circular and it should not use figurative language. This latter stipulation would disqualify as definitions such statements as that alcoholism is an escape from reality. Nevertheless such a statement may or may not have a certain utility. As to the ban on negative statements, its purpose essentially is to avoid circularity of definition, such as that good is what is not bad, and bad is what is not good. On the other hand, if a concept A differs from a concept B in that the former has the characteristics a, b and c, while the latter is composed of the characteristics a, b, c, d and e it would not seem out of order to state, for the avoidance of misunderstanding, that the elements d and e are not present in A; this statement, however, would not be a part of the definition but a commentary of sorts.

The most essential desiderata of definition are given by Kant (*Critique of Pure Reason*): "A formal definition is one which not only clarifies a concept but at the same time establishes its objective reality." He also states that neither empirical nor a priori concepts can be truly defined, but can only be expounded. In a true sense only an arbitrary concept can be defined. Furthermore a concept ex hypothesi is not definable but explainable. It may be said here that alcoholism practically belongs in this latter category.

III.1.2. Alcoholism and its Species

In the preceding chapter, a survey of views held by many nations the world over showed that they have various highly vexatious problems which they term "alcoholism," problems whose seriousness cannot be denied but which would not be designated in America by that term. It would not be doing justice to the nations concerned if one were to belittle those problems by shrugging them off as not representing "alcoholism."

Every country that has alcohol problems has "alcoholism" in the sense in which we are accustomed to think of it in America; but in many of those countries there are other problems arising from the use of alcoholic beverages, and these problems may be so extensive or so grievous that they may overshadow those species of alcoholism for which the term is reserved in America. Furthermore those other problems exist in America, too.

By adhering strictly to our American ideas about "alcoholism" and "alcoholics" (created by Alcoholics Anonymous in their own image) and restricting the term to those ideas, we have been continuing to overlook many other problems of alcohol which need urgent attention.

In this connection it may be mentioned that while in the American alcoholism literature, by and large, alcoholism means true addiction—let us say, for the time being, the type prevalent in Alcoholics Anonymous—there are a number of American students of alcoholism who would include, under that term, heavy weekend drinkers as well as "relief drinkers" who never become addicted. In order to do justice to these international, as well as our own national differences, we have termed as *alcoholism any use of alcoholic beverages that causes any damage to the individual or society or both.* Vague as this statement is, it approaches an operational definition.

It may be said that such a loose definition has little operational value. With such a vague definition we cannot even ask whether alcoholism is an illness. Obviously there are species of alcoholism —so defined—which cannot be regarded as illnesses. One may well say that such a vague definition is useless. But in this uselessness lies its utility, for it forces us to single out species of alcoholism (in

the above sense) and to speak of them in stringent terms. We must
be particularly definite about those forms which we wish to examine
as possibly constituting illnesses. Furthermore, in view of our broad
and vague statement of alcoholism we cannot say that alcoholics
are those who suffer from alcoholism as defined above. We shall
have to make a distinction between alcoholism and alcoholics.

In speaking about the species of alcoholism and alcoholics I shall
give brief descriptions and attach labels to them without any pre-
tension to formal definitions. Only those species of alcoholism will
be described and labeled here that may come at all into consideration as disease processes or symptoms of disease processes. In addition, some statements will be made concerning certain terms that
are frequently used in the formulations of the conception of alcoholism as an illness. Some of those statements may be true definitions,
some may be merely "delimitations" and operational definitions,
and some may comply neither with the formal requirements of definition nor with the desiderata of "delimitation."

For the labeling of the species of alcoholism considered here, I
am taking recourse to letters of the Greek alphabet. Letter symbols
arouse perhaps less misgivings than names which may have different connotations for many students of alcoholism. Of course the
letters can be replaced by word labels according to the preferences
of readers. Nevertheless, adherence to the letter symbols will cause
the least degree of controversy.

Alpha alcoholism represents a *purely* psychological *continual* dependence or reliance upon the effect of alcohol to relieve bodily or
emotional pain. The drinking is "undisciplined" in the sense that
it contravenes such rules as society tacitly agrees upon—such as
time, occasion, locale, amount and effect of drinking—*but does not
lead to "loss of control"* or *"inability to abstain"* (for the latter
two phenomena see section III.1.3.). The damage caused by this
species of alcoholism may be restricted to the disturbance of interpersonal relations. There may also be interference with the family
budget, occasional absenteeism from work and decreased productivity, and some of the nutritional deficiencies of alcoholism, but
not the disturbances due to withdrawal of alcohol. *Nor are there
any signs of a progressive process.*

The relief of bodily pain or emotional disturbance implies an
underlying illness and thus the "undisciplined" use of alcoholic
beverages may be regarded as a symptom of the pathological con-

ditions which it relieves. This species of alcoholism cannot be regarded as an illness per se.

Of course, it is quite possible that in many instances alpha alcoholism may develop into gamma alcoholism, i.e., that it may often
be a developmental stage. On the other hand, it is well known that
this species of alcoholism may be seen in a drinking career of 30
or 40 years without any signs of progression. When we speak here
of alpha alcoholism we mean this latter "pure culture" but not the
developmental stage of gamma alcoholism.

Alpha alcoholism as described here is sometimes called problem
drinking, but that expression just as frequently includes physical
dependence upon alcohol. The terms problem drinking and problem drinker will not be used in the present study.

Beta alcoholism is that species of alcoholism in which such alcoholic complications as polyneuropathy, gastritis and cirrhosis of the
liver may occur without either physical or psychological dependence
upon alcohol. The incentive to the heavy drinking that leads to such
complications may be the custom of a certain social group in conjunction with poor nutritional habits. The damage in this instance is
of course the nutritional deficiency diseases, but impaired family
budget and lowered productivity as well as a curtailed life span
may also occur. Withdrawal symptoms, on the other hand, do not
emerge.

Beta alcoholism too may develop into gamma or delta alcoholism,
but such a transition is less likely than in the instance of alpha
alcoholism.

Gamma alcoholism means that species of alcoholism in which
(1) acquired increased tissue tolerance to alcohol, (2) adaptive
cell metabolism (see below), (3) withdrawal symptoms and "craving," i.e., physical dependence, and (4) loss of control are involved.
In gamma alcoholism there is a definite progression from psychological to physical dependence and marked behavior changes such
as have been described previously (Jellinek, 1946 and 1952b). Alpha and beta alcoholism, as already noted, may develop under
given conditions into gamma alcoholism.

This species produces the greatest and most serious kinds of damage. The loss of control, of course, impairs interpersonal relations
to the highest degree. The damage to health in general and to
financial and social standing are also more prominent than in other
species of alcoholism.

Gamma alcoholism is apparently (but not with certainty) the *predominating* species of alcoholism in the United States and Canada, as well as in other Anglo-Saxon countries. It is what members of Alcoholics Anonymous recognize as alcoholism to the exclusion of all other species. Of course they use loss of control and "craving" as the criteria par excellence but these necessarily involve the other characteristics of gamma alcoholism mentioned above. As I have said before, Alcoholics Anonymous have naturally created the picture of alcoholism in their own image, although at least 10 to 15 per cent of their membership are probably specimens of alpha alcoholism who conform in their language to the A.A. standards. I base this statement on the fact that in a sample of slightly over 2,000 A.A. members I have found 13 per cent who never experienced loss of control. More likely than not only a small percentage of those with alpha alcoholism would seek the help of Alcoholics Anonymous, and almost none of those with beta alcoholism. The latter may be seen most frequently in general hospitals.

In spite of the respect and admiration to which Alcoholics Anonymous have a claim on account of their great achievements, there is every reason why the student of alcoholism should emancipate himself from accepting the exclusiveness of the picture of alcoholism as propounded by Alcoholics Anonymous.

Delta alcoholism shows the first three characteristics of gamma alcoholism as well as a less marked form of the fourth characteristic—that is, instead of loss of control there is inability to abstain. In contrast to gamma alcoholism, there is no ability to "go on the water wagon" for even a day or two without the manifestation of withdrawal symptoms; the ability to control the amount of intake on any given occasion, however, remains intact. The incentive to high intake may be found in the general acceptance of the society to which the drinker belongs, while pre-alcoholic psychological vulnerability, more often than not, may be of a low degree. This species of alcoholism and its underlying drinking pattern have been sufficiently described in Chapter II in connection with the *predominant* species of alcoholism ("inveterate drinking") in France and some other countries with a large wine consumption. For reasons discussed in that chapter, delta alcoholism would rarely be seen in Alcoholics Anonymous, since the alcoholic afflicted with this species of alcoholism does not go through the distressing social and psychological experiences of the gamma alcoholic and manifests only a few of the behavior changes of the latter.

There are, of course, many other species of alcoholism—if it is defined as any drinking that causes any damage—and all the remaining 19 letters of the Greek and if necessary other alphabets are available for labeling them.

Among these other species is periodic alcoholism, which in Europe and Latin America is still designated as dipsomania, a term in disuse in North America. We may denote it as *Epsilon alcoholism* but it will be neither described nor defined here, as it seems to be the least known species of alcoholism. In the course of their periodic bouts, epsilon alcoholics may cause serious damage. I should like to point out that in the last 20 or 25 years a phenomenon which may be called pseudoperiodic alcoholism has turned up. It would appear that some gamma alcoholics who have not benefited to the full extent from the A.A. program or from therapy in clinics or by private psychiatrists are able to resist drinking for 3, 6 or 12 months, but then find no other solution than intoxication, after which they remorsefully return to "sobriety."

Other species of alcoholism (accepting the criterion of damage through drinking) are, of course, "explosive drinking" as well as what the French call "alcoolisation," i.e., the undermining of health and curtailing of the life span (to the exclusion of other "alcoholic complications" and physical or psychological dependence). Then there is the excessive weekend drinking which follows a cultural pattern and causes damage through rowdiness, absenteeism and impairment of the family budget. Still other species cause damage, for instance, "fiesta drinking" and occasional drinking that causes accidents. I do not propose to list, describe or discuss all these species of alcoholism, but should like to point out that the student of the problems of alcohol cannot afford to overlook these behaviors, whether or not he is inclined to designate them as species of alcoholism.

Returning to the question whether alcoholism is a disease, only alpha, beta, gamma, delta and epsilon alcoholism can come into consideration at all. Alpha alcoholism may be ruled out as it is the symptom of an underlying disturbance; this, of course, does not deny that the person suffering from this species of alcoholism is a sick person. As to beta alcoholism, it too must be ruled out, being neither a disease per se nor even a symptom, unless we regard the drinking that produces the damage (certain alcoholic diseases) as social pathology, a rather diffuse concept. No doubt polyneuropathy, cirrhosis of the liver and gastritis are serious diseases, but in this instance they are purely effects of the excessive drinking, and in this species the excess in drinking itself does not indicate any physical or psychological pathology and no dependence develops.

This leaves us with the gamma, delta and epsilon species of alcoholism. The first two of these may come into consideration as diseases, since it is the adaptation of cell metabolism, and acquired increased tissue tolerance and the withdrawal symptoms, which bring about "craving" and loss of control or inability to abstain. These species involve that use of alcoholic beverages which has induced Bacon (1958) to say that "alcoholics do not drink," although Bacon is not thinking merely of the loss of control but, quite rightly, of certain drinking behaviors which precede the loss of control. In gamma alcoholism, the adaptation of cell metabolism and the other characteristics mentioned above indeed represent physiopathological changes analogous to those in drug addiction as well as psychopathological conditions which differ from those of any possible pre-alcoholic psychopathology. With the exception of the psychological changes and the loss of control, which is replaced by the inability to abstain, the same changes are involved in delta alcoholism.

If it should be conceded that morphine, heroin and barbiturate addiction involve grave physiopathologic processes which result in "craving," then they may be designated as diseases (and they are included in the American Medical Association's nomenclature of diseases). The gamma and delta species of alcoholism may be regarded so by the same tokens (and alcoholism is included, too, in the list of the American Medical Association). Of course it is a matter of opinion whether or not such processes are designated as diseases. On the other hand, the presence of the physiopathological changes leading to craving cannot be denied in the addictions, whether to narcotic drugs or to alcohol. The current majority opinion to which the present writer subscribes, and subscribed before it was a majority opinion, is that anomalous forms of the ingestion of narcotics and alcohol, such as drinking with loss of control and physical dependence, are caused by physiopathological processes and constitute diseases.

Whether epsilon alcoholism, i.e., periodic alcoholism, is a disease per se or the symptom of an underlying disease cannot be asserted at our present state of knowledge concerning that species of alcoholism. Pseudoperiodic alcoholism or pseudoepsilon alcoholism is a relapse into a disease, but I must add that the occasion for the relapse is a voluntary one and does not form a part of the disease process, except perhaps in a psychopathological sense.

As I have said before, the definition of alcoholism which I have adopted here, namely that alcoholism is any drinking that leads to any damage, does not permit of designating as alcoholics all those who occasion some kind of damage through their use of alcoholic beverages. I would call alcoholics only those who manifest the alpha, beta, gamma, delta and epsilon varieties of alcoholism. This is admittedly an arbitrary distinction. Some may wish to exclude the alpha or beta alcoholics or both, and others may be inclined to include the "explosive drinkers," the "alcoholized drinkers," or perhaps all who cause any damage through any use of alcoholic beverages. I shall have no quarrel with them as I made these statements only in order to assure what the terms used mean in the present study.

III.1.3 Loss of Control and the Inability to Abstain

In the alcohol literature the term "loss of control" (over the intake of alcohol) is frequently used interchangeably with the expression "uncontrolled drinking." Quite often, however, different drinking behaviors are distinguished by these two terms.

Recovered alcoholics in Alcoholics Anonymous speak of "loss of control" to denote that stage in the development of their drinking history when the ingestion of one alcoholic drink sets up a chain reaction so that they are unable to adhere to their intention to "have one or two drinks only" but continue to ingest more and more —often with quite some difficulty and disgust—contrary to their volition.

American students of alcoholism have taken over this term from the vocabulary of alcoholics, but many years before that European physicians (e.g., Forel, Wlassak, and Bleuler) had observed and described the drinking behavior designated by this term and suggested "das Nichtaufhörenkönnen" as the criterion of "true alcoholism" (Bowman and Jellinek, 1942a).

The description of loss of control will be expanded in section

3.4.4.5. of this chapter and a hypothesis for the mechanism of this phenomenon will be submitted. It should be mentioned at this time, however, that the loss of control does not emerge suddenly but rather progressively and that it does not occur inevitably as often as the gamma alcoholic takes a drink. The loss of control becomes fully established several years after the first intoxication.

In the writings of quite a number of students of alcoholism the expression "uncontrolled drinking" does not denote the behavior described above but rather a deliberate transgression of the social rules (admittedly diffuse rules) relating to amounts, times, occasions and locales of drinking. In order to avoid the suggestion of loss of control in this latter drinking behavior, the use of the expression *undisciplined drinking* seems to be more appropriate, particularly since the drinker in these instances is not deprived of free choice. This undisciplined drinking is characteristic of the alpha alcoholic, but it occurs in the gamma alcoholic too before loss of control is established. Paradoxically enough, after the establishment of loss of control, deliberate, undisciplined drinking greatly diminishes in the gamma alcoholic as he knows or is afraid that the loss of control might bring about serious consequences in situations where that behavior would be most dangerous. As the loss of control progresses, however, the attempt to discipline the drinking occasions may break down.

The loss of control extends over a given drinking bout, after which the gamma alcoholic is able to "go on the water wagon." i.e., to abstain from alcoholic beverages for shorter or longer periods. His starting a new bout is not ascribable to the mechanism of loss of control nor to compulsion, but rather to an impulse whose danger either is not recognized or is "explained away."

The delta alcoholic, on the other hand, is unable to abstain entirely for even a day or two although he can control the amounts he consumes on any given occasion. Loss of control and inability to abstain are thus not interchangeable terms. The differences between these two drinking behaviors are rooted largely in the drinking patterns which have been touched upon in Chapter II.

III.1.4. Craving and Compulsion

The question of craving for alcohol will be discussed in some detail in subsection III.4.4.4. It is desirable, however, to touch upon this concept briefly at this juncture as it enters into the discussion of nutritional and endocrinological theories in the main sections III.4.2 and III.4.3.

In his thoughtful analysis, Mardones (1955) says:

"We can define craving for alcohol as an urgent and overpowering desire to drink alcoholic beverages. Thus, discussion of the nature and origin of this craving can be directed first to the noun 'desire,' and then to the adjectives 'urgent and overpowering'."

In discussing the adjectives which qualify the craving he states:

"The urgency of the desire is a passive condition that is perceived by the individual, and 'overpowering' means inducing an active attitude directed to surmount the obstacles opposing the desire.

"It is obvious that the subjective component can only be recognized in man. There is no doubt that the desire for alcohol is sometimes urgent in alcoholic patients.

"The overpowering character of the desire can only be observed when obstacles stand in the way of its satisfaction. Social life generally raises such obstacles to the satisfaction of the desire for alcohol, making its 'overpowering' nature easily recognizable in human beings."

Mardones points out that in animal experimentation an "overpowering desire" in the above sense has not been demonstrated and that the increased voluntary alcohol intake by animals cannot be equated with craving.

It may be said that an "overpowering desire," i.e., a physical dependence upon alcohol, is shown only in the presence of withdrawal symptoms, and these are late developments in gamma and delta alcoholics. At the beginning of their drinking careers the prospective gamma alcoholics undoubtedly show a greater desire for the tension-reducing effects of alcoholic beverages than other users of alcohol but they do not seem to give any indication of an initial physical dependence. Any etiological theory which postulates pre-alcoholic physiopathological factors that lead from the very start to a larger than average intake of alcohol must give evidence that such an intake constitutes craving in the sense of physical dependence upon the substance.

The term compulsion is frequently used to denote the same drinking behavior which is designated by many as "craving." Psychiatry and psychology offer only nominal definitions of compulsion, namely as that which impels an act contrary to the conscious will. In the sense that a physical dependence can cancel out the conscious will it is not unreasonable to designate as compulsion the behavior manifested in loss of control. But since the term compulsion is, as a rule, regarded as a psychopathological phenomenon it does not seem to cover behavior which arises from the need to alleviate such distressing manifestations as withdrawal symptoms.

III.1.5. Tolerance

Tolerance to alcohol may be defined as a critical level or threshold of alcohol concentration in the blood at which measurable changes occur in nervous functions. A distinction must be made between inherent or initial tolerance and acquired increased tolerance.

The terms tolerance and intolerance to alcohol have been used indiscriminately to designate a variety of phenomena, among them the loss of control. In the present study the term will be used exclusively as defined above. A detailed discussion of tolerance will be found in section III.4.4.2.

III.1.6. Habituation, Sensitivity and Susceptibility

Habituation to alcohol is a term which is frequently used synonymously with tolerance to alcohol but just as frequently to denote the process of physical dependence. Furthermore habituation and forming a habit often become entangled. This state of affairs is confusing and the term habituation will not be employed in the present study except when quoting or paraphrasing writers on this subject.

Sensitivity to alcohol is invoked by some students of alcoholism as a factor in the etiology of "alcoholism." Those who use this term take it for granted that what it means is understood and, consequently, do not define it. The use of the expression sensitivity sometimes creates the impression of some esoteric concept. Occasionally this term is used to denote tolerance. Some students of alcoholism speak of sensitivity when they mean that certain individuals are not able to resist the ingestion of alcohol. It seems preferable to avoid this term entirely, particularly as one can do quite well without it.

Susceptibility is one of the vague characteristics referred to occasionally in the etiology of "alcoholism." Susceptibility means a state of mind in which the individual shows particular readiness to avail himself of the use of a certain substance or to engage in a certain activity. Of course, a person who is suffering from stresses and lacks the ability to cope with them is more "susceptible" to the use of a tension-reducing substance, such as alcohol, than a well-balanced person. The use of the term susceptibility to alcohol contributes little if anything to the description of the alcoholic process unless the term is greatly elaborated. Occasionally, as in the case of "sensitivity," the factor of susceptibility acquires a mystic character through the omission of definition.

III.1.7. Other Terms

Such terms as withdrawal symptoms, adaptive cell metabolism, short-range accommodation, will be discussed in subsections of the main section III.4.4 and do not require any preliminary statements at this juncture.

III.2. The Question of Self-Inflicted Disease and the Ethical Involvements

Although the disease concept of alcoholism requires elucidation in terms of psychological and physiological formulations, the existence of ethical questions in this area cannot be overlooked, and it is most convenient to discuss these aspects first.

That acute alcohol intoxication is a self-inflicted abnormal condition, unless it results from an act of duress or through an accident, has been generally accepted in most of the higher cultures. Seneca, the Roman philosopher and lawyer (4 B.C.–A.D. 65), said "Drunkenness is nothing but a condition of insanity purposely assumed" (Epist. LXXXII). Perhaps similar statements have been made variously before Seneca, as such an opinion is implicit in the legal attitudes which made drunkenness an aggravating element in the commission of crimes in ancient Greek and Egyptian law. (It is still regarded as an aggravating circumstance in various law systems.)

It is, nevertheless, an entirely different matter to ask whether or not a voluntarily assumed or self-inflicted condition obtains in the instance of those species of alcoholism which are currently classified as diseases. While in the latter forms there is a succession of acute intoxications, it does not follow that the same rule applies to them as to intoxications by nonaddictive drinkers.

If it is assumed that certain species of alcoholism have the natures of diseases, it may be further assumed that the act which results in intoxication is outside the volitional sphere of the alcoholic. Nevertheless the loss of control is preceded by a period in which the ground for the disease is prepared and in which the question of impaired volition does not arise.

The question of self-inflicted disease in certain species of alcoholism does, of course, involve ethical considerations which must govern public attitudes toward the alcoholic, including legal thinking on these matters. The latter aspect is of particular importance to the status of the alcoholic in respect to compensation for accidents, unemployment, and so forth.

But is it in keeping with the scientific attitude toward alcoholism to consider the ethical elements? Most scientific writers have not touched upon the subject, but perhaps more because they felt that they could discuss alcoholism relevantly without ethical considerations than on account of a rejection of those considerations. A few scientific writers have at least stated that the ethical elements of "alcoholism" exist and should not be neglected.

Haggard and Jellinek (1942) stated: "However, when we understand the part played by the behavior of the intoxicated person in giving the alcohol problem its rank of capital importance among social issues, it becomes clear that a moral issue is also involved. It is desirable to lay stress on the medical nature of the alcohol problem and to disseminate the recognition of this in the widest possible circles, but it would be a mistake to disregard the moral aspect, for this furnishes a greater incentive for that cooperation by the citizen which is essential to the solution of the problem of alcohol."

In broaching the subject of morals and alcoholism, it seems in order to turn to the Nicomachean Ethics of Aristotle who, in spite of having been dethroned variously, is very much alive in modern formal ethics and thus also to some extent in legal thinking.

The following passages which deal with individual responsibility are of particular interest as they allude to disease and to drunkenness.

"That unrestraint is not strictly a vice (though it is perhaps vice in a sense), is clear; for unrestraint acts against deliberate choice, vice in accordance with it. But nevertheless in the actions that result from it it resembles vice: just as Demodocus wrote of the people of Miletus—

> Milesians are no fools, 'tis true,
> But yet they act as fools would do.

Similarly the understrained are not unjust, but they do unjust things. . . ." (Nicom. Eth. VII. 8, 2/3.)

"An involuntary act is therefore an act done in ignorance, or else one that though not done in ignorance is not in the agent's control, or is done under compulsion; . . . ." (V. 8, 3.)

"But persons under the influence of passion are in the same condition; for it is evident that anger, sexual desire, and certain other passions, actually alter the state of the body, and in some cases even cause madness. It is clear therefore that we must pronounce the unrestrained to 'have knowledge' only in the same way as men who are asleep or mad or drunk. Their using the language of knowledge is no proof that they possess it. . . ." (VII. 3, 7/8.)

"Again, though it is unreasonable to say that a man who acts unjustly or dissolutely does not wish to be unjust or dissolute, nevertheless this by no means implies that he can stop being unjust and become just merely by wishing to do so; any more than a sick man can get well by wishing, although it may be the case that his illness is voluntary, in the sense of being due to intemperate living and neglect of the doctors' advice. At the outset, then, it is true, he might have avoided the illness, but once he has let himself go he can do so no longer. . . . The unjust and profligate might at the outset have avoided becoming so, and therefore they are so voluntarily, although when they have become unjust and profligate it is no longer open to them not to be so. . . ." (III. 5, 13/14.)

"But our dispositions are not voluntary in the same way as are our actions. Our actions we can control from beginning to end, and we are conscious of them at each stage. With our dispositions, on the other hand, though we can control their beginnings, each separate addition to them is imperceptible, as is the case with the growth of a disease; though they are voluntary in that we were free to employ our capacities in one way or the other." (III. 5, 22.)

This latter paragraph of Aristotle, which distinguishes between the voluntary aspects of action and disposition, is of particular importance to the question under consideration. The other salient points are that unrestraint acts against deliberate choice and that "the unrestrained . . . 'have knowledge' only in the same way as men who are asleep or mad or drunk" and that "their using the language of knowledge is no proof that they possess it." Of further interest is the emphasis on the similarity between the growth of "dispositions" and "diseases" in which "each separate addition to them is imperceptible." Applying these principles to "uncontrolled drinking" it would appear that the acquisition of the "disease" is in a limited way voluntary, but that once the disease form is reached it is no different from other diseases, that is, it is not any more in the sphere of volition to terminate it, except through external means. Nevertheless, as will be seen later, even the limited voluntary aspect of the disease in the case of alcoholism is rather elusive and cannot be judged without taking into consideration some sociological aspects of drinking and drunkenness. The attitude of the total abstinence movements is that if alcoholism is a disease it is unquestionably a voluntarily acquired one. From the viewpoint of their philosophy this insistence is entirely justified. These movements are largely rooted in the tenets of the Methodist and Baptist churches and various pietist sects which regard any use of alcoholic beverages as a sin or in any case as immoral. The member of a society in which such an attitude is dominant is warned from the very beginning, and the mere fact that he uses alcoholic beverages suffices as proof positive that any disease which he may acquire from such use is self-inflicted.

In this instance it would be entirely unrealistic to raise the question whether any use of alcoholic beverages is actually immoral or sinful or not. The fact remains that in a society which is oriented by Methodist or Baptist or similar tenets any use of alcoholic beverages is by definition a trespass for which the transgressor must take the consequences.

On the other hand, such denominationally oriented societies do not form islands but are interspersed within cultural groups in which the simple use of alcoholic beverages is not regarded as immoral but constitutes an accepted and rather important social custom. In the intimate social intercourse between cultural groups in which the use of alcoholic beverages is an accepted custom and others in which such use is regarded as immoral, a considerable number of the members of the latter group will tend to conform with the custom of the former. Through that contravention they remain members of their respective churches only in a statistical sense and they become non-practicing or "part-practicing" members of their religious community.

Through their social standing, they may nevertheless remain of some importance in their respective churches. This development constitutes one of the greatest problems of the ministers of such churches and may induce some of these ministers to revise their judgments in relation to the ethical aspects of "alcoholism" as a disease. They will still emphasize the personal responsibility for the acquisition of the disease, but will tend to view it in a milder light and particularly to accept the condition as a disease once it has developed.

One may raise the question of the psychodynamics of the stand of the Puritan churches on the matter of alcoholism, and analyses to this effect have been undertaken by some investigators. Such analysis is no doubt interesting, but not highly relevant to the present discussion. Furthermore, on the goose–gander principle, one may ask also about the psychodynamics of the rejection of the sin conception of alcoholism.

Clinebell (1956) presents the results of a questionnaire survey among Protestant ministers who attended the Yale Summer School of Alcohol Studies. From the 146 questionnaires returned "it seems that the most common view held by these clergymen is that alcoholism begins as a personal sin and ends as a sickness. One who drinks exposes himself to the danger of becoming an alcoholic. Once the drinking has passed a certain point it is out of volitional control and becomes a sickness. He is responsible for having caught the compulsion or illness."

Clinebell believes that this is still an over-simplification of "the causation . . . the early drinking of the alcoholic is part of a total behavioral pattern which is strongly influenced by his damaged personality as well as by cultural pressures."

That alcoholism is a social sin was held by one of the respondents, who said: "Alcoholism is sin only in the sense that it is a sin attributed to society, especially a Christian society—that we have been unable to bring about a world free from the tensions and conflicts of the present day." Another put it this way: "It may be a sin, but it is more a symptom or an evidence of a sinful condition in some parts of our society."

Clinebell says that it is more difficult to grasp the complex ethical problem involved than to define alcoholism; ". . . each person will have to arrive at his own working hypothesis, based on his thinking and feeling about the fundamental problem of freedom, determinism, and personal responsibility."

There are in particular two considerations that render the question of a self-inflicted condition extremely elusive. One is, that in our culture, with the exception of some large subgroups—which, however, do not constitute closed entities—drinking is a custom to which society attaches an astonishingly great importance. In a sociological sense drinking is not an institution, but in some cultures—among them, in America—it comes very near to being one. The second consideration is the insidious nature of alcohol addiction. The

changes toward a pathological process are even more imperceptible
in the case of alcohol addiction than in most disease conditions,
since it develops within the context of an activity that belongs to
the "normal" and even valued behaviors of a society.

One does occasionally find poorly thought out arguments coming
from scientific writers such as, for instance, the eminent Swedish
eugenicist Dahlberg (1947). According to him a person is considered sick when his productive capacity decreases as a result of
involuntary processes occurring in his organism. Furthermore, he
states that if free will is denied, the difference between voluntary
and involuntary becomes meaningless and also the difference between disease and simulation. In that case the alcoholic must be
considered sick, as he is poisoned when he is drunk. If all alcoholics
are sick then all should be treated by physicians, but treatment for
alcoholism as used by physicians has only a partial success. The
superficiality of this argument hardly needs any comment.

In the view of the Roman Catholic Church, "abuse" rather than
drinking is the sin. This is also generally the view of the Anglican
Church, the Eastern Orthodox Churches, the Lutherans with the
exception of some synods, and a few other Protestant churches.

The Roman Catholic moral philosopher, Father John Ford (1951),
expresses the Catholic attitude thoughtfully and eloquently:

"A great many alcoholics (especially the secondary addicts) begin their
drinking by way of harmless self-indulgence. But this indulgence soon
becomes so attractive that it leads to sinful excess. Sins of deliberate
drunkenness become habitual. Little by little one moral ideal after another is allowed to grow dim. Honesty goes. Humility goes. Purity goes.
Increasing selfishness and egocentricity, increasing self-deception; increasing neglect of family, business and friends . . . . At all events my
experience with alcoholics and their own estimate of themselves after
they recover leads me to the conclusion that most of them undergo that
process of moral deterioration for which they are in varying degrees
responsible. I call this a sickness of the soul."

In relation to the question of self-inflicted disease, Father Ford
says the following:

"But supposing alcoholism to be a pathological condition, is it a condition for which the alcoholic himself is responsible? Objectively, many
alcoholics are little responsible for their condition either because their
addiction has a physiological basis over which they never had control,
or because, as in the case of certain primary addicts, they were compulsive drinkers almost from the beginning. They are spoken of sometimes

as addictive personalities. They consider themselves to have been alcoholics from the moment they took their first drink, and they are right."

But Father Ford distinguishes between the neurotic addict and the essential addict:

"Again, objectively, many other alcoholics *are* responsible for their condition because it is the result of long-continued excessive drinking for which they were responsible. To the extent that they foresaw addiction as the end-result or probable end-result of their excess they are responsible for not having prevented it.

"But subjectively, it seems to me, not many alcoholics are mortally guilty as far as the addiction itself is concerned. Very few foresee addiction. Very few believe that they will ever become drunks. There is nothing more insidious and blinding than alcoholic excess. Men and women who are beginning to drink too much are warned by their friends what will happen to them. But they do not believe it. They are convinced that they are going to be different from the horrible examples that are pointed out to them. They succeed in deceiving themselves. Add to this the general ignorance about the nature of alcoholism and the moral confusion with which the majority of them consider the question of excessive drinking itself."

One of the most important comments of Father Ford on the ethical aspects of alcoholism seems to me the following:

"Although the alcoholic may be powerless over alcohol, and unable at times directly to resist the craving for drink, yet it is within his power, generally speaking, to do something about his drinking. He is therefore responsible for taking the necessary means to get over his addiction."

For the elusive question of "alcoholism" as a self-inflicted condition the above discussion must suffice. Any longer exposition of the matter would not diminish the elusiveness except for those who have definitely made up their minds on this question.

Less elusive, but still not quite in the sphere of clear-cut judgments, to my mind, is another ethical aspect of all species of alcoholism. By this I mean that the prospective alcoholic (in whom the disease process has not started as yet), instead of putting out a constructive intellectual and emotional effort to cope with tensions, is taking recourse to the pharmacological effects of a drug which, through its cortical depressant effect, either gives the illusion of having done something about the causes of the tension or alternatively crowds these causes out from the contents of his awareness.

In this instance too some mitigating elements must be considered. One is that the drug used is, as one may say, a domesticated drug to which society has attached a certain prestige value. The other one is that the incipient addict for a long time is not aware of the use to which he is putting alcoholic beverages. For considerable periods the incipient alcoholic associates his feeling of well-being not with the ingestion of the alcoholic beverage but rather with the circumstances under which such ingestion takes place, that is, with certain localities and the companionship of certain persons and, perhaps, with some activities to which drinking is incidental. It is quite some time before it dawns upon the incipient alcoholic that it is the alcoholic beverage which affords him relief and even then he tends to persuade himself that that is not the case.

It is quite a different matter with the "inveterate drinker" or "essential alcoholic" (our delta alcoholic) whose copious intake stems either from the excessive standards of his cultural group or from the deliberate desire to be drunk for the fully recognized pleasure it may afford.

III.2.1. Legal Views

Interesting and important as the legal views on self-inflicted injury or disease may be, in the frame of the present study they can be presented in a fragmentary form only, through quoting one paper which has dealt cogently with this matter.

Lefcourt and Freedman (1949), two lawyers who have studied alcoholism, deplore that "our judiciary today does not approach this problem with understanding born of scientific knowledge and experience, particularly in civil cases involving disability provisions of insurance policies. Uninformed, precedent-conscious judges have castigated the insured by deeming alcoholism as a self-inflicted injury, a non-disease, and beyond the protection of such policies."

The authors refer to the only case of this nature which reached the Supreme Court of the United States. It is the case of Gaines v. Sun Life Assurance Company of Canada. A physician with a yearly income of $18,000 had become, after years of drug consumption, "incoherent, irritable, depressed and slovenly." In 1935 during the period of inebriety he failed to make premium payments. The insurer denied liability for disability payments. A Michigan court found no proof that the physician was mentally or physically ill, and so denied recovery. The court said that as a doctor he "knew" the consequences of his drinking and of drug addiction, and therefore his disability was "self-inflicted." The insured must have known, the court declared,

". . . that the drinking of intoxicating liquor might develop from a harmless indulgence into a baneful disease of chronic alcoholism. It is common knowledge and the warning is evident that indulgence in intoxicating liquors, unless restrained . . . , leads to excessive indulgence and one need not be warned that if continued, the craving for alcoholic liquor may lead to habitual drunkenness and the unfortunate self-imposed consequences."

The United States Supreme Court merely denied certiorari, but in effect endorsed the determination of the Michigan Court.

Lefcourt and Freedman make the following comment on the Michigan decision:

"Such a narrow-minded, temperate opinion of 'restraint' and 'craving' hardly accords with reality, where consumption of alcoholic beverages is commonplace. Surely the sipping of liquor at a social gathering, thought it may lead to chronic alcoholism years later, cannot be later deemed a 'self-imposed' cause of such unfortunate consequences. Yet such court opinions endowed with the virtues of the temperance movement of yesteryear would label alcoholic disability as 'self-inflicted,' and by 'relation back' penalize the insured for ever taking his first drink! . . . To attribute to the alcoholic such an intent to reach a level of mental and physical self-deterioration is to disavow the reasoning in law which led to the establishment of the legal presumption against suicide. Our courts have consistently held that the presumption against suicide is not overcome in such cases as shooting oneself in the head, jumping from a window at a considerable height above the ground, or swallowing a quantity of carbolic acid. This presumption against suicide or an intentional act resulting in death or total disability, should equally apply to the case of the chronic alcoholic, who unquestionably intends to drink intoxicating beverages, but does not 'intend to bring about the condition known as chronic alcoholism'."

The passage relating to the presumption against suicide is correctly stated, but the analogy seems doubtful to me.

Another instance cited by Lefcourt and Freedman is Lynch v. Mutual Life Insurance Company of New York. Parenthetically it may be remarked that this case was also written up in an editorial in a medical journal (*Medical Record*, 1947).

In this case a successful lawyer developed from a social drinker into one who drank to excess. For 3 years he was treated in different hospitals for alcoholism. In 1943 he was moved to his farm where his only activities were the preparation of his own meals and tending to livestock. The insurer did not challenge the fact of disability, but contended that the disability was self-inflicted. A Pennsylvania court concurred with that opinion or, to be more exact, concurred with it in this specific instance. Lefcourt and Freedman greatly deplored this decision but to the present writer a caveat expressed by the court seems to be of much greater significance.

"A caveat must be entered. We do not hold that chronic alcoholism is as a matter of law a self-inflicted injury. Our decision is that the evidence which the trial judge found credible justifies the conclusion that the disability suffered by this insured was self-inflicted. This question has been adjudicated in other jurisdictions under variant policies and facts, and differing conclusions have been announced by the courts. It is difficult to decide where the weight of authority lies. The validity of this judgment will rest upon the facts and the soundness of the reasons which impelled it."

In the case of Hurst v. Mutual Life Insurance Company of Boston, also cited by Lefcourt and Freedman, a Maryland court in 1938 considered medical and psychiatric rationales of alcoholism and rejected the insurance company's contention that alcoholism was a self-inflicted malady:

"There is no evidence on the record legally sufficient for the jury to find that the chronic alcoholism of the insured is the result of his conscious purpose or design . . . . On the contrary the testimony tends to show that he had vainly exercised his will to restrain and control his desire. The result of his disease is a weakness of will and of character which caused him to yield to liquors. The drinking in the first stages was voluntary but there was no testimony that the drinker was then aware of the latent danger in his habit; and so while his consumption of liquor was a voluntary act, yet his ignorance of its insidious effect does not make the act a voluntary exposure of himself to the unapprehended and unexpected danger of the disease of chronic alcoholism. The result of the indulgence of an appetite does not necessarily determine that the result was self-inflicted because if the actor does not apprehend or is ignorant of the danger of his act, he may not be held to have voluntarily inflicted upon himself the consequences."

The progress of medical knowledge on alcoholism slowly influences juridical decisions, but of course prudence demands that there must be a considerable lag between the progress of the two disciplines in this matter. On the other hand, juridical decisions will contribute much toward public attitudes.

As noted in another section of the present study, some of the

American states have passed laws for the establishment of state alcoholism programs and in those laws have expressis verbis incorporated the principle that alcoholism is a disease. Such declarations in a specific legislation, however, do not insure application of the principle in court cases but leave a wide margin of interpretation to the judge.

III.3. Psychological Formulations

Only the theses of students of "alcoholism" will be considered here. The popular writings on this subject, such as Blakeslee's (1952) well-conceived pamphlet, as well as the thousands of educational booklets and leaflets issued by voluntary agencies and state alcoholism programs, important as they are from the viewpoint of educational propaganda, do not contribute toward the clarification of the idea whether or not "alcoholism" is an illness.

Below are given three tabulations which contain statements about alcoholism (a) as an illness in psychological terms, (b) as the symptom of some psychological disorder, and (c) outright rejections of the illness conceptions. Tabulation of statements in terms of physiopathological illness and in terms of addiction in the strict pharmacological sense will be presented in other sections of this book.

EXPLICIT AND IMPLICIT FORMULATIONS OF "ALCOHOLISM"
AS A PSYCHOLOGICAL ILLNESS

Durfee (1938)	Alcoholism is not the result of a sickness, nor the sign of moral degradation, but a pathological expression of an inner need which requires treatment as any physical disease.
Strecker and Chambers (1938)	The alcoholic is sick in his personality. He has a psychic allergy to alcohol.
Moore (1939, 1942a, 1942b)	A mental illness. People do not drink to excess because they choose to do so. The alcoholic is a very sick man with a difficult and dangerous illness.
Seliger (1939)	A psychobiological allergy.
Carroll (1941)	A psychic allergy.
Strecker (1941)	A neurosis of emotional immaturity.
Tiebout (1945)	Alcoholism begins as a symptom, but later develops into a full syndrome which constitutes an illness in its own right.
Simmel (1948)	Alcoholism is an illness [interpreted in psychodynamic terms].

56 E. M. JELLINEK

Wiklund (1948)	Irrespective of whether alcoholism is considered as arising from psychopathology or from social influences, the alcoholic must be considered as sick.
Lolli (1949)	Addiction to alcohol is an illness resulting from lopsided growth: infantile traits in one part of the personality coexist with mature traits in another.
Lolli (1955)	Alcohol addiction is an illness which seeks the blending of psychological and physiological pleasures.
Wexberg (1949, 1951b)	Alcoholism is a disease [interpreted in psychodynamic terms] and a conditioned reflex with components on a pharmacological level.
Hirsh (1950)	Alcoholism is a disease of the total personality.
Kieve (1950)	Alcoholism is a disease and a form of progressive compulsive self-degradation.
Straus and McCarthy (1951)	A condition in which the drinking of alcoholic beverages becomes persistent, repetitive, uncontrollable and progressively destructive of the psychological and social functioning of the individual.
World Health Organization (1951)	Alcoholism (or rather certain forms of it) is a disease process.
McCullough (1952)	An emotional illness.
Reeve (1953)	Recognition of alcoholism as a disease is the most important single factor in the recovery of millions of man hours wasted each year by problem drinkers in industry.
Ullman (1953)	Alcohol addiction is a disease dependent upon a psychological state and made possible by the sociological variable of attitudes toward drinking and by the tension-reducing effect of alcohol.
Vogel (1953)	[Not quite evident that the author means illness, but this idea is strongly suggested.] As a result of insatiability, dependence develops, gradually nullifying all other interests and initiating the familiar vicious circle.
Brunner-Orne and Orne (1954)	A psychological illness viewed primarily as a method of adjustment.
Müller (1954)	Alcoholism is a disease.
Querido (1954)	The craving for alcohol or the inability to control one's drinking, in itself, may be a disease.
Glatt (1955)	Alcoholism is a disease [interpreted in psychodynamic terms].
Rosenman (1955)	Alcoholism is a psychological illness.

American Medical Association, Committee on Alcoholism (1956)	[Statement approved by House of Delegates.] The Council on Mental Health, its Committee on Alcoholism, and the profession in general, recognize this syndrome of alcoholism as an illness which justifiably should have the attention of physicians.
Button (1956a, 1956b)	A process in which the original reasons for drinking ultimately become unimportant to the drinker and the once painful act of drinking and hangover become relatively gratifying. The organism adapts itself physically and psychologically to chronic drunkenness.
Conger (1956)	Alcoholism is interpreted in terms of a reinforcement theory of learning, but not to the exclusion of physiopathological and psychopathological factors.
Lazarus (1956)	Alcoholism is a psychobiological malfunction which manifests itself in craving for alcohol.
Pfeffer (1956)	Alcoholism begins as a symptom of anxiety and becomes a clinical syndrome with psychological, physical and social symptoms.
Wilkins (1956)	Alcoholism belongs to the deprivational stress diseases, in both their psychological and physiological aspects.
Kruse (1957)	Alcoholism is a pathological process even in its initial stages. It has finally come to be recognized as a disease.
Sessions (1957)	An illness of that aspect of man frequently described as spiritual.

FORMULATIONS OF "ALCOHOLISM" AS A SYMPTOM OF A
PSYCHOLGICAL ILLNESS

Explicit Formulations

Monsour (1948)	A symptom of underlying personality structure and psychoneurotic conflicts.
Brocklehurst (1949)	Secondary (compensatory) alcoholism is a symptom of personality dysfunction.
Laidlaw (cit. Texon, 1949)	Alcoholism is a symptom of compulsion neurosis.
Newton (1949)	A symptom of a neurosis of predominantly hysterical type.
Réquet (1950)	A symptom of neurosis.
Osborn (1951)	Alcoholism, from a medical point of view, is more a symptom than a disease.
Larimer (1952b)	Alcoholism, like hypertension, is not a disease but is symptomatic of underlying pathology.

Lemkau (1952)	A symptom of social unrest and psychological and possibly physiological maladjustment.
Berner and Solms (1953)	In neurotics, alcoholism is often a symptom which will later be replaced by other symptoms.
Sherfey (1955)	The drinking of the alcoholic represents a symptom of various illnesses.

Implicit Formulations

Diethelm (cit. Texon, 1949)	It has not been determined as yet whether there is a physiological craving or a psychological compulsive need in alcoholism.
Perrin (1949)	In a certain proportion of alcoholics, symptoms of personality conflicts predominate; in another proportion, environmental influences.
Wall (1953)	The drinking of the alcoholic is only a part of the problem of the personality.

The following references pertain to papers which postulate frustrations, tensions, anxieties and various maladjustments in the etiology of "alcoholism," but they neither mention the term illness nor suggest an illness conception. It is inferred, therefore, that they think of "excessive" drinking as a relief from the above mentioned traits. In other words, they regard alcoholism as symptomatic of the psychological factors. Some of these authors may hold that "alcoholism" is an illness, but they have given no indication of such an opinion: Acevedo Castillo and Calvo (1949), Berreman (1950), Bertagna (1953), Cathell (1954), Deshaies (1946–1947), Duchêne et al. (1952), Figuerido (1947), Forizs (1953, 1954), Meri (1948), Mueller (1949), Ødegard (1952), Oltman and Friedman (1953), Orelli (1952), Peters (1955), Rommelspacher (1953), Schaefer (1954), Schultz (1953), Seliger (1949), J. A. Smith (1954), Stefanacci (1953), Tähkä (1954), Teirich (1952), Wallinga (1956), Wyss (1949), Zurukzoglu and Nussbaum (1952).

REJECTION OF THE ILLNESS CONCEPTION OF "ALCOHOLISM"

| Dahlberg (1947) | If all alcoholics are sick, then all should be treated by physicians, but treatment for alcoholism, as used by physicians, has had only a partial success. |
| Björk (1950) | Alcoholism is due to defective superego development and is therefore a moral question. In its destructive aspects, alcoholism must be viewed as a crime. |

Giscard and Giraudon (1951)	Alcoholism is a sign of a weak character. The treatment of alcoholism should be combined with punitive measures.
McGoldrick (1954)	Alcoholism is no more a disease than thievery, or lynching; like these, it is the product of a distortion of outlook, a way of life bred of ignorance and frustration.
Brown (1955)	The designation of alcoholism as a disease limits and poorly describes the phenomenon which makes the man a problem, namely his behavior.
Lewis (1956)	Alcoholism is not a disease entity, but disease may be a useful label for it.
Lake (1957)	There is no such thing as "alcoholism." Physiologists have not discovered either a physiological craving or a specific physiological cure. Many remedies help but always in conjunction with some promotional or social condition. Nobody has dissected alcoholics and found in them anxiety or fear or bashfulness.

A perusal of the above tabulations may give the impression that there must be a great deal behind the brief sloganlike excerpts. Unfortunately, that is true of not more than 20 per cent of the papers cited in the first two lists, and those papers will be discussed in much greater detail as will some other papers that were not listed because they did not lend themselves to the tabular presentation. The fact remains that in 80 per cent of the papers cited, there is little depth behind the label, disease.

"There are questions which in practically every paper on alcoholism receive brief mention, but the discussion is never carried beyond the stage of casual suggestion. Nevertheless, these suggestions are repeated so frequently that they tend to become accepted as well-established theories in spite of the fact that they have not been examined as to their implications and involvements." (Jellinek, 1944.)

Wexberg (1951a) has expressed this idea more graphically: "In no other area of research and social or medical endeavor have slogans so extensively replaced theoretical insight, as a basis for therapeutic action, as in alcoholism. The emotional impact of the statement, 'Alcoholism is a sickness,' is such that very few people care to stop to think what it actually means."

In line with this predominant vagueness is the fact that there are no particular differences between the psychiatric or psychological ideas on which the verdict, "disease," is based and those which

lead to the conclusion, "symptom." There are, fortunately, thoughtful exceptions on both sides.

Vagueness, here, refers to the lack of any attempt, in the majority of theses, to explain a pathological process in the terms of those
psychological traits or functions which are invoked as important
factors in "alcoholism." In their concern over the important psychological factors—which in many "alcoholics" are present at the start
of the drinking career, and in many others not—there is a tendency
on the part of writers on alcoholism to forget about the alcoholic
process. This process is thought of, all too frequently, merely as
drinking getting worse and worse. The possible role of alcohol—
which, in the quantities absorbed and the high frequency of intake,
represents a powerful drug—is entirely neglected. The clinical picture of certain species of alcoholism is so incomplete that, with the
fewest exceptions, no analysis has been attempted of "craving" or
"dependence" or "compulsion;" nor has it seemed necessary to most
writers to describe and explain acquired increased tolerance, withdrawal symptoms, loss of control, or the major behavior changes,
not to speak of such matters as the changes in the drinking pattern.
Craving is often inferred on the grounds that if the "alcoholic"
drinks again and again, in spite of disastrous experiences, there
must be a craving or compulsion present. The acquired increased
tolerance is boiled down to the drinker's learning, anticipating and
compensating for the effects of alcohol. One hears of withdrawal
symptoms almost exclusively in papers on the treatment of acute
intoxication. Except for solitary drinking, changes in the general
and drinking behaviors are mentioned only by a few students of
alcoholism who use Jellinek's "phases" or their own modifications
of it.

The same remarks apply to psychoanalytic conceptions of alcoholism. Even the most recondite psychodynamic theory cannot account for many of the essential aspects of "alcoholism." It is good
to hear such an outstanding analyst as Alexander (1956) saying:

"Exclusive preoccupation with the psychodynamic factors and the
cultural influences entails the danger of overlooking an important factor
that might be decisive in the most malignant cases. I mean the physiologic constitution. There are clinical observations that suggest the importance of the individual's physiologic constitution, particularly in the
malignant cases. The range of susceptibility to alcohol in different persons is strikingly great. There is no proof that this can be explained
solely from the differences in personality structure. Moreover, in the

advanced cases the craving for alcohol has a great similarity to the craving in drug addiction, in which the physiologic adaptation to the drug is well established. This explains the uncontrollable power of the craving."

It is of particular interest that those psychiatrists and analysts who have gone to the pains of elaborating a psychological exposition of "alcoholism" as an illness, have not been able to do so without taking recourse to conceptions of alcoholism as a drug addiction in the full pharmacological sense. As will be seen later, Wexberg leaned so heavily on the pharmacological aspects that his psychological explanations of the process crumbled without his noticing it.

Pfeffer (1956), too, adapts his ideas of the psychological process of alcoholism to a basic addictive process in the pharmacological sense: "Alcoholism may be regarded as an addiction, as evidenced by loss of control over the use of alcohol, change in tolerance, a withdrawal syndrome and the relinquishing of all other interests in favor of a preoccupation with the use of alcohol. . . . These are the usual over-all criteria used to determine whether or not a substance is an addicting one."

There are others who consider that alcohol needs to be taken into account in the "illness of alcoholism," but who do not allude to a pharmacological addictive process. Thus Vogel (1953) says that in discussing the problem of alcoholism, the first major problem is to define the role that alcohol plays. And Aamark (1955), who sees alcohol as the cause of the loss of control, feels that if alcoholism is conceived of as a disease, it must be distinguished from health by some definite signs. It is significant that small amounts of alcohol create the desire for more in the alcoholic so that soon he is unable to control his consumption.

There are a fair number of students of alcoholism who conceive of it as a drug addiction pure and simple, but these will be discussed in a separate section.

The rejections of the illness conception are not more carefully thought out than the positive psychological formulations of it. Furthermore, the rejections frequently display a strong emotional tone. Interestingly enough, the most strongly worded negative formulations stem from lay therapists rather than from physicians.

Of the psychological traits and functions that are emphasized as etiological factors in various species of alcoholism, anxiety is perhaps the most prominent. It may be noted that this trait was first reported on by Magnus Huss (1852), who was not a psychiatrist but an internist. He was struck by the frequent occurrence of this emotion in the "chronic alcoholics" at his hospital.

As anxiety is a harassing state and as alcohol is undoubtedly a tension-reducing substance, it is quite understandable that the latter should be sought in instances of gross anxiety. This may be particularly the case when an individual has not learned to use other means for the reduction of this troublesome state of mind, and when social custom facilitates the use of alcoholic beverages.

Horton's (1943) anthropological study has clearly shown that there is a statistical contingency between the degree of anxiety generated by subsistence insecurity and the fear of institutionalized witchcraft on the one side and the degree of tribal drunkenness on the other.

Masserman and Yum (1946) have provided some experimental evidence that the paralyzing anxiety arising from a conflict situation in cats can be overcome to a degree through ingestion of alcohol which solves the conflict situation. This experiment shows that use of alcohol is doubtlessly a *possible* means of anxiety reduction, but not that anxiety is a necessary precondition for the use of that substance.

It must be considered, furthermore, that the use of alcohol to a degree of intoxication may itself precipitate strong anxiety, and there is much clinical evidence to this effect. As a matter of fact, other symptoms may arise from such anxiety. Thus, the great prevalence of anxiety in some species of alcoholism is not per se evidence of its existence in a pre-alcoholic phase. In an important proportion of "alcoholics," however, gross anxiety in the premorbid state can be traced. In this relation it may be mentioned that Horton (1943) has noted that "counteranxieties," e.g., the fear of breaking sex taboos, may inhibit the seeking of relief of anxiety through intoxication.

Frustration, with its emotional consequences (among them anxiety), is one of the most frequently mentioned conditions for starting the frequent and large intake of alcoholic beverages. However, not variation in degrees of frustration but rather differences in capacity to cope with frustration would account for relief drinking.

Wexberg (1951a) expressed the opinion that it was indeed justifiable "to consider a low frustration threshold as one of a variety of personality traits which may—but do not necessarily—predispose to addiction. This low frustration threshold is not likely to be caused by addiction. . . . There is some evidence in the dynamics of many alcoholic patients that they were less able to 'take it' than the average person a long time before they started drinking to excess. When something went wrong, when they failed to attain a goal they had been hoping for, when a girl walked out on them, they became desparately unhappy to the point that they 'just had to' do something about it. . . .

"It must be made clear at this point that the low frustration threshold, important as it may be, is not regarded as the one and only feature constituting the prealcoholic personality. It may not even be indispensable, though I am inclined to believe that it is. Another feature . . . is aim-inhibited hostility. . . .

"It is true that one group of alcoholics answers the description of the schizothymic, and for these alcoholics it may be assumed that an innate factor at least contributes to their low frustration threshold. This, however, obviously holds only for a minority of cases."

The concept of frustration tolerance is used by a number of students of alcoholism, e.g., Vogel (1953) and Wellman (1955a, 1955b). It would be difficult to trace the first usage of this expression, but I have heard it, read it, and used it for the past 20 years.

Wexberg's contention that the low frustration threshold is not likely to be caused by addiction, may be questioned. The demoralizing effect of frequent high degree intoxications may greatly undermine the resistance to any form of the hardships of life.

The idea of frustration tolerance may be extended to tension tolerance in general, or in other words, to the ability to cope with tensions. The most common form of pre-alcoholic vulnerability is a low capacity for handling tensions. Nevertheless, this should not be generalized either to the several species of alcoholism nor to all individuals of a given species of alcoholism.

The common designation of escapist for "alcoholics" only brings under one heading the drinking for relief from frustrations, anxieties, suppressed hostility, and any other forms of tension. This is what one may presume is meant by Bird (1949) when he speaks of escape from internal reality.

While all these characteristics can create a favorable terrain for the development of the process of alcoholism, they do not explain the process itself, nor are they the exclusive terrain for "alcoholism." In the delta alcoholic ("inveterate drinker" or "primary addict"), who predominates in the viticultural countries and who exists in America too, the cultural patterns of a nation or a cultural subgroup play a greater role than individual vulnerabilities. Furthermore, it must be granted that pre-alcoholic physiological anomalies may constitute the starting point, at least in some specific, as yet not identifiable, proportion of "alcoholics."

The element of pleasure produced by alcohol as an etiological factor of "alcoholism" is also quite common and of course the euphoria-producing nature of a drug does play a decisive role in its addiction-forming capacity. On the other hand, its role in initiating the process of alcoholism is questionable. Wexberg (1951a) says:

"Of course, we have already established the fact that extreme lust for some specific pleasure—'craving'—is a common attribute of all addicts, *secondary* to addiction: progressive destruction of other values (personality metastasis) leaves the specific chemical satisfaction, whatever it may be, as the only survivor. However, the possibility exists that there might be such a thing as primarily increased lust for pleasure, which, together with a multiplicity of concurring factors, would account for addiction. . . .

"We have no right to postulate a pre-alcoholic pleasure-craving personality as predisposing to alcoholism. Such a theory would imply measurable libido, which, it is suggested, is not a workable hypothesis."

That the pleasure element is rather a product which perpetuates drinking than one which initiates it, is expressed also by Pohlisch (1954):

"It is not escape from reality, but a positive assertion of existence that causes people to drink; when the feeling of well-being produced by alcohol is experienced repeatedly, a habitual need for pleasure will develop. The more a people use alcohol as a substance for pleasure, the greater the danger of developing alcoholism for those who originally show no psychiatric abnormalities. But there are also those whose personalities are abnormal, and who will become alcoholics because they seek not pleasure but a toxin."

Apart from such isolated manifestations of forms of psychological vulnerability, neurosis is suggested by many students of alcoholism as the basis of various forms of alcoholism; but as no specific alcoholic neurosis has ever been shown, the pre-alcoholic existence of such a personality disorder cannot be used in order to show that "alcoholism" is an illness. The argument cannot go beyond heavy drinking as a symptom of a given neurosis. Minor vulnerabilities may, under some circumstances, initiate the heavy use of alcoholic beverages. The problem or situation which is "solved" by alcohol need not be on the neurotic level. The problem-solving function of alcohol can be accepted even if one rejects the assumption that all or even most alcoholics have either a neurotic or a psychopathic origin. If one asserts that the source of alcoholism is "entirely of an economic nature," that, for example, the slum dweller is "forced" to frequent the tavern in order to escape his dreary environment and is thus "forced" to become alcoholic, one runs up against the fact that not all the slum dwellers of the world become alcoholics, but only 5 or 10 per cent of them. One cannot say, therefore, that economic conditions "forced" them but rather their inability to cope with this economic condition through those emotional or intellectual means which hundreds of thousands of their fellow sufferers successfully used. Thus, above and beyond the economic factors, which undoubtedly play a large role, there must be a personality factor which avails itself of the function of alcohol.

While Wexberg's paper on "Alcoholism as a sickness" (1951a) is a most thoughtful document and the only one in the alcohol literature that constitutes a major effort to explain "alcoholism" as a psychological illness, he actually does not show the development of the illness in psychological terms but demonstrates only the psychological elements that facilitate development. On the other hand, he has pointed out some of the criteria of an illness conception.

He distinguishes eight possible meanings which may attach to "alcoholism as a disease." Of these meanings only five are of relevance to the present discussion. These are: (a) that excessive drinking produces mental, emotional or personality changes which result in sickness of the person involved; (b) that uncontrolled excessive drinking represents a compulsion comparable to those in obsessive–compulsive neuroses; (c) that alcoholism is based on, and caused by, some preexisting biochemical condition in the body, such as allergy or adrenal cortex insufficiency; (d) that alcoholism is based on *specific* deviations (from the normal) of the total personality which make a person an alcoholic even before he knows there is such a thing as liquor; (e) that "uncontrolled" excessive drinking (loss of control) per se is a sickness.

Wexberg accepts formulation (a):

"Apart from organic deterioration, however, it is taken for granted that prolonged excessive drinking produces what may be legitimately called an alcoholic personality which appears to be specific and closely correlated, in many cases, with excessive drinking. There is no need to look for organic factors which may account for the typicality of the clinical picture. The far-reaching identity of the experience of progressive alcoholism may account for the uniformity of personality changes in alcoholics: their progressive loss of interests in life; their loss of emotional stamina which makes them 'go to pieces' for minor reasons; their irritability; their lack of persistence of effort in work and otherwise; their dishonesty . . . their loss of 'sense of honor'; their superficial sentimentalism and tearfulness; their callousness toward suffering caused by them; their indifference toward human relations and other cultural values and so forth. It is entirely justified to consider these characteristics as a syndrome quite typical for many alcoholics—though certainly not for all of them—and describe it as the disease 'alcoholism'."

Jellinek (1953) has pointed out that while Wexberg has described a syndrome, all that the latter author's formulation amounts to is that prolonged excessive drinking *produces* a disorder which may be called alcoholic deterioration. That this is "produced by excessive drinking" implies the pharmacological process of addiction, and in another paper (Wexberg, 1951b) the implication becomes explicit. This will be discussed later. Wexberg has recognized the significance of behavior changes but he has not isolated the most significant changes, nor has he made adequate conclusions as to disease process.

According to Jellinek (1953) the importance of the changes in psychological and social behavior is that they lead to changes in drinking behavior. The excessive drinker who has been using alcohol intoxication as a means of "problem solution," while still continuing that use is, in addition—and probably more prominently—using alcohol to remedy the psychological, physiological and social stresses and strains generated by heavy drinking. Only when this occurs in conjunction with acquired increased tolerance, withdrawal symptoms, inability to abstain or loss of control may the excessive user of alcohol be termed an *alcohol addict* and his drinking behavior regarded as a disease process.

It seems that some species of alcoholism show a progression which strongly suggests a true disease process, but apparently as yet no one has given proof that a specific disease condition gives rise to the heavy drinking at the beginning of the alcoholic career. For the initiating phase, the postulation of psychological and cultural factors seems adequate, but not beyond that.

Wexberg takes exception to etiological theories which postulate a physiopathological origin as he maintains that the pathology referred to by the proponents of such theories is a consequence and not a cause of the heavy drinking. It will be shown later that such an argument is not necessarily valid.

The psychoanalytic conception of alcoholism is not noted for its clarification of the illness conception of "alcoholism." The relevant psychodynamic theories have been reviewed by Bowman and Jellinek (1942a), Gibbins (1953) and Higgins (1953). Since then nothing of particular interest has been produced in that field.

The gist of these theories which, according to Higgins (1953), are based on Radó and Knight, may be schematized as a threat of oral narcissistic deprivation followed by anxiety which leads to drinking and to elation. Higgins does not dispute the existence of such a mechanism but believes that a threat to the satisfaction of oral narcissistic needs is not always the primary initiating agent. This modification of theory is based on interviews with 52 patients at the Cincinnati General Hospital. He grants that alcohol is used to diminish the awareness of anxiety, but the anxiety may arise from a conflict over sadistic genitosexual or other impulses or from activation of psychological defense mechanisms against such impulses. Also, alcohol may facilitate the operation of defense mechanisms. His revised hypothesis is that

"A predisposed person (and the predisposition may represent fixations at various levels of personality development) is confronted with a difficult life situation; the 'difficult life situation' may or may not be one which has as its primary component an 'oral threat'; an attempt is made through drinking to handle the anxiety aroused by this conflict. The drinking may serve as a defense through various channels: it may bring diminished awareness of internal or external stress, or it may facilitate defenses previously inhibited."

What Higgins calls "predisposition" is nothing but a greater proneness to alcoholism than is shown by others, and is merely a suggestion of the function of alcohol in highly vulnerable persons. Thus, as far as the illness conception is concerned, the psychodynamic theories of "alcoholism" do not go beyond what the nonanalytic psychiatric and the formal psychological theories have to offer.

Button (1956b), who endeavored to validate psychodynamic hypotheses through psychometric tests, offers an elaborate schema of the psychodynamic factors in "alcoholism." However, he notes that

"The same constellation of factors might very well result, in another person, in nonalcoholic behavior. The control groups used for various parts of the psychometric and experimental conditions whose results led to the present theory are varied; in no case did statistically significant or nonsignificant differences between the alcoholics and the controls imply that the behaviors in question were specific for either alcoholics or nonalcoholics. Thus, while the present schema does seem to be descriptive of a putatively representative sample of male alcoholics, it is not possible to say that it might not just as well describe some other clinical syndrome."

In the case of the alpha alcoholic (as distinguished from the addictive gamma and delta alcoholics) psychological explanations are sufficient, as with him relief drinking on a large scale is the beginning as well as the end. His drinking remains symptomatic throughout his drinking career and there are no noticeable changes of a neurophysiological nature, such as occur in the addictive species of alcoholism, and many fewer behavioral changes. For the addict, more explanation must be given than merely what alcohol accomplishes for his troubles. In the absence of an interpretation beyond symptomatic relief, the illness conception is not substantiated by psychological and psychiatric arguments.

Among the French students of alcoholism, the predominating etiological idea is still social custom and "habituation." Lately, however, an increasing number of French psychiatrists and other physicians have come to a consideration of individual psychological elements. Prominent among those students is Deshaies (1946–1947) according to whom the various possible motivations leading to alcoholism include imitation of accepted customs; "derivation," or the carrying over of conflicts and solving them by means of drinking; compensation for feelings of inferiority; aggression to satisfy desires for punishment; and morbid impulses. The latter occur in the defective or psychasthenic personality for which alcohol increases tension instead of relieving it. The hedonistic tendency of the individual, combined with social customs and polarized by a toxicophilic attitude, creates the basis for alcoholism.

Generally, French physicians—to the extent that they consider psychological vulnerability at all—do not intend to infer that "alcoholism" is a psychological illness, but wish to imply the symptomatic nature of heavy drinking. Among them are Bertagna (1953),

THE DISEASE CONCEPT OF ALCOHOLISM

Desruelles and Fellion (1951), Dublineau and Honoré (1955), Duchêne (1949), Duchêne, Schutzenberger, et al. (1952), Lemieux (1949), Réquet (1950), Royer (1953) and to some extent Dérobert (1953). There are, however, exceptions, and they are on the increase. Fouquet (1951, 1952; Fouquet and Clavreul, 1956) is one of the few French physicians who speaks of alcoholism as an illness per se, but while he assigns a role to psychological factors, he leans toward physiopathological conceptions and will be considered later. Laurent (1958) and Paris (1958) are much more emphatic, even evangelistic, about the illness conception.

Quite frankly, the majority of psychiatric and psychological writers, Americans or others, who assert that alcoholism is an illness have not gone to the trouble to analyze the matter, but take it for granted that this is a well-established fact.

About all that 80 per cent of the psychiatric writers mean by their statements is that alcoholism is not a moral depravity or weakness of volition, but that the alcoholic is suffering from some undefined condition which either "compels" him to drink or makes it impossible for him to utilize alcohol "correctly." Other investigators, however, have been more explicit. The greatest effort has been made by those who have spoken of alcoholism as a "psychological addiction."

III.3.1. "Psychological Addiction"

At this juncture it may be in order to repeat that—for the purpose of the present study—alcoholism has been very broadly defined as any drinking which results in any damage to the individual or to society. Further, two species of alcoholism have been singled out which may be particularly considered in the light of the conception of "alcoholism" as an illness.

One species involves loss of control, which extends to the amount consumed on a given occasion, while the ability to determine the initiation of a new bout, i.e., the ability to abstain for shorter or longer periods, remains intact. This occurs predominantly in the gamma alcoholic.

In the other species the ability to abstain from alcoholic beverages even for one day is lost, but the drinker retains control over the amounts he consumes. This is predominantly characteristic of the delta alcoholic.

The first species is the predominant one in America and the

Anglo-Saxon countries of the world, but not to the exclusion of the second. The second species is predominant in the viticultural countries (most of them Latin countries), but not to the exclusion of the first.

In the instance of the second pattern, alcoholic beverages are ingested every day in such a way that small quantities of alcohol are present in the blood stream at practically all times of the day and night. After several years of such drinking, a day of abstinence brings about withdrawal symptoms, although the drinker may show frank intoxication only on scattered occasions. I am postulating (in section 4.4.4 of this chapter) that this behavior is evidence of adaptive cell metabolism. Thus, there is no need to ask whether this pattern may be viewed in the light of the addictive processes as discussed below.

On the other hand, the question arises whether "loss of control" can be explained in terms of the addictive processes and, if so, how this affects the question of the "disease" nature of this particular species of alcoholism and how it modifies the idea that "alcoholism is not in the bottle, but in the man."

These two species of alcoholism are the only ones of which one may legitimately speak in terms of addiction. In other species of alcoholism, including alpha alcoholics, as defined for the purpose of the present study, the use of the word addiction is purely metaphorical.

There are papers which deal with the truly addictive species of alcoholism, but nevertheless apply the term addiction figuratively and, on the other hand, a considerable number of papers discuss these species in terms of pharmacological addiction but use the expression "alcoholism" instead of addiction.

Of those papers that deal with the etiology of "alcoholism"— not counting papers which pertain to some highly specific experimental aspect only—and that are considered in the present study, about 35 per cent use the term addiction or its foreign language equivalents.

The majority of American students of alcohol problems prefer the less specific designation alcoholism and there is a scattering of preference for the term problem drinker which has found much greater favor in magazine and newspaper articles.

The term "alcohol addiction" is rejected by some investigators in this field because they do not see in "alcoholism" any characteristics which would suggest an addictive process, either in the psychological or in the pharmacological sense. Others have an outright aversion to the label addiction in connection with alcohol because they fear an identification with drug addiction. In order to avoid any possible equation with the drug addictions they may go so far as to deny the occurrence of any phenomenon which could be equated with elements of drug addiction. Thus, as I have pointed out elsewhere (Jellinek, 1953) some psychiatric writers on alcoholism deny the occurrence of withdrawal symptoms. It would seem that more than a few students of alcoholism bend far over backward in order to escape any possible tainting of alcoholism—which is related to a highly valued social custom—through contamination with anything suggesting the despised use of narcotics.

Such an attitude is understandable to some extent, as narcotics addiction is frowned upon in the American culture to a considerably greater degree than in European countries. The narcotics habit or the use of narcotics is regarded here as so reprehensible that Dwight Anderson (1942) advocated that the term alcohol addiction should not be used, in order not to offend the "alcoholic" who was about to accept treatment. This warning made an impression at least on some therapists, although to my knowledge many members of Alcoholics Anonymous speak of themselves as alcohol addicts. I used the term alcohol addiction in 1942 and thoughtlessly repudiated it in 1946, but later reverted to that usage.

The use of the term alcohol addiction may or may not indicate that the employers of this term regard the form of alcoholism that they may have in mind as a process similar to the one operative in the various drug addictions. In other words the expression addiction in connection with alcohol does not necessarily imply a pharmacological connotation.

In everyday language, the word "addicted" is used mainly as defined in Webster's New International Dictionary:[2] "given up or over (to); devoted (to)." And addiction denotes "state of being addicted; indulged inclination; also habituation, esp. to drugs."

Actually the word addiction is used ordinarily in a "psychological" sense, and applied to activities in which obviously no pharmacological process is involved, as for instance, a "theater addict."

In psychology and psychiatry too, it is quite customary to speak

[2] Webster's New International Dictionary of the English Language, 2d ed. Springfield, Mass; Merriam; 1958.

of such behaviors as gambling, kleptomania and nymphomania as addictions (e.g., Gabriel and Kratzmann, 1936) although the mechanisms of a pharmacological process are obviously not involved in those behaviors.

A distinction must be made between alcohol addiction as conceived in a purely psychological sense and a strict pharmacological conception of an addiction. This latter conception involves such criteria as acquired increased tissue tolerance, adaptive cell metabolism, withdrawal symptoms, and craving; in the case of alcohol addiction (gamma alcoholism) loss of control must be added, unless the addiction is of the type which involves only the inability to abstain (delta alcoholism).

In my opinion, the term addiction should be applied only in those instances which comply with the above criteria even if the conception is entirely psychological. But in the latter case, the psychological hypotheses must give a reasonable tentative explanation of all the critical phenomena.

The strict pharmacological conception of addiction, on the other hand, does not exclude factors on the psychological and sociological levels, particularly in the preparation of the terrain on which addiction develops.

It is thus acceptable in psychological and psychiatric parlance to speak of a "psychological" addiction to alcohol; acceptable, that is, if one should be able to talk reasonably about this process in terms of symbolic factors.

It must be pointed out that in a number of papers which use the expression alcohol addiction, "psychological" addiction is implied without the writers' seeing the necessity of explaining the symbolic process which could account for the loss of control or for the inability to abstain, as they assume that it is evident what "psychological" addiction is.

Some writers on alcohol addiction find it sufficient to refer to frustrations, guilt feelings, inferiority, resentments and generalized tensions to justify the postulation of a dependence upon alcohol on a symbolic level. While the emotions named above may satisfactorily account for the individual's seeking of relief through the action of alcohol, they do not cover without further elaboration the loss of control or the inability to abstain from alcohol, either of which should be among the criteria for employing the term addiction. But, of course, these writers either do not require a stipulation of such criteria, as they think of addiction in the vernacular sense, i.e., as one's "being given over" to the use of alcohol, or else they feel that the critical behaviors can be accounted for by simple symbolic processes which are self-evident.

Thus Ullman (1952), speaking of the "psychological mechanism of alcohol addiction," says:

"It is suggested that the formation of an addiction is dependent upon a psychological state made possible in part by the sociological variable of attitudes toward drinking and the physiological fact of the tension-reducing effect of alcohol. It is posited that (a) when a person is highly motivated to drink or there is some emotional arousal with regard to drinking, and (b) such drinking is accompanied by a stress situation, and (c) these circumstances occur on several occasions when a sufficient amount of alcohol is imbibed to produce a tension-reducing effect, then alcohol addiction will result."

It must be granted that such symbolic mechanisms as Ullman suggests are part of the picture, and they are an important part, in leading up to the process of addiction. On the other hand, they do not explain the addictive characteristics, namely, the loss of control in which the continued ingestion of alcohol brings about effects opposed to the objects of the drinker, nor do they explain acquired increased tolerance, withdrawal symptoms, and so forth.

Diethelm (1951), who operates with the conceptions of resentment, anxiety and tension, does not fall into the above category of investigators, as he and his associates relate the symbolic factors to nonsymbolic factors (certain chemicals in the blood stream) which may—but do not necessarily—explain the behaviors in the addictive species of alcoholism.

There are, however, proponents of a symbolic process in alcohol addiction who proceed to hypothesize the mechanism of such a process even as far as loss of control is concerned.

Simmel (1948) distinguishes the social drinker, the reactive drinker, the neurotic alcoholic and the addict. In his conception, if the ego of the neurotic alcoholic regresses beyond the phallic, oral and anal stages to its earliest ego state, the alcoholic becomes an addict. This, of course, implies a severe psychopathological process which hollows out the personality and impairs the learned restraints. Nevertheless, the loss of control—if one has seen it in the course of a drinking bout—does not seem to be explained by this suggested psychodynamic process.

Lolli (1955) stresses that while the "symptomatic drinker" (alpha alcoholic) wishes to escape from a certain condition, the addict is seeking to create a condition in which a blending of "pleasures of the body and mind" results and an attempt is made to maintain the blood alcohol level at a point where these pleasures are experienced. This suggestion seems rather attractive, but there still remains to be explained what the mechanism is that makes it impossible after the loss of control to maintain the desired blood alcohol level, while before the loss of control such an attempt is usually successful.

According to Straus and McCarthy (1951):

"Whereas all addictive drinkers can be classified as pathological drinkers, not every pathological drinker is an alcohol addict. The borderline psychotic, the epileptic, the social psychopath may drink and be conspicuous because of drinking. Yet the pathology in personality is not primarily addiction to alcohol. In fact, in many cases there may be no evidence at all of this form of addiction.

"An essential criterion of addiction is insatiability. It is this phenomenon—the persistent seeking for the unattainable in the fantasy world of alcohol—which distinguishes the alcohol addict.

"Alcohol addiction may be defined as a condition in which the drinking of alcoholic beverages becomes persistent, repetitive, uncontrollable and progressively destructive of the psychological and social functioning of the individual."

The drinking behaviors of the nonaddictive and the addictive pathological drinkers are excellently differentiated, but it is not suggested how the uncontrollable drinking comes about nor are the other criteria of addiction covered. The insatiability, which is not an initial phenomenon but rather a later development, is a manifestation of the process but not the process itself. In this connection, it may be mentioned that Vogel (1953) emphasizes that insatiability is the criterion of addiction par excellence.

Wexberg (1951b) considers in his psychological hypothesis some pharmacological elements. As the initial phase of the process he sees a need for relaxation which is met by the effect of alcohol. The gratification of the need develops into "a mechanism with functional autonomy." From the experience of "pleasurable slackness" stems a desire for repetition and with the repetition the desire is enhanced until it becomes a compulsion. The establishment of the habit is seen as a conditioned reflex with components on the "biological level," such as acquired increased tolerance and withdrawal symptoms. Nevertheless, these pharmacological phenomena may be influenced, in his view, by "mental processes." He propounds the idea that in general the higher mental functions are of sufficient strength to prevent repetition, but nòt strong enough to outweigh the functional autonomy of the mechanism of the cycle: tension—drug—relaxation. This, he believes, explains the phenomenon that the alcohol addict can resist the first drink, but not the second and subsequent ones.

This is a sophisticated and meritorious explanation of the loss of control on the symbolic level, but as he admits that acquired increased tolerance and withdrawal effects of a pharmacological character are operative, and as these elements are sufficient to bring about the loss of control, or the inability to abstain, the suggested autonomous functional mechanism does not seem to be more than a *reinforcement* from the symbolic plane.

The elements of a learning theory can be seen in the above exposition although not presented in the frame of reference of formal psychology. As a matter of fact, informal allusions to a learned drinking response are numerous in the etiological literature. And these allusions embrace the essential elements of learning, namely, repetition of an activity motivated by a gratifying experience.

A presentation of the psychological learning theory as applied to drinking was given at the Yale Summer School of Alcohol Studies in 1944 by Professor Leonard W. Doob but his lecture did not appear in published form.

From Masserman's (1946) classical experiment with cats there emerged certain findings that could be formulated in the terms of learning. These leads were taken up experimentally by Conger (1951) and summarized, together with some general principles of the learning process, in another paper (1956). In view of the great significance of the learning theory to all species of alcoholism some passages from Conger's later paper are quoted here.

"The basic assumption of a reinforcement theory of learning is that the learning of an association between a stimulus and a response requires the presence of some sort of reward or reinforcement. Reinforcement, in turn, is defined in terms of drive reduction, . . . drive . . . being a state of tension arising from an unsatisfied need. . . . Through experience, the drinking response becomes learned, . . . [and it] is learned *because* it leads to a reduction in drive. . . . [In other words] the drinking response is learned . . . because it is rewarding."

This, as the author himself points out, corresponds to the frequently emphasized contention that alcohol reduces tension, worry and anxiety.

Conger's three experiments with rats, set up in order to answer some of the questions that emerged from Masserman's investigation, had significant results. They

"seem to have several implications for a drive-reduction or reinforcement theory approach to alcoholism. . . . It may be that alcohol tends to decrease the strength of learned drives while leaving primary drives relatively unaffected. . . . On the other hand, it may be that this effect of alcohol is specific to the drives involved, irrespective of their being learned or primary. . . . It does appear, as suggested by these experiments and by clinical observation, that one of the drives most vulnerable to alcohol is anxiety. If so, we can see some of the ways in which two of the most important alcohol problems, that of *learned addiction*,[3] and the related problem of differential effects of alcohol upon individuals, may be better understood."

Conger's findings are significant and his interpretations are highly relevant to the understanding of the process that precedes the addictive phase of drinking. But "learned addiction" is conceivable only if the term alcohol addiction is used in the same sense as "gambling addiction." The criteria of addiction, in the proper pharmacological sense, are not fulfilled in animal experiments. Animals do not reach a stage of senseless intoxication, they do not exceed the aim of alcohol intake by quantities which bring about a cancellation of the adaptive functions of alcohol. Such results do not occur in animal experiments as reported to date, although at least one experiment is suggestive (Sirnes, cited by Mardones, 1955). Nevertheless, they could be brought about in animal experiments of very long duration. If any drinking behavior similar to that observed in alcohol addicts had occurred in the rats, the experimenter would have had to take recourse to additional concepts in order to explain the change in behavior.

Conger (1956) recognizes that there is a puzzling aspect to, let us say now, excessive drinking instead of addiction, and he offers a tentative explanation of it.

"If we asume that drinking is learned because it is reinforced, one apparent exception is offered by the man whose drinking is, at least

[3] Italics mine.

socially, more punishing than rewarding. The man who is alienating his boss, his wife, and his friends hardly seems to be socially rewarded for drinking. However, two factors should be considered here. One is the immediacy of reinforcement. Immediate reinforcements are more effective than delayed ones. This learning principle is called the gradient of reinforcement. It may be that, according to this principle, the immediate reduction in anxiety more than compensates for the punitive attitude of the man's wife the next morning. The other factor is the amount of drive and conflict. The personal anxiety-reducing effects of alcohol may, if the anxiety is great enough, constitute greater reinforcement than the competing social punishment."

This last sentence is perfectly acceptable, but the category of behavior involved in the argument is far removed from the loss of control in which the anxiety is not reduced but magnified.

There remains the fact that a learning theory of drinking in the well-defined terms of psychological discipline is essential to all species of alcoholism, including addiction. The learning process so ably described and interpreted by Conger is a prerequisite to bring about the conditions which are necessary for the development of addiction in the pharmacological sense.

The learning theory, as Conger readily admits, does not exclude any other etiological theories; it can be complementary to any of them. Neither would it conflict with a disease conception of one or the other species of alcoholism.

What has been said here of the importance of the learning process as bringing about necessary conditions for the emergence of addiction holds true for many of the symbolic (psychological) mechanisms which have been suggested as etiological factors in alcohol addiction. The most inveterate pharmacologists would not deny that symbolic factors are at work in creating the terrain for the development of addiction in the strict pharmacological sense; as a matter of fact, they insist on the psychological factors for the initiating process.

The papers on alcohol addiction in the psychological sense are mainly relevant to the initiating process of addiction. As far as the addictive process itself is concerned, the psychological hypotheses at best offer some significant contributions to the reinforcement of pharmacological developments through symbolic factors.

The psychological hypotheses are of greater relevance to alpha alcoholism than to alcohol addiction with its stringent criteria.

III.3.2. Public Health Views

Somewhat more definite elements are introduced into the illness conception through Querido's exposition of alcoholism as a public health problem and Gordon's treatment of the matter in epidemiological terms.

Querido (1954) applies the broad principles of public health work to "alcoholism."

"In the biological–clinical field the attempt will be made to realize what may be called the public health program in its narrower sense: case finding; the detection of ill persons and germ carriers; the provision of adequate treatment and sufficient facilities for isolation and hospitalization; training of doctors and ancillary personnel. . . .

"We have now reached the stage in which we are not only able to carry out this kind of work when attempting to free mankind from scourges caused by the attack of biological agents but also when noncontagious pathological conditions play a role. Alcoholism may be considered in this category. Although perhaps in principle not different, in these cases the problem becomes at the same time more and less complicated. Less complicated because one link in the chain of causes —the life cycle of the extraneous agent—is missing; more complicated, however, because a larger number of links in the chain of consequences must be traced in the human behavior itself and is, therefore, more difficult to understand, isolate and evaluate.

"Emphasis tends to shift from the biological–clinical toward the psychological field, from the psychological toward the socioeconomic category of factors which are not readily understood and handled by the public-health authority, and the results might appear to be less exact and less spectacular. . . .

"In the first place there must be agreement on the concept that alcoholism is a disease or at least a complex of symptoms representing a pathological condition.

"Let us try to be very clear on this point. That alcohol causes many diseases, somatic as well as psychic, need not be emphasized. But that the craving for alcohol or the inability to control one's drinking in itself might be a disease is perhaps not as readily understood in all its implications."

The modifications of the public-health approach to noncontagious pathological conditions bring one nearer to the understanding of some of the difficulties inherent in the outlook upon the various species of alcoholism.

As a public-health man, Querido is well aware of the psychological and socioeconomic elements which enter into practically every problem in the health field and he puts them into the proper perspective.

"We cannot enter into a rationally planned combat [of public health problems] without knowing why the community in question lacks a safe water supply or adequate footwear and what are the specific impediments to realizing these provisions. As you will see when following this line of reasoning, we inevitably meet the social equilibrium mentioned above. . . .

"From the fact that in this argument social factors are considered as links in a chain of circumstances, it follows that these factors cannot be regarded as final causes per se but must be evaluated in relation to the other conditions which bring forth the undesirable consequence. In fact, the chief purpose of public health activity, should it be successful, will be to analyze the various conditions and to trace their interrelations. . . .

"We can distinguish (a) the biological–clinical factors related to the dead and living agents in man's surroundings and to his somatic reactions to these agents; (b) the factors arising from psychological attitudes and human interrelations; and (c) the social and economic factors, the influences arising from the specific, self-created part of the surrounding world.

"When such an analysis has been made in a given case the next step is to find out not which of these sets of factors might be the most important as a causative influence—for this is a sterile question without inner meaning—but rather, in which field do the conditions most favoring the changes necessary for achieving the desired results lie."[4]

It may not be said that Querido's considerations greatly clarify the idea of "alcoholism" as an illness, but they facilitate the discussion of the subject.

The same applies to Gordon's (1956) epidemiological formulation of alcoholism:

"That alcohol has the capacity to produce physical and mental abnormalities consistent with a concept of disease is a justifiable premise. That it involves groups of people in sufficient numbers to be recognized as a mass disease is equally evident. The inference follows that there is an epidemiology of alcoholism irrespective of its present state of development, for epidemiology has to do with disease as manifested in populations. The essential restriction is that alcoholism be viewed as a medical problem."

[4] To this may be added the suggestion of Wilkins (1956) concerning the need for statistical and experimental study aimed at the identification of such significant variables as exposure to opportunity to develop the habit, favorable climatic, familial and cultural factors.

Gordon proposes for alcoholism a "biologic gradient," a concept which has been useful in understanding mass disease. In this gradient the abstainers represent, "in analogy with infective processes," the immune and susceptible part of the population. The social drinkers correspond to the population without apparent infection, "lacking clinically discernible disease, but nevertheless infected." The problem drinkers display a typical infection with relatively minor effects, while "addictive drinkers" are analogous to the classical form of a given infection. In most instances of disease the biologic gradient is a dynamic system. According to whether it tends to be dynamic or static, significant variations may be found from one society to the other, as well as within a given society at different times.

Studies of this nature may contribute to the isolation of socioeconomic and biological factors. A beginning has been made through surveys of drinking customs and attitudes toward drinking and drunkenness in a number of European countries. The results of those surveys, commissioned by the European Regional Office of World Health Organization, are now being analyzed.

III.3.3. Summary of Psychological Formulations

At least half of the psychological formulations on "alcoholism," deal with it either explicitly or implicitly as a symptom of underlying psychological disorder. The other half designate it as a psychological illness, but do not succeed in explaining the process of "alcoholism" and its major manifestations through psychological mechanisms. They remain at the level of the explanation of the covert motivations for the use of alcoholic beverages in larger amounts and with greater frequency than is practiced in so-called social drinking. In other words, in spite of using the term illness, they do not achieve more than the interpretations which term "alcoholism" a symptom. It may be said that as far as the initiating stage of alcohol addiction goes, the psychological formulations are much more satisfactory than the physiopathological ones, but this refers to the initiating mechanisms only and does not extend to the later developments.

Most of the psychiatric and psychological papers do not even consider the role that alcohol itself may play in the process and, as a matter of fact, do not even consider the elements of what they call a "progressive disease." Some of the students of alcoholism who deal with it as a "psychological addiction" do attempt to explain the developmental process in psychological terms, but either they do not succeed or they take recourse to concepts pertaining to drug addiction in the strict pharmacological sense. On the other hand, some of these papers have given an excellent account of those psychological factors which reinforce the pharmacological development of addiction and give them a specific coloring.

Generally, the psychological formulations apply much more to the alpha alcoholic than to the alcohol addict and by definition, at least by the definition used by numerous writers on alcoholism, as well as in the present study, the alpha alcoholic may be a sick person; however, his illness is not drinking, but some underlying personality disorder.

Common deficiencies of all psychological formulations are that, deliberately or unintentionally, they point up alcohol addiction and alpha alcoholism as *the* problems of alcoholism and, especially, that they do not recognize that there are species of alcoholism in which psychological vulnerability plays a minor role, while the major factors may be cultural or socioeconomic combined with the specific effect of alcohol itself. This leads to the unfortunate slogan, that "alcoholism does not lie in the bottle, but in the man." The role of the "bottle" may be predominant in certain alcoholics (gamma and delta alcoholics), while the "man" may be the predominant factor in others. Of course, both are present in any species of alcoholism and the question reduces itself to the predominance of one or the other.

These last remarks anticipate some of the following discussions, but it seems desirable to state them at this point.

In view of the vagueness and inadequacy of the psychological formulations one may wonder what considerations induce the proponents to speak of alcoholism in terms of an illness per se. It would seem that one main inducement for this is the consideration that an "alcoholic" cannot regain the lost control, as even after years of abstinence the "compulsion" sets in on resumption of drinking. There enters, also, a recognition of the fact that such behavior changes (often designated as personality changes) as take place in the course of alcoholism cannot be explained in the terms of "a good man turning into a bad man" and on recovery into a good man again, but that there must be a grave disease process and at least its arrest to account for these behavior changes. These considerations seem to be of considerable value, but unfortunately the psychological and psychiatric formulations do not explain them in the terms of their respective disciplines.

III.4. Physiopathological and Other Physical Formulations

In 1939 Bowman asked the question in relation to alcoholism: "Will psychiatry have to reorient itself to a physiological approach to many of the problems which heretofore have been regarded as purely psychological?" At that time physiopathological formulations, except for suggestions of alcoholism as an allergy, were rather scarce, although some vague allusions had been made since the turn of the century, e.g., Wagner von Jauregg (1901).

In the 1930's it was found that many of the diseases of chronic alcoholism, such as polyneuropathy and some of the alcoholic encephalopathies, were attributable to vitamin deficiencies. These deficiencies were not extended to the etiology of "alcoholism" itself, but perhaps Doctor Bowman saw the possibility of such an extension. Furthermore, he may have been thinking of the development of new techniques, e.g., autoselection between water and alcohol solutions by animals (Richter, 1926), which to some extent made the experimental exploration of alcoholism possible.

In the past 20 years a number of elaborate physiopathological etiologies have been proposed which have put the protagonists of the psychological etiologies on the defensive; sometimes a too aggressive defensive. While some vagueness still adheres to the newer etiological hypotheses, a much greater effort in the construction of rational—even if unsatisfactory—explanations has been put forward by its exponents than by the representatives of the psychological school. This has resulted in a battle which has brought about at least some clarification of psychological hypotheses.

In addition, a number of new techniques have been made available which certainly have given an impetus to new exploration. Some of those new techniques, e.g., tagged isotopes and microelectric methods, have been only slightly exploited and promise a new crop of experiments and hypotheses. Furthermore, the technique of autoselection has been considerably refined.

Two major physiopathological hypotheses and a number of minor ones have emerged. The major ones are concerned with nutritional and endocrinopathic etiologies. The minor ones range from vague mentions of unknown physiological factors (I, also, have indulged in the guessing game) to positive statements on identifiable biochemical factors and less demonstrable brain damage.

If any of these hypotheses should be fully substantiated there can be no question about the illness nature of "alcoholism." If an organic lesion or a physiological anomaly can bring about an anomalous form of alcohol ingestion, the latter must be regarded as a disease process, and this irrespective of *whether the lesions or the physiological anomalies are preexistent to "alcoholism" or acquired through initial heavy alcohol intake.* The questions are whether such preexisting or acquired anomalies can be demonstrated, whether or not a craving, compulsion, physical need or dependence (or whatever it may be called) can be postulated either at the beginning of heavy drinking or at some later stage, and whether or not a reasonable contingency between the latter and the former can be shown. Up to the time of this writing no such proofs have been given, but the trends are promising.

A number of physiopathological or physical etiologies are tabulated below in the briefest form, and some of them will be discussed in more detail and subjected to critical analysis.

FORMULATIONS OF ALCOHOLISM IN PHYSIOPATHOLOGICAL AND PHYSICAL TERMS (IN THE PAST 20 YEARS)

Allergy

Silkworth (1937) — An allergic disease coupled with emotional factors.*

Alcoholics Anonymous (1939, 1955) — Psychological factors are important, but there is also a physical component, believed to be an allergy.*

Cowles (1941) — A chemical allergy with a specific reaction on the meninges.*

Lemere, Voegtlin et al. (1943) — An innate susceptibility to alcohol which is akin to food allergy or drug idiosyncrasy.* [This hypothesis was later abandoned by the authors.]

Brocklehurst (1949) — In one type of alcoholic there is an idiosyncrasy to alcohol.* The seat of the disturbance is in the lining of the fourth ventricle in the medulla.

Randolph (1950, 1956) — A masked food allergy.* Certain food allergens, whose manifestations must be counteracted through specific alcoholic beverages, create a craving for alcohol.

*NOTE: Formulations of alcoholism in terms of a *psychological* allergy are given in the preceding section.

Biochemistry–Physiology

Davidson (1939)

Alcohol causes physiological imbalance of stimulation and depression of the integrated nervous system, and creates a continuous urge for repetition of the excitation due to the mediated pleasure and the necessity for discharge.

Dent (1941, 1955)

A chemical disease. An imbalance between front and back brains. Alcohol, by depressing front brain function, helps to escape anxiety. Frequent recourse to such escape establishes a conditioned reflex.

Lecoq (1942–1957)

Alcoholism is characterized by a neurohumoral syndrome (toxic factor). The role of alcohol is the disruption of the nutritional balance and the generation of acidosis, an exaggerated cholesterol–urea relation and pyruvicaemia. These factors are responsible for inability to abstain.

Tuck (1943)

Alcohol addicts should be considered as physiological problems rather than as psychiatric ones. Nutritional deficiencies overshadow all other factors.

Jellinek (1945–1953)

Heavy drinking is initiated by psychological or social factors; later a physiological X factor accounts for a disease condition outwardly manifested through loss of control.

Diethelm (1948)

Alcoholism is a pathological reaction rather than a disease. This reaction occurs as a symptom in well-defined disorders or as a major deviation in psychoneurotics.

Feldman (1951, 1955)

From the medical point of view the chronic alcoholic is an individual suffering from considerable humoral and hypothalamic disturbance.

Fleetwood and
Diethelm (1951)

The factors of tension and resentment in alcoholism are related to two distinct cholinergic substances.

Fouquet (1951)

There are three factors that must combine to make an alcoholic: (1) a psychological factor implying some pathology of personality; (2) a biological factor which permits the ingestion of alcoholic beverages without notable ill effects and accompanied by euphoria; and (3) a "toxic" factor which develops gradually after years of drinking through the creation of humoral disequilibrium and which manifests itself as craving for alcohol.

Dérobert (1952)

Excess quantities of alcohol lead to incomplete oxidation and the resultant substances, particularly pyruvic acid, produce a series of aggressions against the organism. This explains the mechanism of dependence upon alcohol.

Izikowitz (1952)	Initial heavy use of alcohol is psychologically motivated, but the desire for more alcohol always has a somatic basis whose nature is not known.
MacLeod (1952)	There may be an interaction between alcohol and certain systems involving acetylcholine resulting in an exaggeration of the intoxicating effect of alcohol.
Breit (1953)	The uncontrollable craving which distinguishes the chronic alcoholic from other types of drinkers has a physiological basis.

Brain Pathology

Little and McAvoy (1952)	On the basis of electroencephalographic studies it must be concluded that there is a cerebral condition predisposing to alcoholism.
Lereboullet et al. (1954), Pierson and Kircher (1954a, 1954b), Pluvinage (1954), Courville (1955), Skillicorn (1955), Tumarkin et al. (1955), Kircher and Pierson (1956), Lemere (1956)	Brain damage from alcohol and nutritional deficiencies can explain to a large extent the essential pathology of alcoholism, namely, the permanent loss of control over drinking.

Nutrition

Mardones (1951) as well as Mardones and various associates (1942–1955)	Alcoholism may be rooted in nutritional deficiencies, such as lack of a specific factor N_1 in the diet and thiamin deficiency. There seems to be a biochemical lesion in one of the steps of metabolism.
Brady and Westerfeld (1947)	The deficiency or lack of dietary factors, particularly vitamins and some unknown factors contained in the liver, may bring about a demand for alcohol.
Williams (1947–1954) as well as Williams and associates (1949–1955)	A genetotrophic disease. An inherited pattern of individual metabolic peculiarities which cause an increased requirement of vitamins and other substances which are operative in intermediary metabolism.
Sirnes (1953)	Cirrhosis of the liver and other liver injuries may cause a need for alcohol, perhaps through the prevention of the normal functions of Mardones' factor N_1 in the body.
Zarrow and Rosenberg (1953)	Liver damage may result in an alcoholic drive.

Vallee and various associates (1955, 1956, 1957)	Zinc metabolism and alcohol dehydrogenase (a zinc metalloenzyme essential in alcohol metabolism) are linked to the pathogenesis of liver cirrhosis.*

Endocrinology

Berman (1938)	Alcohol acts as a sugar substitute in people whose emotional tensions result in hypoglycemia.
Goldfarb and Berman (1949)	Alcoholism in some persons is a self-perpetuating progressive disease in which the organism first invites the noxious agent because of its helpfulness in stimulating needed secretory responses and then requires the same agent with increasing constancy to achieve the desired result, because of its proclivity to produce pluriglandular dysfunction.
Smith, J. J. (1949)	A constellation of pituitary–adrenal and gonadal dysfunctions are preexistent to alcoholism and set up a demand for alcohol.
Tintera and Lovell (1949)	Hypoadrenocorticism, which is preexistent to alcoholism in some alcoholics and acquired by others, sets up a need for alcohol.
Lovell (1951)	A constellation of neurosis and sensitivity to alcohol, the latter being detrimental through endocrinophies.
Tintera (1956)	Alcoholism is a symptom of a glandular disorder with hypoadrenocorticism underlying the condition.

III.4.1. Miscellaneous Hypotheses

The sodium chloride deficiency discussed by Silkworth and Texon (1950) has not been included, as I do not see that the authors related it to anything but the craving evidenced in *acute* intoxication.

III.4.1.1. Alcohol Allergy. In one form or another the matter of allergy to alcohol has been presented at various times since Toulouse's study in 1896 (cited by Cheymol and Thuillier, 1950) by a number of proponents. The idea was in abeyance for a considerable time until it was revived by Silkworth (1937) and from 1939 on it became widely spread through the book "Alcoholics Anony-

---

* Although these observations were not extended by Vallee and his associates to loss of control or physical dependence upon alcohol, it seemed pertinent to mention their findings in this table. The vulnerability of alcohol dehydrogenase to metabolic insults by high concentrations of alcohol and "the participation of zinc in the dehydrogenation of ethanol in the metabolism of post-alcoholic cirrhosis" may be of great relevance to Sirnes' hypothesis (above).

mous" and members of the fellowship of the same name, although the conception of "alcoholism" as an allergy did not find much support from psychiatric quarters. Some psychiatrists used the term metaphorically, as a "psychological allergy," as they found it useful in briefing alcoholic patients on their condition.

Haggard (1944) presented a potent critical study, showing that this particular conception of alcoholism went against medical logic. More recently, Robinson and Voegtlin (1952) in a definitive experimental study entirely refuted the allergy hypothesis. Their conclusions are quoted below.

"On the basis of the completely negative results obtained in tests of serum from over 50 rabbits and from 17 human subjects, including 2 abstainers, 5 normal drinkers and 10 alcohol addicts, it has been concluded that ethyl alcohol stimulates neither the development of detectable amounts of an antialcoholic antibody nor a detectable allergic reaction. Admittedly, because of necrotic reactions, most of the rabbits were given alcohol in a more dilute form than was used by other investigators. However, negative results were obtained also when serum from a group of rabbits prepared exactly according to the original and to the modified intramuscular routes was tested. . . .

"Failure to confirm claims that ethyl alcohol stimulates production of an antialcoholic antibody is not surprising. Serotherapy apparently does not modify the effects of alcohol in an alcohol addict in the same way that a conventional antiserum neutralizes the effect of its homologous antigen in an organism. Instead, serotherapy is supposed to create a revulsion to alcoholic beverages similar to some manifestations of gastric allergy. Sapélier and Dromard gave ethyl alcohol to their serum-producing animals, but its purity was not stated. All other reports on serotherapy for alcohol addiction are based on the use of autogenous serum or serum from animals which had received alcoholic beverages. That ethyl alcohol is repulsive to the alcohol addict after serotherapy has not been shown. Therefore, if serotherapy does stimulate some sort of gastric allergy, there is no evidence that ethyl alcohol is the specific agent. Skin tests for 'tolerance' to alcohol distinguish between those resistant and those susceptible to the effects of the test without distinguishing between normal and abnormal drinkers. If ethyl alcohol were antigenic, such tests ought to distinguish between normal and abnormal drinkers."

This discussion of the allergy view has not been presented here in order to persuade Alcoholics Anonymous to abandon their conception. The figurative use of the term "alcoholism is an allergy" is as good as or better than anything else for their purposes, as long as they do not wish to foist it upon students of alcoholism.

The idea of "masked food allergy" (Randolph, 1950, 1956) does not seem to have had any acceptance and the present reviewer cannot comment on it as he was not able to understand its exposition.

III.4.1.2. Etiologies in Terms of Brain Pathology. That brain damage occurs as a consequence of heavy alcohol intake is a common contention to be found in the alcohol literature of the past 150 years. On the other hand, it has been pointed out that with the exception of Marchiafava's disease (Lolli, 1942), no *specific* brain pathology has been found in alcoholics, i.e., no changes beyond those which occur in nonalcoholics of the same age, although Courville and Myers (1954), as well as Bennett, Doi and Mowery (1956) and also Lemere (1956) postulate alcoholic specificity. While it is extremely difficult to establish brain pathology of alcoholic origin, this is by no means a proof that such damage does not occur. Those who have disregarded this hurdle have invoked alcoholic brain changes largely as etiological factors in the alcoholic psychoses, but have not extended the idea to the etiology of the alcoholism itself and in particular to the loss of control. Recently, however, a hypothesis has been presented which assumes that brain damage acquired in the course of initial heavy alcohol intake may produce in the course of time those characteristic behaviors which distinguish "alcoholism" from ordinary drunkenness.

Following on the encephalographic observations by Gelma and co-workers (1952) of apparent cerebral atrophy in alcoholic patients with Korsakoff's psychosis, other French investigators (Pluvinage, 1954, Lereboullet, Pluvinage and Vidart, 1954, Pierson and Kircher, 1954a, 1954b, Kircher and Pierson, 1956) made air encephalograms in numerous nonpsychotic alcoholics and found similar indications of atrophty, i.e., enlarged cerebral ventricles. These investigators suggested that such brain lesions—usually though not always irreversible—might explain the recalcitrance of some alcoholics to treatment. In the United States, Tumarkin, Wilson and Snyder (1955) found enlarged cerebral ventricles in a group of seven rather young male alcoholics (aged between 25 and 38 years). Since in these cases the lesions presumably could not be attributed to age, the personal and familial histories of the patients were scrutinized carefully, but no common explanatory factor emerged—other than the excessive drinking of these men. Tumarkin and his co-workers therefore theorized that some of the injury to the cerebral cortex from repeated severe intoxication involves a permanent and possibly cumulative loss of cells and nerve fibers. This, they surmised further, could result in loss of tolerance to alcohol, in psychological changes such as impoverished judgment, and in subsequent inability to control drinking. Still another American investigator, Skillicorn (1955), found abnormal pneumoencephalograms, particularly enlarged ventricles, in six alcoholics to whom attention had been drawn by the development of rather early cerebellar ataxia (at ages between 39 and 55 years). Although Skillicorn warns of the danger generally of inferring cerebral atrophy from the evidence of pneumoencephalography, in his cases the great extent and severity of the lesions seemed to justify such an inference; he also speculated on the possibility of repeated severe intoxication as the cause. In their later report of additional pneumoencephalographic findings in alcoholics, Kircher and Pierson (1956) made the further suggestion that the phenomenon of craving in these patients might be explained by assuming that alcohol imparts tonus to a brain with a cortical atrophy.

Most recently Lemere (1956), apparently on the basis of some of these reports, has favored this sort of explanation of the etiology of alcoholism. He believes that cerebral cortical atrophy is the end product of gradual dissolution of large numbers of cells and that there must be thousands of alcoholics with intermediate stages of such damage, but that current methods are inadequate to demonstrate cellular loss. Lemere proposes that this brain damage from alcohol and the indirect effects of nutritional deficiencies and head injuries can explain to a large extent the essential pathology of alcoholism, namely, the permanent loss of control over drinking. In order to reinforce this hypothesis, he cites the well-established fact that the higher cerebral areas and thus their functions are most subjected to the effects of alcohol and that the cells constituting those areas are also the first to be anesthetized by alcohol. Thus Lemere feels it is justified to assume that, with progressive destruction of the frontal cortex, less alcohol will be required to produce that stage of anesthesia where control is lost. Once alcohol enters the alcoholic's system, "there is an immediate paralysis of the control centers of the brain," and this would explain why the loss of control over drinking is permanent. He concedes, however, that usually the alcoholic will be able to function normally provided he does not drink. In Lemere's view, the metabolic pattern of the brain cells changes after prolonged use of alcohol and the presence of alcohol becomes a necessity for optimum brain functioning. Sudden withdrawal of alcohol throws the brain cells into disequilibrium which brings about a cellular craving for alcohol.

That atrophies do not emerge suddenly but are products of gradual developments is of course true. How gradual the process is cannot be said, and as Lemere points out, present techniques cannot detect the destruction of a relatively small number of cells in a mass of billions. It is, however, a question whether such destruction has any perceptible effect. Frequently, much more marked brain changes do not show any correlation with behavior changes.

Lemere's rationale for the contingency between the organic lesion and the loss of control, which seems to parallel the suggestion of Kircher and Pierson (1956) that enlarged ventricles are determinant of alcoholism, is much more plausible than the rationale of some of the other physiopathological etiologies which have been discussed, but the argument is far from invulnerable. Lemere admits that as long as the recovered "alcoholic" does not ingest alcohol he can function normally. As a matter of fact there is the evidence of at least 200,000 recovered alcoholics who not only function normally but pursue their goals with great energy and discernment. If the loss of control stems from a destruction of cells of the frontal cortex and if this loss of control over drinking is permanent, but all other functions remain, or become normalized, one would have to assume that alcohol selects a tiny area whose only function is the control of alcohol intake (not fluid intake in general); and that, of all other possible brain damage, this is the one which is irreversible. In fact, however, Kircher and Pierson (1956) have found that some of these lesions are reversible. The fact that not all recovered alcoholics return to fully normal functioning, of course, does not detract from this criticism.

Lemere also says that the metabolic pattern of the brain cells changes in such a way that the presence of alcohol becomes a necessity for their optimum functioning and that withdrawal of alcohol causes a disequilibrium. This idea is in conformity with the classical pharmacological conception of drug addiction—that the toxic substance in the course of time is integrated into the cell metabolism, where its sudden absence brings about upheavals in the form of withdrawal symptoms. This integration into cell metabolism, which in a way is also related to acquired increased tissue tolerance, need not and cannot be explained on the basis of the loss of a relatively small number of cells.

While Lemere's hypothesis is limited to lesions subsequent to heavy alcohol intake, there is a hypothesis which postulates a cerebral anomaly preexistent to alcoholism. Based upon electroencephalographic studies of their own and others, Little and McAvoy (1952) come to the following conclusions:

". . . There is general agreement that progressive degrees of intoxication produce slowing in the electroencephalogram of the normal individual, and that patients with disorders of chronic alcoholism and evidence of structural brain change exhibit a variety of paroxysmal and nonparoxysmal abnormalities in their electroencephalograms. [And in another passage they say] Funderburk has indicated that in his patients in whom alcoholism appeared to be the primary difficulty, the alpha index tended to be low, while those in whom the alcoholism was a secondary problem tended to show normal alpha activity. Our experience agrees with this impression, and this together with other findings would tend to substantiate the suggestion that the poor alpha type of record in alcoholics may be the result of the cerebral condition predisposing to alcoholism and not the result of the alcoholism itself."

Too much depends here on the differential dignosis between primary and secondary alcoholism. The criteria of differentiation would have to be clearly set out and the compliance with those criteria would have to be shown. That was not done in Funderburk's two-page report. Furthermore, assuming that the classifications were perfect, there would still remain the question whether the differences in the alpha indices did not merely denote absence or presence of neurosis or other psychological deviations. In this connection it is also interesting to note that in Skillicorn's six alcoholics with abnormal pneumoencephalograms the electroencephalograms were normal in every case.

III.4.2. Nutritional Etiologies of Alcoholism

Without stating it in so many words, the proponents of the nutritional deficiency etiologies of alcoholism have taken their cues from two facts. First, that alcohol—in contrast to other calorigenic substances—requires for the first steps of its metabolism the initiating action of the liver with its elaborate enzyme system; and second, that many organic complications of "chronic alcoholism" are associated with vitamin deficiencies. It does not seem far-fetched to infer that enzyme deficiencies in general, and vitamin deficiencies in particular, may not only be acquired through heavy alcohol intake but may also be preexistent to alcoholism and may have some role in the pathogenesis of that condition.

The basic technique in the exploration of this idea is to administer to animals diets in which various or all vitamins are lacking (of course, with control diets) and to present them with a choice of pure water or an alcohol solution, with provision for the measurement of consumption. This technique of "auto-selection," as mentioned before, originated with Curt P. Richter, who used it for other purposes. In the later course of the experiments, the various vitamins, etc., lacking in the basic or deficient diet are separately or jointly supplied.

The proponents of nutritional deficiency etiologies assume that in the prospective alcoholic a "need" or a craving for alcohol exists from the very beginning or that such a "need" can develop into a craving.[5] Some believe that the "need" for alcohol may be a seeking of additional calories. Another assumption is that voluntary increased intake of alcohol is evidence of such a "need" or craving and that the increased alcohol ingestion seen in some animal experiments is at least akin to alcoholism in humans.

The first experimental investigation of the effect of vitamin deficient diets upon the voluntary intake of alcohol by rats was carried out by the Chilean pharmacologist and nutritionalist, Professor Jorge Mardones (Mardones and Onfray, 1942). Four or 5 years later, his findings were checked by Brady and Westerfeld (1947). The latter, with other associates, subsequently reported their experimental findings in numerous papers. More recently the question was limited to the effect of cirrhosis of the liver and other liver damage by Sirnes (1953) and by Zarrow and Rosenberg (1953).

The work of Mardones and his associates may be summarized briefly, partly in their own words.

"In 1942, Mardones and Onfray showed that rats maintained with a diet deprived of thermolabile elements of the vitamin B complex (autoclaved yeast as the only source of this complex) increased their alcohol intake under conditions of self-selection. They reported also that the level of alcohol intake dropped when the animals were given a supple-

[5] Mardones (1955) has modified his views on this particular point.

ment of untreated dried yeast, or liver, or meat or wheat germ, but not when they received supplements of thiamin alone or of thiamin together with other pure vitamins of the B complex. My associates and I suggested the existence of a new thermolabile factor and we called it factor N. Subsequently it was observed in our Laboratory that factor N was actually composed of a least two elements: one thermolabile, identified with thiamin, and another thermostable, called provisionally factor N_1" (Mardones, 1951).

Mardones ascribed the increased voluntary alcohol intake to the lack of the specific factor, N_1. This effect may be enhanced by thiamin deficiency. Further experiments reported upon by Mardones, Segovia et al. (1954) would indicate that factor N_1 may be composed of thioctic acid and at least one more unknown component. Mardones suggested that the fundamental metabolic fault was in the pyruvate–acetyl coenzyme A step of metabolism. This assumption is supported by the findings of Varela, Penna et al. (1953) in human alcoholics. However, Mardones did not make any farther reaching claims as to the nature of alcoholism.

It should be mentioned that in all their experiments Mardones and his associates found that certain strains of rats were more prone than others to respond to N_1 deprivation with an increased alcohol intake. Thus there is a possible genetic factor at play in the preference for alcohol. It may be recalled that some genetic factor was suggested by Richter and Campbell (1940) in relation to the alcohol taste threshold of rats.

The investigations of Brady and Westerfeld (1947) and of Williams and his associates (various papers between 1948 and 1956) confirm the findings of Mardones as to the increased voluntary intake of alcohol by rats maintained on diets deficient in vitamin B complex. On the other hand, there were differences in alcohol intake when diets were supplemented with various vitamins. Mardones (1951) agrees with Williams in respect to the genetic factor, but cannot agree with him on the details of the "trophic" factors "because since [Williams and his associates] always worked with diets containing autoclaved yeast, they could not observe the N_1 deficiency."

Williams (1947) presented a working hypothesis on the etiology of "alcoholism" which he later termed a genetotrophic disease (Williams, Berry and Beerstecher, 1949a, 1949b). This hypothesis was based on Williams' own theories concerning individual genetically transmittable metabolic patterns and the instinctive seeking of animals to remedy errors of metabolism through an increased ingestion of various substances, as well as on the findings of Mardones (although the latter were not mentioned).

The arguments of the genetotrophic theory of Williams and his associates have been concisely summarized by Popham (1953): "(a) The presence of one or more partial genetic blocks leads to (b) diminished production of one or more specific enzymes; this results in (c) corresponding impairment of ability to utilize one or more nutritional elements, which means that (d) the individual has an augmented requirement for these elements and that he possesses (e) the distinctive metabolic pattern which predisposes to alcoholism."

The work of Williams and his associates has become much better known than that of Mardones, not only in professional circles but also among the interested lay public, because of the great publicity which attached to his investigations. This fact is due largely to his biochemical surveys of human alcoholics, the more explicit extension of findings in animals to human alcoholism, the prediction of the feasibility of detecting "potential alcoholics" by means of biochemical tests, and the application of his ideas to the treatment of alcoholic patients. (In this latter area the available information is meager, but dramatic.)

It may be mentioned here that in clinical testing (4 members of Alcoholics Anonymous and 8 controls) Beerstecher, Sutton et al. (1950) reported 6 statistically significant differences between recovered alcoholics and control subjects among 60 variables measured. These 6 variables were: sodium (saliva), hippuric acid (urine), uric acid (saliva), uric acid (urine), gonadotropin (urine) and citrulline (urine). From this study Williams and his associates concluded: "Thus, the data strongly indicate that compulsive drinkers possess certain common metabolic features."

Popham (1953) has pointed out that 3 of the 6 "significant" differences had probability values of .05 and that "if 3 values of .05 or less were to be expected, as many as 6 such values out of 60 would occur by chance more than 10 per cent of the time. In other words, there are no grounds for surprise, from the standpoint of probability, when 6 of the differences between 60 pairs of means for the same pair of samples prove to be 'significant' in the conventional sense."

Popham's argument is relevant but not conclusive. There are statistical and experimental means for testing the validity of Williams' findings, and the experimental test would be the more potent. If the observation of the same 60 variables were to be repeated on a similar pair of samples and if the same 6 variables should show differences as great or greater it could hardly be doubted that such differences exist between alcoholics and nonalcoholics. But the findings would still not support the conclusions. First, the findings do not justify the assumption that such differences in metabolic patterns exist in the premorbid state; and second, there is no rationale that would connect such differences with the genesis of a "need" for alcohol. Wexberg (1950) has voiced somewhat similar critical points. His objection, however, that one may not speak of an appetite for alcohol because most alcoholics do not like the taste of it, is not relevant.

Williams' 1947 exposition of his working hypothesis represents the best effort for the elaboration of an etiology of alcoholism. Furthermore, that paper is a vast improvement over any formulation of hereditary factors in alcoholism presented theretofore, although some of its premises and deductions are open to grave doubts. Williams rightly took issue with those who want to exclude hereditary factors for fear that "nothing can be done about heredity" and he pointed out that the existence of hereditary factors does not preclude ameliorative action. He said that in the past both hereditary and environmental factors had not received the simultaneous study necessary for progress in the field and added that a one-sided approach was doomed to failure. In the subsequent studies, however, Williams and his associates became entirely one-sided.

Among the salient features of the genetotrophic theory of alcoholism is metabolic individuality that is largely genetically determined. (One would have to be biologically unsophisticated in order to doubt the existence of individual metabolic patterns.) Other features of Williams' etiological theory of alcoholism are that there is a "need" or craving or appetite for alcohol in certain persons and that this "need" results from nutritional faults, largely anomalies in their enzyme systems. Furthermore the existence of this "need" is assumed to be present in the pre-alcoholic (premorbid) state.

Neither Williams nor anybody else has ever shown that a craving or need for alcohol exists in the pre-alcoholic state of alcoholics. Williams (1947) regards as "one of the evidences for the existence of metabolic individuality in relation to alcohol . . . the fact that there is a wide variability among individuals in the amount of alcohol required to bring about signs of intoxication or impairment of function." He refers to Jetter, who found in 1,000 subjects that 10.5 per cent were diagnosed as intoxicated at blood alcohol concentrations of 0.05 per cent but that 6.7 per cent were adjudged "sober" at 0.4 per cent. What Williams overlooked in this instance is that increased tissue tolerance can be acquired in the course of time, particularly if daily use of excessive or even of medium amounts is involved. Thus, those who were diagnosed as intoxicated at 0.05 per cent may have been persons little accustomed to the use of alcohol.

One of the important points in all critiques of the genetotrophic theories is the lack of rationale for a connection between enzymatic anomalies and a craving for alcohol.

Another point mentioned in the various critiques of the genetotrophic theory is that the elements of the metabolic pattern of alcoholics as found by Williams are "not causes but consequences" of alcoholism and thus do not play a role in its etiology. This argument emerges in practically every printed and oral discussion of his theory. At first hearing this argument sounds relevant, but it does not do justice to the development of the alcoholic process. While it is obvious that the consequences of initial heavy use of alcohol cannot account for an initial need or seeking of the substance, the consequences of initial heavy drinking could still have an effect on the later development of the alcoholic process, namely on the loss of control and the inability to abstain. In the subchapter on the addictive species of alcoholism a suggestion will be made as to the role of some sequels of heavy alcohol intake in the development of crucial changes in the later stages of the process of alcohol addiction.

A few words must be said in relation to the ethnic aspects of Williams' genetic theory. His main ethnic argument is the nonalcoholism of the Jews and he sees in this the working of hereditary metabolic patterns to the exclusion of cultural factors. The importance of the latter, however, is becoming more and more clear (e. g., Snyder, 1958), while there is no evidence bearing on the biological facts. Popham (1953) has cogently pointed out that if differences in alcoholism rates between the Irish and the Jews were to be accounted for genetically, then the great variations in alcoholism rates among various countries of western Europe and between geographic areas of the United States would also have to be explained by the distribution of genetic factors.

The most potent doubt concerning the conclusions emanating from the animal experiments of Mardones and of Williams and his associates is cast not by critical analysis of premises and arguments involved in the interpretation of the experimental results, but by an inspired experiment performed by Lester and Greenberg (1952), and verified by Mardones, Segovia et al. (1955).

Lester and Greenberg followed the pattern of administering first normal diets and later diets depleted of vitamins, but instead of giving two choices of fluid, i. e., pure water and a 10-per-cent alcohol solution, they offered also a third choice in the form of a sucrose solution. When this third choice was allowed, the rats diminished their alcohol intake and showed a preference for the sucrose solution. Interestingly enough, the alcohol intake was also markedly diminished when the third choice was a saccharin solution instead of a sucrose solution. Thus the preference for a sweet solution could not be attributed to a replacement of alcohol calories by sugar calories; the important characteristic was apparently the sweetness. On the other hand when the third choice was solid sucrose the decrease in the voluntary intake of alcohol was not clear cut.

Mardones and his associates obtained essentially the same results when they duplicated the procedures of Lester and Greenberg. In addition, Mardones and his co-workers gave as a third choice a solution of pure B vitamins and this did not significantly change the alcohol intake.

Lester and Greenberg concluded that the increased voluntary intake of alcohol by rats does not represent a craving for alcohol, and that the rat experiments both of Mardones and of Williams are not applicable to alcoholism in humans. It may be noted that rats which increased their voluntary intake of alcohol did not exhibit those phenomena that are associated with the picture of alcoholism.

Mardones, Segovia et al. (1955) acknowledged ". . . that the observed preference for alcohol is not actually a craving. Consequently, it cannot be regarded as an exact mirror of the desire for alcohol observed in alcoholic patients." On the other hand they do not believe that the results obtained with three choices of liquid intake "necessarily invalidate all the observations made in studies of preference between two choices." I agree with this opinion and do not feel that the findings of either Mardones or Williams are irrelevant to alcoholism.

Williams, Pelton and Rogers (1955) stated: "The fact that laboratory rats, unlike alcoholics, will turn from alcohol consumption to sugar consumption indicates either that there is no parallelism between alcohol consumption in rats and humans, or else that there are metabolic differences between rats and humans which may modify the parallelism which does exist. We think that the latter alternative is worthy of consideration."

No doubt vitamin deficiency, whether produced by alcoholism or by experimental conditions, brings about a certain physical discomfort which rats tend to compensate for rather through a sweet fluid than through alcohol which—although it can bring some relief from physical discomfort—does not have for rats any prestige value or symbolic meaning as is the case in human subjects. The implications of this phrasing, of course, will not appeal to those who reject social factors in the genesis of alcoholism.

In summary, the nutritional theories of Mardones, their elaboration by Williams into a genetotrophic theory, and the experimental results of both these investigators, all represent a significant advance in the thinking about alcoholism. It will require much research with entirely different techniques and excursions into many related aspects before one can adjudge the proper place of their findings in the total picture of alcohol addiction. Some suggestions will be offered in a later section of the present study.[6]

The premises and investigations of Mardones as well as Williams come nearest to a true conception of alcoholism as a disease. They postulate nutritional anomalies, biochemical lesions and metabolic faults as underlying the craving or physical need for alcohol, even though Mardones concedes that the increased voluntary intake of alcohol by rats does not represent a craving.

Irrespective of whether such anomalies exist in the premorbid state or whether they are acquired in the course of heavy alcohol intake and, after their emergence, bring about radical changes in the drinking behavior, such a process may be legitimately desig-

---

[6] More than a year after the covering of the present study, Professor Roger J. Williams (1959a, 1959b) postulated an alcohol "appestat," a control mechanism which governs or misgoverns alcohol intake. In spite of this he adheres to his genetotrophic theory, but it is not evident how the two theories hang together.

nated as a disease process. By the same token liver damage as an underlying factor, as postulated by Sirnes and some of his followers, would fall into the category of disease processes, and again irrespective of whether such damage is preexistent to alcoholism or represents acquired damage (through heavy alcohol intake) which alters the course of the drinking behavior.

The above remarks are made with the reservation that the premises and the relevance of the findings must be verified or the findings must be brought into some other connection with the process of alcohol addiction.

III.4.3. Endocrinological Etiologies

There are in the alcohol literature—particularly in papers by French investigators of polyneuropathy and delirium tremens—numerous allusions to possible endocrine factors in alcoholism. Many years ago I pointed out (Jellinek, 1942) that no actual study of the possible endocrine aspects had been carried out, but that there were sufficient suggestive data to justify a systematic study. Gross (1945) presented a working hypothesis which was based solely on the resemblance of certain symptoms of alcoholism to some manifestations of endocrine dysfunctions.

The first thorough clinical survey on this matter was carried out by J. J. Smith who reported on it at a meeting of the American Association for the Advancement of Science in 1947, but a "preliminary report" was not published until 2 years later, followed by other clinical and experimental papers (J. J. Smith, 1949, 1950, 1951a, 1951b).

Smith claimed a pituitary–adrenal constellation as the etiological factor of alcoholism, and similar findings with modified formulations of the adrenal factor were presented by Goldfarb and Berman (1949), Tintera and Lovell (1949), Lovell (1951), and Tintera (1956). These hypotheses, which, except for those of Goldfarb and Berman, were presented not as hypotheses but as proven relations, caused considerable interest, new experimentation and criticism. The pertinent literature will be reviewed here.

J. J. Smith (1949) says that alcoholism "manifests itself primarily as a behavior problem" but that the behavior did not seem to him to constitute the disease; the disease was, rather, an underlying metabolic disturbance. His conception of alcoholism stems from his "observation of the biochemical and clinical similarity between

Addisonian crisis and delirium tremens." He explains this in terms of Selye's (1946) adaptation syndrome to repeated stresses, and refers to experimentally induced exhaustion of the adrenal cortex through stresses of various kinds. ". . . Stimuli associated with alcoholism lead to various stages of adrenal cortex insufficiency." Delirium tremens, which he regards as "one of the possible end states of alcoholism," shows the same biochemical changes as Addisonian crisis, namely, "in both conditions plasma potassium and nitrogen are increased, sodium and chloride are decreased, and there is hemoconcentration as well as marked acidosis and, frequently, a low blood sugar level."

Smith refers to other similarities and assumes that "the existence of identical pathological processes must be presumed."

Following this reasoning, he has treated patients manifesting delirium tremens and acute alcohol intoxication with desoxycorticosterone and whole adrenal cortex extract, and found improvement "beyond that expected in the usual treatments."

He also makes reference to similarities with the clinical picture of pantothenic acid deficiency and the correlation of the latter with adrenal cortex damage.

Smith investigated the background of alcoholic patients (with acute intoxication) and, as evidence of "good accord with the accepted findings in adrenal cortex insufficiency," lists the following results of his investigation: lymphocytosis in a "considerable number of patients;" expanded or contracted blood volume in "many alcoholic patients;" low blood chloride level in 10 per cent of 150 patients; significantly low glucose level in the blood in 58 per cent of 115 patients; subnormal plasma ascorbic acid in 71 per cent of 153 alcoholic patients; significant elevation of total blood lipids in 26 per cent of 39 patients, and a significant elevation of total blood lipids in 18 per cent of the same 39 patients.

In the same paper Smith reports on his study of behavior patterns in 1,800 male alcoholics from a clinical point of view:

"From this study it appears that there is a certain constitutional type of individual who becomes an alcoholic or problem drinker. Only members of certain ethnic groups appear to fall into this category: the Celtic and Scandinavian peoples seem most susceptible to this disease, whereas the Semitic and the Chinese peoples, although not teetotalers, are seldom affected. The ethnic incidence of alcoholism is usually explained on cultural, religious, climatic, sociological or psychological grounds. It seems, however, that a biogenetic explanation is more plausible. The Celts, the Scandinavians, the Semitic people and the Chinese generally tend to marry within their own groups. If alcoholism is the symptom of a metabolic defect, the tendency to which is transmitted genetically, it should be found pooled in a close-knit ethnic group, and should occur rarely in an ethnic group in which this biogenetic susceptibility is not present."

In his survey, Smith also finds that the alcoholic demonstrates a consistent community pattern. This pattern he also regards as indicative of endocrinopathies. The alcoholic "is usually single, or separated, or divorced. If married he has few if any children. This lack of children does not seem to be a function of economic status, because it is found quite as commonly among well-to-do alcoholics as among low-income alcoholics. The peak incidence of the severest phase of alcoholism is in the early 40's." Smith relates this age datum to a "common denominator," namely, "the incipient male climacteric."

From an experimental study (J. J. Smith, 1951a) he infers that alcohol stimulates the adrenal cortex as indicated by a significant drop in ascorbic acid. Later (J. J. Smith, 1951b) he concludes that since 75 per cent showed a deficient eosinophil response to epinephrine and only 36 per cent to adrenocorticotropic hormone (ACTH) the disturbance "appears to reside . . . at the pituitary or hypothalamic level." And in another paper (J. J. Smith, 1950) he states that the treatment of the acute forms of alcoholism is no longer a problem. Adrenal cortex extract controls acute intoxication and Korsakoff's psychosis, while delirium tremens and hallucinosis are successfully treated with ACTH. He also expresses the opinion that available evidence indicates that endocrine dysfunction precedes alcoholism. Patients who are treated with adrenal cortex extract and other hormones remain sober and feel well. However, they are not able to drink normally; thus the treatment of addiction to alcohol is not really solved as yet. But a few years later (J. J. Smith, 1953) his outlook on therapeutic success of hormonal treatment is optimistic without reservation; it is "the only treatment which offers the alcoholic prompt, specific therapy for the various phases of acute as well as chronic alcoholism."

This is J. J. Smith's case for alcohol addiction as a manifestation of a metabolic pattern which precedes alcoholism and which involves the interactions of the pituitary, adrenal and gonadal systems. This represents a constellation in which the outstanding feature is exhaustion of the adrenal, which is secondary to a pituitary deficiency.

Before presenting related etiological theories of others, some critical comments raised by various investigators and remarks of the present reviewer pertaining to the contributions of J. J. Smith will be considered. Some of these criticisms apply equally to the contributions of Tintera and Lovell, which will be reviewed later.

In view of the fact that Smith endeavors to explain the *entire* process of alcoholism through endocrine dysfunctions and that he proposes hormonal therapy as the treatment par excellence, some of the criticism is naturally quite stringent.

The targets of criticism are largely some speculative points raised by Smith in favor of an adrenal–gonadal insufficiency; his extension of his therapeutic argument from acute intoxication to "chronic alcoholism;" the inadequacy of eosinophil response; lack of proof of preexisting endocrinopathies; and the lack of a rationale for the engendering of an initial craving for alcohol by endocrinopathies.

My own remarks shall be restricted to those points which have not been covered by others. Smith's claim that well-to-do alcoholics have as few children "if any" as do the poorer alcoholics, and that both groups have fewer children than average, runs entirely counter to all experience on this matter. Haggard and Jellinek (1942) tabulated the results of American, Swedish, Finnish and French surveys and in all these countries the average number of children in alcoholic families exceeded the average found in temperate families of the same economic status and in the same periods.

As to his ethnic arguments the comments made in connection with Williams' genetotrophic theory apply.

His statement that delirium tremens represents a possible end stage of alcoholism belongs with other common misconceptions about alcoholism. Of course, delirium tremens is so dramatic in its manifestations, as well as so dangerous in nature, that it impresses one as being the culmination of the alcoholic process. Actually it frequently occurs long before gross deterioration has set in, and may be followed by several recurrences or by long periods of alcoholism without any obtrusive developments.

Furthermore, the possibility of the occurrence of delirium tremens as a withdrawal symptom would force one to rethink the role of adrenal dysfunction in that disease. This is not to say that in a withdrawal symptom the adrenals could have no role. To the contrary, that would be quite conceivable, but not in the sense of Smith's theories.

Wexberg's (1950) potent criticism must be considered at some length, but it suffices to make a selection of his comments. Wexberg agrees that alcoholism is a metabolic disease (and I should like to add that any drug addiction involves metabolic changes), but he says that it is

". . . an entirely different matter to believe—as Smith apparently does—that (according to Williams) the alcoholic possesses a metabolic individuality which predisposes to addiction. Nowhere in Smith's article, and nowhere else in the literature, to our knowledge, have facts been brought out to support this theory. It would require studies of large numbers of young, nonalcoholic individuals and the establishment of a premorbid metabolic type which, in follow-up studies, would show a significant correlation with alcoholism. It would require control studies which would show (a) that there were not substantial numbers of individuals of the same metabolic type who did not become alcoholics, and (b) that there were not substantial numbers of alcoholics who never exhibited this metabolic type.

"A metabolic pattern found frequently among confirmed alcoholics, without the controls mentioned above, is most likely to be secondary to alcoholism and not a predisposing factor."

Wexberg extends this criticism to the report by Tintera and Lovell (1949) too:

"Since the clinical material of these investigators consisted of alcoholic patients, how could they possibly differentiate . . . a hypoadrenocortical constitution allegedly predisposing to alcoholism, and those whose hypoadrenocorticism was secondary to their alcoholism? Did they use the necessary controls mentioned above? In view of the fact that they worked with alcoholic patients, it seems that they did not. In addition, there is no evidence that low tolerance to alcohol, which supposedly is found in nonalcoholic hypoadrenocortical individuals, has anything to do with alcohol addiction, as the latter usually leads to increased rather than decreased tolerance."

Returning to Smith, Wexberg continues:

"He has failed to submit controls necessary to prove his point, and to answer the following questions:
"1. How many nonalcoholic individuals of the same age exhibit the same findings as those listed under his points 1 to 8?
"2. What is the explanation for those alcoholics who do not show the signs of adrenal cortex insufficiency mentioned—e.g., the 90 per cent

who do not have a low blood chloride level, the 43 per cent who have a normal or increased blood sugar level, the 74 per cent whose total blood lipids are normal?

"3. What are the biochemical findings in patients who have not taken a drink for 6 months, a year, or more? Do they not come back to normal?

"It appears to me that these questions must be raised as part of our constructive criticism of the physiopathological school of thought on alcoholism."

Below follow excerpts from some papers which confirm Smith's findings to some extent, but not in relation to the main points of his claims.

Owen (1954a) collected data on 27 patients with delirium tremens. Their adrenal cortex reserve status was determined by means of the eosinophil response to a test injection of ACTH. Adrenal cortex insufficiency seemed to be related to prolonged alcoholism rather than to any of the phenomena of delirium tremens.

Forbes and Duncan (1951) studied the effect of a single intoxicating dose of alcohol (4.5 to 9 g. per kg.) on the concentration of cholesterol and ascorbic acid in the adrenal glands. The results were clear-cut and the number of experimental and control animals adequate. Alcohol intoxication "imposes a condition of stress on the organism which results in a depletion of these adrenal constituents." These results confirm J. J. Smith only to the extent that alcohol affects adrenal function, but in no way supports his idea that adrenal hypofunction is the cause of alcoholism.

Voegtlin (1953) reports that in a controlled study the administration of adrenal steroids and ACTH had a dramatic effect on the immediate sequels of excessive indulgence in alcohol and the craving for liquor quickly subsided. On the other hand, this apparent specificity in the acute stage "was not evident in respect to the chronic disorder of alcoholism" and to Voegtlin this suggests

"that the underlying pathological physiology is different in these conditions. In this connection it is noteworthy that our laboratory studies have failed to reveal consistent evidence of characteristic alteration of adrenal function in alcoholic patients. Also, the failure of our relapsers to enjoy normal drinking certainly should be considered as strong evidence that the adrenal drugs, as administered during this study, have not corrected a hypothetical abnormality which is the cause of addictive drinking."

Jellinek (1953), too, has pointed out the fallacy of extending the meaning of therapeutic success from acute states to mechanisms between bouts. Beutner (1951) outrightly denies applicability to the treatment of addiction. He found large doses of adrenal cortex extract effective in the treatment of the withdrawal or hangover stage of alcoholism, but useless in the treatment of the addiction itself.

On the other hand, Thimann (1951) reports that of 27 patients to whom adrenal cortex extract was administered 27 per cent maintained sobriety for 2 to 19 months, 1 patient improved and 41 per cent were outright failures. The comparison of these percentages suggests that there may be "a preponderance of the psychologic factor in Antabuse in contrast to the predominantly pharmacologic mechanism in ACE." These "psychological factors" must, of course, be seriously considered in therapy. As Steck (1951) points out, proponents of the biological methods look down upon psychological methods and this is dangerous, as the success of the new treatment is at least in part due to the psychological value of "new methods." That value dwindles as the method becomes routinized.

Sherfey and Diethelm (1953), who reviewed the use of various drugs in treatment of alcoholic patients, state that adrenocorticotropic hormone is beneficial in some instances for the physical manifestations of alcoholism, but there is no indication that it is a specific cure of alcoholism.

Johnston (1954), in a therapeutic experiment, found that

"There were no significant differences in the clinical responses of alcoholic patients treated with Lipo-Adrenal Cortex, thiamin hydrochloride or a placebo. It must be pointed out, however, that the 300 patients in this experiment had a median of 3 days of dryness before contact with the clinic. In a similar experiment with patients who had stopped drinking only just prior to clinic contact there might well be differences in the response to the 3 types of treatment."

As to arguments based on the eosinophil response, the following may be noted:

Dowden and Bradbury (1952) believe that the subnormal eosinopenic response of the alcoholic group to epinephrine suggests the possibility of some deficiency in the production or release of corticotropin by the pituitary. They feel that further study is necessary to determine whether alcoholics are less responsive to other stress agents, but the above findings tend to confirm the clinical impression that adrenal cortex extract is beneficial in the treatment of the acute alcoholic "hangover" stages.

Mann (1952), on the other hand, found in 78 male and in 17 female alcohol addicts that the analysis of the responses to the epinephrine stress test showed normal pituitary adrenal function in 59 patients (62 per cent). An abnormal response occurred in 11 patients (12 per cent), while 25 patients (26 per cent) exhibited a less striking subnormal reaction to the stress, i.e., a decrease of 40 to 50 per cent in the eosinophil level.

In the group of 11 subjects who showed the most clear-cut abnormal response, 9 had been classified as neurotic, 1 as schizoid and 1 as having an organic psychosis.

A general picture, however, emerges from the results. The fact that over 60 per cent of the group displayed normal reactivity to the stress employed suggests that a defect in the pituitary–adrenal axis is not a characteristic of alcoholic patients generally.

The unreliability of eosinophil responses for diagnostic purposes has been pointed out repeatedly. Thus Kark (1952), in reference to the work of Dowden and his associates, cautions that eosinophil responses are not necessarily indicative of pituitary or adrenal cortex insufficiency. Analysis of 702 4-hour response tests in 284 subjects indicates that the epinephrine test is of little value in the diagnosis of adrenal or pituitary disorders.

The critical remarks may be concluded with the comments by Gottesfeld and Yager (1950):

"At the present time there is no direct evidence that individuals with the so-called character neuroses, if exposed to the pattern of alcohol addiction, develop a specific new hormonal or physiological demand which is met only by alcohol. Although the adrenals have been shown to play some role in the general changes which occur in the alcoholic, and there is evidence of degenerative changes in testicular tissue, as well as of alterations in the glucose tolerance curve, it must be pointed out that similar changes have been noted in the random population of state hospitals in nonalcoholic patients. Much has been made of the avidity for sugar during periods of abstinence from alcohol, but this is again a matter of popular gratification and cannot definitely be interpreted on the basis of physiological principles."

With these critical comments in mind the other contributions to the endocrinopathic etiology of alcoholism may be reviewed. Tintera and Lovell (1949) distinguish two major groups of alcoholic patients: (1) younger males of asthenic type with smooth skin, gynecomastia and hypotension, displaying hypoglycemia, low ketosteroids and low androgens, i.e., hypoadrenocorticism with low tolerance to alcohol; and (2) individuals without preexisting hypo-adrenocorticism who, through alcoholic overindulgence, cause eventual damage to the adrenal cortex and to other associated glands involved in carbohydrate metabolism. Continued drinking further decreases the blood sugar; liver glycogen stores become depleted and fatty degeneration of the liver occurs, "Then the liver is unable to detoxify the estrogens and sex changes found in alcoholism result. . . . The entire process is reversed by the administration of adrenal cortical hormone."

The therapeutic claim for the use of adrenal cortex extract is presented later by Tintera (1956) with even greater vigor. He states that a controlled administration of adrenal cortex extract will change the personality of the alcoholic to a worthwhile, uninhibited, productive, useful individual.

Lovell (1951), in his book "Hope and Help for the Alcoholic," gives a prominent role to psychological factors and a "sensitivity" to alcohol which is linked with adrenal anomalies. He tries to assign different weights to these factors in different alcoholics.

"All the factors that cause the disease known as alcoholism—the immaturity, frustrations, fears and sensitivity to alcohol—are mingled in different proportions in every alcoholic. While the general pattern is repeated over and over again, the individual variations are infinite, as numerous as the actual number of alcoholics. In some the emotional disturbance seems to be more important than the allergy-like reaction of the body to liquor. In others, the physical factors seem to be dominant.

"But in none of them can any single factor be considered the sole cause. We never see an alcoholic who is simply sensitive to alcohol yet has no neurotic symptoms at all. We never see an alcoholic who is simply neurotic without any sensitivity to alcohol. Nor is the neurosis simply exaggerated immaturity or frustration or fear or any other single emotional disturbance. . . . The alcoholic is afflicted with a neurosis plus a sensitivity to alcohol. The sensitivity is the physical basis of his disease; without it his neurosis will not lead to compulsive drinking. On the other hand, the sensitivity in the absence of a neurosis probably will make an abstainer rather than an alcoholic."

A psychiatrist in his private practice, of course, sees predominantly the secondary addicts whose serious personality difficulties make him seek the psychiatrist. Others, however, have seen many non-neurotic addicts with minor psychological vulnerabilities, particularly in the viticultural countries. The contention that neurosis is a sine qua non of "alcoholism" cannot be accepted. Furthermore, the "sensitivity" to alcohol is not defined, but remains a vague concept which could suggest tolerance to alcohol, or susceptibility (another vague concept) or any of many other reactions.

While Lovell wishes to do justice to the question and concedes that the physical factor (adrenal dysfunction) may be preexisting in some "alcoholics" and acquired in others, and while he assigns the initiating role to the neurosis, the time aspects become somewhat conflicting: "In diagnosing these psychosomatic troubles it is easy to put the cart before the horse, since they react so closely upon each other. However, it is probably safe to say that the horse is the neurotic situation and the cart is the glandular imbalance."

Later, however, he says that "alcoholism is much more the expression of a physical condition already existing than merely the result of heavy drinking."

As to the rationale of endocrine imbalance causing the loss of control and other essentials of the addictive use of alcoholic beverages, Lovell remains unconvincing. "Alcohol in these cases is no more the cause of alcoholism than sugar is the cause of diabetes. The alcoholic simply is not able to handle liquor normally. . . . In the alcoholic, the cause is a failure of the adrenal glands to produce sufficient amounts of hormone."

The analogy between diabetes and "alcoholism" is, in this instance, not particularly felicitous. In the case of diabetes, the inability to "handle" sugar means that a glandular (pancreatic) dysfunction inhibits the metabolism of that substance resulting in a physiologically noxious accumulation of sugar in the organism. But in the case of alcoholism there is no evidence that the metabolism of alcohol is impaired. Neither the absorption nor the oxidation or other means of elimination of alcohol seem to proceed at rates different in addictive users than in small users of alcohol, nor is there at present any evidence that the intermediary metabolism of alcohol has any specific deviations in "alcoholics." Furthermore, relations between alcohol metabolism and various modifications of adrenal functions have not been shown.

The joint and individual contributions of Tintera and Lovell do not represent reinforcements of Smith's theories but rather seem less evidential than the latter.

Goldfarb and Berman (1949) have given much thought to rationales and to placing the roles of endocrinopathies in alcoholism into their proper perspective. They hypothesize that the stresses of high alcohol intake cause an adrenal hyperfunction which through exhaustion leads ultimately to a hypofunction. The adrenal anomalies are thus not preexistent to heavy drinking, but result from it. On the other hand, once these dysfunctions are established they add to the initial psychological incentive for an increased use of alcohol, and bring about some behavioral changes which give "alcoholism" a certain coloring. Goldfarb and Berman do not claim to have covered the entire phenomenon of the addictive use of alcohol by this theory. Although one may not subscribe to all their interpretations, it is well worth while to quote these investigators' conclusions (based on clinical observations and a critical review of the pertinent literature) at some length:

"The basic premise of our hypothesis is that alcohol, apart from its anesthetic action, provokes in many individuals an alteration of the neuro-endocrine homeostatic mechanism. Initially this consists of facilitation of adaptive reaction (increased range and intensity of emotional response), possibly leading to basic solutions of social and sexual problems. This constitutes an affective–intellectual integration serving to defer symptoms of neurosis or psychosis. . . .

"Our clinical impressions, together with a review of experimental data, lead us to believe that alcoholism, directly or indirectly, produces endocrine insufficiency especially of the adrenal cortex. Alcohol appears to be in itself a 'stressful agent.' By its anesthetizing effects on the central nervous system it can predispose to the nonspecific stresses of trauma, malnutrition and infection, each of which predisposes to the others and to financial privation. The latter, in turn, increases the possibility of malnutrition and, following on alcoholism as it does, invites social disapproval and self-condemnation which add to already present emotional stress in the individual. Social disapproval and self-condemnation (loss of love) also follow upon the 'disgraces' associated with public intoxication and its sequels, including medical care, hospitalization or legal prosecution. . . .

"The repeated exposure to stress results in stimulation of the pituitary (via adrenal medullary secretion, sympathetic nervous system pathways or other paths) with consequent repeated adrenal stimulation and eventual glandular exhaustion. An antagonism between alcohol and sexual hormones may lead eventually to relative gonadal failure. This possibly throws an additional burden on the adrenal cortex.

"At the same time malnutrition serves to withhold dietary constituents necessary for normal adrenal cortex function and repair, e.g., ascorbic acid.

"An organism prone to alcoholism seems to be one that needs the initial effect of alcohol as a "stressful agent" in order to make temporary adaptations to an environment with which it cannot cope adequately.

This need may be either on the basis of neurosis (with intermittent relative adrenal cortex "fatigue") or on the basis of other constitutional or acquired factors. The initial use of alcohol may be fortuitous; its choice after the original introduction is predetermined. Continued excessive use of alcohol is itself a means of constitutional alteration.

"Alcoholism, then, by this hypothesis, is in some persons a self-perpetuating progressive disease in which the organism first invites the noxious agent (alcohol) because of its helpfulness in stimulating needed secretory response of the adrenal cortex and then requires the same agent with increasing constancy to achieve the desired result because of its proclivity to produce pluriglandular dysfunction."

Some of the above statements—particularly the last paragraph quoted—are somewhat obscure and thus less useful. The full process of alcoholism is not explained either through the psychological nor psycho-endocrine mechanism, but evidently that was not the object of the authors, who merely endeavored to clarify the adrenal contribution toward the process.

III.4.3.1. Summary of Endocrinological Etiologies. A preexisting, genetically determined endocrine pattern in "alcoholism" has not been established, nor has an "initial craving" for alcohol been shown by proponents of the endocrine etiological theories of alcoholism.

On the other hand, there is ample evidence to show that large alcohol intake exerts an exorbitant stress upon the adrenals, and that there is a fairly high incidence of adrenal damage in alcoholics.

There is, of course, overwhelming evidence of the effect of such damage on behavior quite independent of alcohol studies. It is not conceivable that such damage should not have repercussions in alcohol addiction.

Yet there is no plausible rationale for a craving for alcohol as a result of such damage, nor is any rationale for the loss of control inherent in the endocrine anomalies.

The endocrinopathies may have a role in the mechanism of withdrawal symptoms, but as those symptoms are the same as in morphine and heroin addiction it would have to be known whether those addictions cause adrenal changes.

In the section on alcohol addiction in the strictest pharmacological sense, a possible role of endocrinopathies in the addictive process will be tentatively suggested.

III.4.4. Alcohol Addiction in the Pharmacological Sense

Alcohol addiction in the psychological sense was discussed in Chapter III.3 and it was said that the use of the term addiction in those instances could be regarded only as a figure of speech. Furthermore in Chapter III.1.2 distinctions among various species of alcoholism were made, and gamma and delta alcoholism were singled out as those species that probably constitute true disease processes and which, by pharmacological standards, could be regarded as addictions.

It will suffice to repeat here that the main difference between gamma and delta alcoholism is that the former leads eventually to loss of control but not to inability to abstain and that the latter produces inability to abstain but may allow control over the amount of consumption, at least within certain limits. These differences seem to be determined by the drinking patterns. In the gamma species the drinking pattern is largely that of consuming highly concentrated spirits in a brief period of time, but in the delta species large total daily amounts of beverages low in alcohol content are consumed in small, nonintoxicating portions over 14 to 16 hours of the day. It was also suggested that the differences in the drinking patterns were largely determined by social attitudes, the predominance of certain sources of alcohol and, in certain areas and social gradings, by economic factors.

Otherwise, however, the gamma and delta species of alcoholism showed the same addiction processes, namely, acquired increased tissue tolerance, subsequent increase in the amounts of alcohol required, and adaptation of the cell metabolism to alcohol, evidence of which is seen in the drastic withdrawal symptoms which in their turn lead to the manifestation of craving, i.e., physical dependence.

The tendency of many students of alcoholism, particularly those who are psychiatrically oriented, to neglect the above-mentioned processes and their reluctance to see alcoholism as an addiction analogous to drug addictions has been mentioned previously. Because of this tendency psychiatric and psychological theories have failed to explain the later developments of the alcoholic process, although these theories seem to be valid for the initial phase of gamma alcoholism and for the entire picture of alpha alcoholism.

Proponents of nutritional etiological theories and of endocrine etiologies of alcoholism have also neglected the questions of acquired tolerance, withdrawal symptoms and other aspects of the pharmacological process of addiction.

On the other hand there are more than a few students of alcoholism, among them some psychiatrists, who have paid adequate attention to the pharmacological addictive process. Some of them have made that process the axial structure of the picture of alcoholism or, more exactly, of some of its species. It is remarkable that the proponents of alcoholism as a drug addiction have given more consideration to psychological and cultural components than many other students of alcoholism. Perhaps it is due to this reasonable attitude of these students toward psychological and cultural factors that their basic ideas on the addictive nature of some species of alcoholism have not been noticed by other students of alcoholism. It has become the predominant impression that the view of alcoholism as an addiction in the pharmacological sense became obsolete some 50 years ago.

It is probable that some of my closest associates would be surprised on re-reading some of the ideas that I expressed in 1942. Bowman and Jellinek (1942a) in their discussion of alcohol addiction said:

"There are . . . physiological theories which may be called etiological, although not in the strictest sense of the word, i.e., they do not deal with the initial factors which start the process, but rather explain the genesis of one of its stages. These physiological theories relate to the factors which, after years of excessive drinking, lead to a physical dependence upon alcohol. This physical dependence is regarded by many as the criterion of addiction. However, such a theory does not explain why the person had been drinking to excess for years; any theory of the etiology of addiction must answer this question, i.e., must show the driving forces, psychological or physiological, which cause this drinking. Furthermore, addiction in the sense of physical dependence is, as we have explained before, a criterion of secondary addiction. In the primary addict, the dependence upon alcohol is practically immediate and is psychologically motivated although not necessarily without any physiological component: his inability to give up alcohol is to all intents an initial phenomenon. The secondary addict is initially not dependent upon alcohol and simply does not give it up because he does not seem to have any reason to do so. In the course of years, habituation develops; this makes him physically dependent and this physical dependence may then be rationalized into psychological dependence. The fact remains, however, that he now is an addict and, as far as medicine and society are concerned, he presents the same problem as the primary addict. This, and the fact that secondary addicts are probably much more numerous than primary addicts, lends importance to physiological theories of the genesis of such dependence. The importance of such theories, however, should not obscure the fact that they do not touch upon the initial causes. What these theories do explain is the physiological process of habituation, but not the necessary conditions for such a habituation."[7]

Below are tabulated formulations of alcoholism in terms of addiction in the pharmacological sense. Most of these formulations will come as a shock to those who believe in the obsolescence of the idea of alcoholism as a true addiction and who do not recognize that alcohol itself plays more of a role in the process of alcoholism than just that of causing intoxication.

FORMULATIONS OF ALCOHOLISM (IN THE PAST 25 YEARS) IMPLYING
A PHARMACOLOGICAL PROCESS OF ADDICTION

Adams (1935)	Alcohol is one of the addiction producing drugs; the characteristics of addiction are tolerance, craving and the withdrawal syndrome.
Lévy (1935)	"Accoutumance," i.e., adaptation of the organism to alcohol, is of great importance.
Bumke and Kant (1936)	The alcoholic is an addict in the sense of the morphinist.
Fleming (1937 and 1952)	True alcohol addiction is characterized by specific craving and associated with real habituation. Any individual—no matter how healthy or well organized he may be—who drinks heavily enough and long enough will become addicted.
Bowman and Jellinek (1942a)	Physical dependence upon alcohol exists mainly in the "secondary addict." (See above, page 112.)
Griffin (1942)	Symptomatic drinking is distinguished from "true addiction."
Carter (1943)	Alcoholic patients who are "handicapped by alcohol addiction" are distinguished from those who are not. The latter can make "social adjustments."
Felix (1944)	From the psychiatric point of view the alcoholic and the drug addict differ chiefly in that they use different drugs.

[7] If I were to rewrite the above today I would not use the expression "habituated" and I would label as secondary addict the alcoholic whom I called in 1942 primary addict and vice versa. The relabeling would be in accordance with the majority usage. On second thought, I would not make such distinctions as primary and secondary addicts.

Myerson (1944)

The drinker who builds up early tolerance to alcohol is in danger of becoming a heavy drinker and, from there, becoming addicted to alcohol.

Deshaies (1946–47)

If to the search for pleasure and toxiphilia there is added an organic adaptation ("accoutumance")— which may be normal or pathological—the *alcoholomanic* (addictive) stage is reached.

Page (1947), also
   Page, Thorpe and
   Caldwell (1952)

Four main types of alcoholics are distinguishable; among these a small group (one in six or seven heavy drinkers) become "habituated" to alcohol.

Reichard (1947)

Physical dependence, or the physiological change produced by prolonged dosage with certain drugs, can be ascertained only by the occurence of the abstinence syndrome. This has been reported in association with withdrawal of barbiturates, alcohol and paraldehyde. Habit formation should not be confused with addiction; the former is a type of activity so well learned that the acts involved are carried out with little or no conscious attention.

Wexberg (1949 and
   1951b)

Psychological mechanisms are highly important, but in the late stages of alcoholism biological factors [which are largely the phenomena of addiction in the pharmacological sense] operate.

Lundquist (1951)

Alcoholism is distinguished from abuse of alcohol. The former is present when a physical dependence on alcohol and craving exist; the latter, where the user of alcohol causes social damage (e.g., neglect of family) or damages his health.

Meerloo (1952)

In the initial phases there is a general urge for pleasure followed by repetition of the primary experiences. In the third phase, however, addiction becomes specific (to alcohol or another drug) and is reinforced by pharmacological dependence.

Pohlisch (1954)

The process of alcohol addiction is comparable to the pharmacological processes operative in all drug addictions.

Isbell, Fraser et al.
   (1955)

Experimental evidence of acquired increased tissue tolerance and of the emergence of withdrawal symptoms are manifestations of physical dependence.

Wellman (1955a)

Alcohol is the important etiological factor in alcoholism.

Alexander (1956)

In spite of the highly significant psychodynamic processes which initiate and explain many features of alcoholism, there are certain phenomena, such as

	increased tolerance and withdrawal symptoms, that are characteristic of the pharmacological role of alcohol, and are features of addiction.
Himwich (1956)	The case for psychological mechanisms is strong. But there is also a physiological mechanism; for the cells of the body—and especially those of the brain —require the presence of alcohol for their function, as indicated by the grave disturbances that develop on the withdrawal of alcohol. This viewpoint places alcohol in a class with morphine and the barbiturates as a substance for which a physiological need can be created.
Hoch (1956)	Alcohol acts like a narcotic which is incorporated in the metabolism of the nervous system.
Pfeffer (1956)	"Loss of control over the use of alcohol, change in tolerance, a withdrawal syndrome and the relinquishing of all other interests in favor of a preoccupation with the use of alcohol" are all criteria of an addiction.

The following subsections of Chapter III.4.4 deal with an elaboration of the criteria of the addictive process.

III.4.4.1. The Position of Alcohol in Relation to Drug Addiction. Certain drugs are referred to as habit forming and a warning to this effect must appear on the bottles or packages in which those drugs are sold. The warning, of course, implies that the drug in question through its pharmacological properties can, so to speak, force a habit upon the user. In other words, the forming of the habit is attributed primarily to the drug and only to a much lesser degree to the individual. Such was the connotation of "habit forming drug" until recently.

In 1952 the Expert Committee on Drugs Liable to Produce Addiction of the World Health Organization changed the broad nomenclature of drugs coming within the competence sphere of the committee.

Parenthetically it may be mentioned that the above named committee periodically reviews various drugs and makes recommendations to the Commission on Narcotics of the United Nations Economic and Social Council concerning drugs that, on account of their addiction producing properties, require international control of production and sales. It is this latter branch of the U.N. that implements the control while the W.H.O. Expert Committee on

Drugs Liable to Produce Addiction is only the source of recommendations upon which the Commission of the Economic and Social Council of U.N. takes action.

The W.H.O. Expert Committee on Drugs Liable to Produce Addiction, in their third report (1952), established three categories of drugs according to whether the pharmacological properties of the drug or the psychological reactions of the user are predominant.

The first category includes drugs that (with some variation due to differences in the duration of administration and in doses) will always and in all individuals produce through their specific pharmacological action an irresistible need for the drug, dependence and drug addiction. The use of these drugs cannot be interrupted without causing troubles on the physiological as well as psychological levels. These drugs which formerly had been designated as habit forming drugs were now designated as *addiction producing drugs*. The pharmacological effect of these drugs is of primary importance in producing addiction while the personality structure of the user is secondary. Such drugs require international control on account of their noxious effect upon the individual and society.

In the second category are those drugs which do not produce an irresistible need, but through their pharmacological effects which certain individuals regard as desirable lend themselves easily to the formation of a psychological habit. The administration of such drugs can be interrupted without evoking characteristic troubles. In this instance the psychological reaction of the user is primary and the pharmacological effect secondary. Such *habit forming drugs* are not socially dangerous and they do not require rigorous control.

The third category comprises "some drugs whose pharmacological action is intermediate in kind and degree between the two groups already delineated so that compulsive craving, dependence and addiction can develop in those individuals whose psychological make-up is the determining factor, but pharmacological action plays a significant role."

The nature of control relating to these drugs is made dependent upon the extent of damage that they may produce. Drugs of type one—outside of their legitimate medical use—always "cause individual and sociological damage and must be rigidly controlled." Drugs of type two "cause no sociological damage and do not need rigid control." Lastly, concerning drugs of type three, while individual and sociological damage may develop "the damage is not general" and the "type and degree of control of this group are better left at present to national consideration."

The labels which were tagged on to the three categories of drugs, especially the transfer of the term "habit forming drugs" from the first category to the second, may give rise to differences of opinion, but any polemics concerning the labels should not obscure the fact that the classifications as described are valid irrespective of their names.

The above revision of the classification of certain drugs was made before the W.H.O. Expert Committee was ever called upon to consider the matter of alcohol as a drug.

It should be made clear that the problem of alcoholism is a subject of study by the W.H.O. Expert Committee on Mental Health which from time to time has an Alcoholism Subcommittee composed of psychiatrists. On the other hand the chemical substance ethyl alcohol requires the consideration of pharmacologists and is, therefore, also in the domain of the section on addiction producing drugs.

At the first session of the Alcoholism Subcommittee of the Expert Committee on Mental Health in 1950 it was felt that there were some questions relative to alcoholism that could not be answered competently by psychiatrists, but needed the expert opinion of pharmacologists, physiopathologists and biochemists. In consideration of this point the Alcoholism Subcommittee made a recommendation that "a subcommittee on alcohol (as opposed to alcoholism) should be set up under the Expert Committee on Drugs Liable to Produce Addiction," in order to study certain pharmacological aspects of ethyl alcohol (World Health Organization, 1951).

In 1953, this suggestion was acted upon and an Expert Committee on Alcohol (not subcommittee) was convoked to consider among other questions, concepts pertaining to the pharmacological position of alcohol, i.e., to determine whether or not ethyl alcohol belonged in any of the three categories distinguished by the Expert Committee on Drugs Liable to Produce Addiction.

After the committee reviewed the questions of tolerance to alcohol, acquired increased tolerance, withdrawal symptoms, and "tissue adaptation," they arrived at a formulation based largely upon quantitative rather than qualitative differences between the addictive properties of ethyl alcohol and those of morphine, morphine derivatives, some synthetic drugs and the barbiturates.

In view of the facts that excessive alcohol intake is a source of grave social damage and that under certain circumstances (heavy, continual intake over long periods) "compulsive craving" may result, ethyl alcohol could not be classed among the merely habit forming drugs (type two).

On the other hand the comparison with the morphine group and other addiction producing drugs (type one)—which was brilliantly presented by Professor Leonard Goldberg[8]—showed that ethyl alcohol could not be grouped with those drugs either.

While the continued use of drugs in the morphine group produces a tolerance to amounts 20 to 100 times above the therapeutic doses and well above the usual lethal dosage, the acquired increased tolerance to ethyl alcohol surpasses the inherent or initial tolerance not more than 3 or 4 times. The incidence of addiction in users of heroin is practically 100 per cent, and among users of morphine around 70 per cent, but among users of alcoholic beverages it is only 10 per cent at a maximum. Furthermore, addiction to drugs in the morphine group sets in after approximately 4 weeks of continued use, but addiction to alcohol requires a very high intake over a period of from 3 to 20 years. Lastly the committee thought that the withdrawal symptoms in "alcoholism" were milder and less persistent than in the recognized addiction producing drugs. (This latter conclusion, however, was modified in a joint committee of psychiatrists and pharmacologists in 1954.)

Alcohol thus does not comply sufficiently with the definition of addiction producing drugs to be classed among them. Most important, the criterion of producing addiction in nearly all users is not fulfilled.

In consideration of all the points enumerated above, the Expert Committee on Alcohol agreed on the following statement:

"Alcohol must be considered a drug whose pharmacological action is intermediate in kind and degree between addiction-producing and habit-forming drugs, so that compulsive craving and dependence can develop in those individuals whose make-up leads them to seek and find an escape in alcohol. With this substance the personal make-up is the determining factor but the pharmacological action plays a significant role. Damage to the individual may develop, but does so in only a minority of users. The social damage that arises extends, however, beyond these individuals themselves" (World Health Organization, 1954).

* To my knowledge his presentation has not been published.

The deliberations of the Expert Committee on Alcohol pointed up the need for a joint discussion by psychiatrists and pharmacologists. The World Health Organization, therefore, convoked in 1954 a Committee on Alcohol and Alcoholism.

This committee discussed such matters as craving, withdrawal symptoms, loss of control, and alcoholic amnesias, and reviewed the former committee's classification of alcohol as intermediate between addiction producing drugs and habit forming drugs. They agreed with this classification, but felt that the intensity of the withdrawal symptoms had been underestimated (World Health Organization, 1955):

"The discussion of this question by the present Committee also brings out the fact that, though many of the events observed in alcoholism are parallel to many of the phenomena observed in opiate addiction, many important differences exist. The Committee feels, however, that recent evidence makes it appear that there is more resemblance between the responses to the withdrawal of alcohol and of opiates than was previously realized.

"It is now clear that, following discontinuation of alcohol after a prolonged period of very heavy drinking, severe withdrawal symptoms, which in a limited proportion of cases include convulsions or delirium, or both, may occur. These latter symptoms are more dangerous to the life of the individual than are any of the manifestations of withdrawal of morphine. When serious symptoms follow the withdrawal of alcohol they persist almost as long as do those following the withdrawal of opiates.

"Even though a marked degree of physical dependence on alcohol, as manifested by withdrawal symptoms, can develop, it occurs only after a prolonged period of very heavy drinking. In contrast, a considerable degree of physical dependence on morphine can appear after administration of therapeutic doses over a period of 21 to 30 days. Moreover, the attitude of both the individual and society to the use of alcoholic drink is entirely different from their attitude to the use of opiates. The first is widely on sale; it is consumed in public, and its use is generally considered to be normal and is even sometimes encouraged. The sale of opiates, on the contrary, is controlled or clandestine, and they are generally administered by injection. Their use by the addict is always concealed. This use for non-medical purposes is generally considered extremely abnormal and reprehensible. Feelings of guilt for use and condemnation by society are therefore far greater in the second case than in the first. Finally, it is a well-known clinical fact that, although treatment of alcoholics is far from achieving satisfactory and lasting results in every case, the proportion of such results is much greater than among opiate addicts.

"These observations all lead to the conclusion that, although there exist so many clinical and biochemical analogies between alcoholism and opiate addiction, one must make a clear distinction between them, both in medical practice and in the medico-social or legislative measures concerning them."

The deliberations of the two committees bring out unequivocally that in a minority of users acquired increased tolerance to alcohol takes place, and "compulsive craving" and "dependence upon alcohol" can develop "which manifests itself in severe withdrawal symptoms." Thus the criteria of true drug addiction are fulfilled in some species of alcoholism.

The fact that these processes occur only in a relatively small minority of users, and then only after years of continual excessive drinking justifies the classification of alcohol as intermediate between the addiction producing and the habit forming drugs. Nevertheless, in the instance of that minority who go through the above-mentioned processes, it is justified to speak of alcohol addiction in the pharmacological sense of the word.

One may ask why addiction to alcohol occurs in a relatively small minority of users only. The process of addiction to alcohol requires the continual consumption of large amounts of alcoholic beverages over many years. Such drinking behavior, however, is not favored by our culture. Consequently, mainly those are liable to expose themselves to the risk of alcohol addiction who have a special individual inducement, such as inability to cope with tensions, or who are placed in one of the small cultural subgroups which accept a high alcohol intake as the norm.

Both committees emphasized that only a small minority of the users of alcoholic beverages became addicted to alcohol while 70 to 100 per cent of the users of heroin and other narcotic drugs developed addiction. I should like to point out, that, at least in Europe and the Americas, this "small minority" is probably 20 times greater than the number of addicts to all other drugs. The social damage originating in alcohol addiction is thus incomparably greater than that from the so-called addiction producing drugs.

Furthermore, it must be taken into account that there are also those who use excessive amounts, but nevertheless not sufficiently and not sufficiently frequently to trigger off the process of tissue adaptation, but who nevertheless impair their health and may cause some social damage.

It must be considered, however, that in some alcoholics no true addiction develops, in spite of the frequent ingestion of large quantities of alcohol. It may be that in these instances some factors protect the nervous tissues against adaptation to alcohol.

At this juncture it may be in order to repeat that—for the purpose of the present discourse—alcoholism has been very broadly defined as any drinking that results in damage to the individual or to society. Further, two species of alcoholism have been singled out for the question whether or not they constitute an illness, or rather a disorder in the medical sense.

One species involves loss of control that extends to the amount consumed on a given occasion while the ability to determine the initiation of a new bout, i.e., the ability to abstain for shorter or longer periods remains intact.

In the other species the ability to abstain from alcoholic beverages even for 1 day is lost, but the drinker retains control over the amounts he consumes.

In the instance of this latter pattern alcoholic beverages are ingested every day in such a way that small quantities of alcohol are present in the blood stream practically at all times of the day and night. After several years of such drinking, a day of abstinence brings about withdrawal symptoms, although the drinker may show frank intoxication only on scattered occasions. I have postulated (see Chapter III.4.4.4) that this behavior is evidence of adaptive cell metabolism. Thus there is no need to ask whether this pattern may be viewed in the light of the addictive processes as discussed above.

The great differences in time and amounts as involved in alcohol addiction on the one side and drug addictions on the other side play an important role in obscuring the identity of the addictive processes. Perhaps most important in this connection is the great difference between times necessary for the development of alcohol addiction and of the drug addictions. In a conversation Dr. David Lester suggested that, in the instance of ethyl alcohol, adaptation of the cell metabolism is much slower on account of its similarity to normal metabolites.

III.4.4.2. Acquired Increased Tolerance to Alcohol. It is a common observation shared by laymen and students of alcohol problems that as the use of alcoholic beverages is repeated often, the user shows smaller reactions to the same amounts of ethyl alcohol. The diminishing alcohol effect, which is termed increased tolerance in scientific discussion as well as in everyday conversation, may become more pronounced as repetitions become more frequent, and as the amounts used increase.

Aside from this tolerance trend, which develops over a long period of time, there is a certain accommodation of the nervous system to the effect of a given blood alcohol concentration that takes place within half an hour or an hour of a single drinking occasion. This phenomenon, which can be observed only in the laboratory, has some interrelations with acquired increased tolerance, but cannot be assumed to have the same mechanism as the latter. This "short-range accommodation to alcohol" will be discussed separately in section III.4.4.5.

Mention must be made also of "decreased tolerance" which is frequently mentioned as a manifestation of highly advanced, late "alcoholism." Descriptions of this phenomenon are based not on laboratory tests but on subjective statements of alcoholics. It may involve not tolerance but rather the gastric inability to ingest large amounts of alcohol on account of gastritis, which is common in late alcoholism. On the other hand, there may be a true decreased tolerance due to brain injuries and other severe physical trauma or to a high degree of sugar depletion. These forms of decreased tolerance need not be considered in the present discussion.

The term "tolerance to alcohol" has been invoked by many writers on alcoholism in order to explain various manifestations of the use of alcoholic beverages. Conversationally, the term is used to denote the individual consumer's ability to ingest certain amounts without giving the appearance of "drunken behavior."

In scientific discussion, of course, the term is generally—but not always—used in a much stricter sense. Yet there is an interchangeable usage of "tolerance" with such terms as "habituation," "susceptibility," "capacity," "sensitivity," and so forth. Furthermore, the term "tolerance" is frequently used in conflicting or obscure ways.

Persons with low tolerance are thought by some to be particular risks for development of alcoholism, but the same risk is attached by other writers to individuals with high tolerance to alcohol. These contentions are by no means conflicting. Cogent arguments may be given for both sides. The person with a low initial tolerance to alcohol, of course, experiences tension reduction after rather small amounts of alcohol and thus a conditioning to the utilitarian use of alcohol is easily established. The European alcohol literature recognizes the "alcohol intolerant drinker" as a member of a special group not to be confused with those having a "pathological reaction to alcohol." The "alcohol intolerant" drinkers do not necessarily drink small amounts, as a matter of fact their intake may increase considerably as their frequent, severe intoxications demoralize them. The fairly high incidence of "alcohol intolerant drinkers" claimed by European authorities is, however, far from being a well established fact.

On the other hand the drinker with very high initial alcohol tolerance may constitute a risk for addiction, as his gradual acquisition of increased tissue tolerance might go unnoticed for a long time.

There are also such distinctions as "psychological tolerance," "tissue tolerance" and "gastric tolerance" and this latter term may be equated with "capacity."

Capacity and tolerance are related phenomena, but a distinction should be made between them. There is a much smaller ability to hold down given quantities of alcoholic beverages at the time when an individual begins to use alcoholic beverages than later—irrespective of whether the person in question becomes intoxicated or not. The capacity for holding larger amounts increases with time —again without necessarily implying a decreased tendency to become intoxicated. Capacity for alcohol can increase faster than tolerance, and the lag may become greatly pronounced in the course of developments. Goldberg (1952) attributes the loss of control to the lag between capacity and tolerance, but this suggestion does not seem to explain many of the manifestations of the loss of control, particularly the appearance of withdrawal symptoms at a diminished rate of alcohol intake.

In the case of the addiction producing drugs (morphine, heroin, etc.) one speaks only of "acquired tolerance" as apparently no particular differences in tolerance to these drugs exist among individuals before continued use. On the other hand, it is well known that even from the very start of the use of alcoholic beverages individuals may react quite differently to the same amounts of alcohol per kilogram of body weight. On account of this fact it is necessary to distinguish between, on the one hand, what may be called initial tolerance or inherent tolerance or essential tolerance, and on the other hand, the tolerance developed through the use of alcoholic beverages, that is, acquired increased tolerance. A W.H.O. committee (1954) suggested the term "acquired increase of tolerance to alcohol."

Acquired increased tolerance to alcohol is not to be equated with "habituation," although tolerance belongs in that complex of phenomena to which the term habituation attaches.

At this point a more stringent discussion of the term "alcohol tolerance" is necessary as well as a clarification of the question of psychological tolerance versus tissue tolerance.

There is a difference between tolerance as judged in a social situation and tolerance as thought of in the research laboratory. Both ways of viewing the question are relevant to the problem of alcoholism, but for the sake of clear discussion it is desirable to distinguish between them.

In the ordinary social drinking situation there is no way of determining blood alcohol concentration, nor is it possible to make objective tests of the effect of the alcohol consumption of various individuals on their psychological and physiological functions. All that is accessible to observation at a banquet or a cocktail party are the amounts that a participant consumes and the apparent effects that these amounts have on his total behavior. The judgments of the apparent effects by the participant observers may be colored by their particular standards and, occasionally, by their own degree of alcoholization, but a certain validity attaches to them nevertheless.

In the social drinking situation the observation and its interpretation are made in terms of the amount of alcohol consumed and its effect on a given drinker with reference to the effects of the same amount on another given drinker or on the fictitious "average drinker."

"Mr. A has a much greater alcohol tolerance than Mr. B, as each of them had half a bottle of wine, but Mr. A did not seem affected in any way, while Mr. B got flushed and engaged in rather silly conversation." That Mr. B may weigh 40 to 60 pounds less than Mr. A, or that the latter was drinking right after he had eaten, while B may have been drinking on an empty stomach, are matters which are not considered.

On the other hand, the observer in the laboratory always takes cognizance of factors that influence the effect indirectly by modifying the rate of absorption and, therefore, the magnitude of the blood alcohol concentration.

While the physiologist may, in certain instances, talk of tolerance in terms of the effects of certain amounts of alcohol as modified by the rate of absorption, as a rule he will mean by tolerance the degree of impairment of a function corresponding to definite concentrations of alcohol in the blood, let us say of 0.3 per mil or 0.5 per mil, irrespective of the amount of alcohol from which such concentrations may have resulted.

As far as the social drinking situation is concerned, it is justified to talk about tolerance in terms of given amounts without further considerations. The tolerance that is judged in these latter terms may be spoken of as apparent tolerance, while the expressions true tolerance, intrinsic tolerance, or essential tolerance may be applied to tolerance with reference to the magnitude of blood alcohol concentrations. It matters little what terms are chosen to distinguish between meanings of tolerance so long as some distinguishing labels are used consistently (Jellinek, 1952a).

For the measurement and some quantitative data on acquired increased tolerance to alcohol as reflected in tests on "occasional drinkers," "moderate drinkers" and "heavy drinkers," reference is made here to the basic work of Goldberg (1943, 1952).

"The alcohol tolerance of an individual may be established through the determination of the smallest blood alcohol concentration at which he shows a perceptible change in a given psychological function. If, on the other hand, alcohol tolerance of a group of individuals—such as an ethnic group, or a group of abstainers—is investigated, the criterion will be the smallest blood alcohol concentration at which 50 per cent of the individuals show perceptible changes" (Goldberg, 1952).

In an investigation of this question, Goldberg used the following objective tests:

(a) *Flicker test*—Determination of the fusion frequency of the eye to intermittent light through the use of an apparatus producing a flickering light, adjustable for varying flicker frequencies and light intensities.

(b) *Blink test*—Establishment of the threshold stimulus for the blink reflex through a graded jet of air against the cornea.

(c) *Quantitative Romberg*—Recording of standing steadiness through photographic and planimetric measurement of the deflections of a source of light attached to the subject's head and shoulders.

(d) *Finger coordination test*—Coordination of finger movement tested by dotting on a target.

(e) *Subtraction test.*

(f) *Bourdon test*—Comprehension and concentration tested by marking letters in a standardized text.

Only tests a, b, and c will be considered here as they do not involve any question of learning or psychological compensation. Apparently at blood alcohol concentrations above 1.0 per mil acquired increased tolerance plays less and less of a role in the reaction to alcohol.

The data in Table 3 show that a certain level of alcohol in the blood was necessary in order to produce symptoms of intoxication, and this level or threshold varied from one test to the other and, within limits, also between different individuals. For occasional or moderate drinkers the threshold in one series averaged 0.2 to 0.4 per mil for the Flicker and Blink tests. It may be mentioned that in practical road tests with automobile drivers the threshold for the impairment of driving was 0.35 to 0.40 per mil.

The findings that the blood alcohol concentration must be over a certain threshold in order to produce symptoms of intoxication and that the increase in the degree of impairment has a logarithmic relationship to the blood alcohol level explain the frequently made observation that a drinker may show no symptoms of intoxication after a certain amount of alcohol, but may be markedly intoxicated after a just slightly greater amount (Goldberg, 1952).

A W.H.O. Committee on Alcohol (1954) agreed "to regard tol-

TABLE 3.—*Percentage of Cases with Positive Quantitative Test of Intoxication at Different Blood Alcohol Concentrations, Classified according to Drinking Habits (Adapted from Goldberg, 1943)*

	Blood Alcohol Concentration per mil	Flicker	Blink	Romberg
Occasional drinkers	0–0.50	71.3	86.5	49.9
	0.51–1.00	100.0	100.0	97.4
Moderate drinkers	0–0.50	9.7	65.6	30.9
	0.51–1.00	99.8	99.7	94.6
Heavy drinkers	0–0.50	0.0	4.5	8.9
	0.51–1.00	69.2	69.2	46.1

erance to alcohol as the capacity of the organism to function with alcohol in the blood without measurable deterioration in nervous function." The committee further stated that

"considerable individual differences in tolerance to alcohol in this sense exist [and have] been demonstrated in experimental work upon animals and man. Various functions of the nervous system have been tested by suitable procedures, such as fusion frequency determination, the use of the pursuit meter, electro-encephalography, quantitative measurement of standing steadiness, and many others. By administering different amounts of alcohol, and following by serial determinations both test performance and blood alcohol concentration, it has been possible to correlate the response of the organism, as measured by these tests, to blood alcohol concentration.

"Such experiments have demonstrated that there is a critical level or threshold of alcohol concentration in the blood at which performance begins to show deterioration. This threshold is characteristic of the individual tested and of the particular test employed. Tolerance to alcohol can thus be measured by that concentration of alcohol in the blood at which a demonstrable effect on the performance of a given test of nervous function first becomes apparent.

"Since this precise method of measuring tolerance to alcohol exists, it was considered that the term tolerance should not be used in other senses such as, for example, the following: (a) the amount of alcohol required by an individual to produce euphoria; (b) the amount of alcoholic beverages ingested by an individual without the appearance of signs of intoxication; (c) the mere ability to ingest large quantities of alcohol irrespective of whether such quantities result in intoxication or not.

"The main reason for the rejection of the above forms of usage was because they relate the effects of alcohol to dosage. This is undesirable since variation in the rate of absorption and other aspects of the metabolism of alcohol, as well as the period over which ingestion takes place, may change the relation between dosage and blood alcohol levels. . . .

"It has been shown that to produce the same effects, as measured by objective tests, a higher blood alcohol level is required in habitual heavy drinkers than in moderate drinkers and abstainers. That this increase of tolerance is acquired is shown by its disappearance after a period of abstinence.[9] There is, furthermore, experimental evidence that in animals subjected to prolonged administration of large doses of alcohol the blood alcohol level required to produce the same symptoms must be increased. . . .

---

[*] There is no exact knowledge concerning the time necessary to abolish acquired increased tolerance. It appears that the time period may vary from individual to individual and that the variation may be related to differences in the extent of the acquired increase and the time involved in achieving it.

"Prolonged heavy intake of alcohol does not decrease the rate of absorption nor does it increase the rate of oxidation or excretion of alcohol. There is no evidence to show that the permeability of the haemato-encephalic barrier to alcohol is lowered. Two other possible explanations have been put forward for the increase in resistance to alcohol.

"Conditions may arise that make the nervous system more resistant to alcohol, or the individual may compensate for the effects of intoxication through the process of learning. Frequently, these two possibilities are regarded as though mutually exclusive, but it does not appear necessary to make this assumption. No doubt continued experience with the effects of alcohol can enable an individual to offset them to a limited degree. However, in view of the results of experiments with objective tests both in man and in animals it is the opinion of the committee that, although the biological mechanism of the change is not fully understood, the total phenomenon cannot be accounted for solely by compensation based on learning, and in addition requires for its explanation a changed physiological response of the organism to alcohol.

"The committee felt that special emphasis should be laid on the fact that acquired increase of tolerance to alcohol was of a lower order of magnitude than the corresponding phenomenon known to occur with addiction-producing drugs of the morphine type. The morphine addict may develop (an increase of) tolerance enabling him to withstand several times the lethal dose. An increase of this degree has not been observed with alcohol" (World Health Organization, 1954).

In the case of the experiments of Goldberg, discussed above, "psychological tolerance," i.e., learning and compensation, is out of question; and in view of the fact that neither a lowering of absorption rate nor an acceleration of oxidation of alcohol occurs in alcohol accustomed subjects, the acquired increased tolerance must be regarded as true tissue tolerance. This by no means implies a denial of the role of learning and psychological compensation in the development of acquired increased alcohol tolerance. In some cases learning is not only possible, but even evident.

The most decisive datum for the postulation of acquired increased *tissue* tolerance to alcohol is the cross tolerance of alcohol addicts and other heavy drinkers to certain anesthetics, such as ether and chloroform. It is the common experience of surgeons that alcoholic patients require much more of these substances than do others in order to produce surgical anesthesia. Of course this cross tolerance could not come about unless the increased tolerance to ethyl alcohol were acquired tissue tolerance; no learning or psychological compensation can account for this phenomenon.

The surgical experience in this matter is so general that experimental confirmation is hardly necessary. Nevertheless, evidence from animal experiments can be offered too. The French pharmacologist, Lévy (1935), has shown conclusively that rats highly accustomed to alcohol required 28 per cent more alcohol (intravenously) to produce a 3-minute period of anesthesia than did abstinent rats.

The data of Goldberg (discussed above) and the cross tolerance to ether and chloroform should suffice to establish the fact that much of the acquired increased tolerance to alcohol is tissue tolerance, but some additional material is offered here.

Newman (1941) has shown in two groups of habituated dogs, that there is definite development of tolerance. The habituated animals in the first group were compared with normal controls and showed a markedly greater ability to control their neuromuscular apparatus than did the controls at the same blood alcohol levels. They were then taken off alcohol and after 7 months had lost the acquired increased tolerance. The second group was compared before and after habituation and again demonstrated the acquisition of tolerance to alcohol. As there is neither any slowing of absorption in habituated subjects nor any speeding up of alcohol metabolism, "by process of elimination we must conclude that this acquired tolerance to alcohol is a tissue tolerance."

Allan and Swinyard (1949) conclude that the electroshock seizure threshold may be used as a graphic measure of "tissue tolerance" to ethyl alcohol. This is based on the administration of 1 to 4 g. of alcohol per kg. of body weight to rats. After a first dose the threshold increased 20 per cent in rats given 1 g. of alcohol and practically 100 per cent in those given 4 g. The initial increase was followed by daily decreases in the threshold until normal values were reached after 3 weeks.

"A standardized oral dose of 1.25 g. of ethyl alcohol per kg. of body weight was administered to 10 male hospital attendants and 10 hospitalized male alcoholics.

"(1) The blood alcohol curves during the experiments were largely the same in both attendants and patients.

"(2) EEG frequencies shifted between 0.7 and 3.0 c.p.s. toward slower ranges (average 1.4–1.5 c.p.s.), and the amplitudes at the same times increased by about 50 to 100 per cent. There was no statistically significant difference between the two groups, although the frequency drop seemed a little less in the patients than in the attendants.

"(3) In the patients the maximum EEG changes coincided with maximum blood alcohol concentration, whereas in the attendants, who were significantly younger and less accustomed to alcohol, the EEG changes remained on the average 45 minutes after the maximum blood alcohol concentrations. This was probably due to the drowsiness that followed direct intoxication in the attendants.

"(4) The patients were in every way less affected by the alcohol, although their blood alcohol concentrations were slightly higher. The drop in EEG frequency was not as great nor as protracted (difference not statistically significant) and the pulse reactions were less pronounced (almost significant) and less complex."

The above findings are borne out by the data of the experiment carried out by Wikler, Pescor, Fraser and Isbell (1956) to which reference has been made before. Their EEG data furnish additional evidence of the addictive properties of alcohol in the sense that partial tolerance and pharmacological dependence developed in association with prolonged continuous intoxication. "The partial restitution of control patterns during the early part of chronic intoxication reflects metabolic tolerance." Later, when blood alcohol levels may rise and clinical symptoms may remain the same or decrease, EEG changes decrease, reflecting "tissue tolerance."

In summary it may be said that while the user of alcoholic beverages may learn to some extent to anticipate the effect of alcohol on some psychological functions and to compensate for them consciously or unconsciously, there is a limit to such compensation; furthermore there are certain functions (discussed above) in which compensation cannot account for lowered reaction to alcohol, and acquired increased tissue tolerance is an inevitable conclusion. Tissue tolerance of course may be assumed only after prolonged regular alcohol intake.

It should be added that the acquired tolerance to alcohol remains of a much lower degree than the tolerance that occurs in addiction to the morphine type drugs and to the barbiturates. Furthermore, there are no acceptable data that would indicate an increase in the lethal blood alcohol concentration either in humans or infrahuman animals.

III.4.4.3. The Withdrawal Syndrome. The only criterion for the development of physical dependence upon alcohol, or upon any other substance, is the emergence of certain disturbing symptoms on the abrupt cessation of the ingestion of the substance in question. These untoward manifestations are known as withdrawal symptoms and form an entire syndrome.

As a matter of fact, the appearance of withdrawal symptoms is not limited to abrupt cessation of intake.

"Withdrawal symptoms may be defined as those manifestations which appear either after cessation of drinking or even after an abrupt decrease in the rate of intake, either of which, in the opinion of the Committee, constitutes a 'withdrawal.' It follows that such symptoms are not present as long as a sufficient degree of intoxication is maintained and that the symptoms can be relieved by alcohol or by some drug with similar pharmacological effects (e.g., paraldehyde, barbiturates and chloral hydrate)" (World Health Organization, 1955).

That the mere *decrease* of the level of alcohol (or of an addictive drug) in the blood may provoke withdrawal symptoms has been emphasized by many observers (e.g., Page, 1947; Pohlisch, 1954; Bell, 1956; and Isbell, Frazer et al., 1955).

In the case of alcohol some psychiatrically or psychologically oriented students of the problem have either denied the occurrence of withdrawal symptoms, or—more frequently—in their discussion of the development of "alcoholism" have omitted any mention of such symptoms.

Those psychiatrists who deny the existence of withdrawal symptoms do not mean that such behaviors as mentioned above are not observed in acute intoxication, but believe that they are of psychological origin. In the psychiatric literature on alcoholism, with few exceptions, the affirmative use of the term "withdrawal symptoms" implies that the author assumes their physical origin.

Psychiatrists who reject the idea that alcoholism is an addiction in the pharmacological sense place great weight on the psychological explanation of the "apparent" withdrawal symptoms. The reason for this emphasis is that the admission of true withdrawal symptoms would imply the acceptance of a pharmacological process of addiction in alcoholism (Jellinek, 1953).

It may be said that the above attitude pertains largely to those psychiatrists who do not see alcohol addicts in states of acute intoxication, but receive the sobered-up patients with a view to treating their "alcoholic behavior."

It is of interest to note that some of the proponents of physiological etiologies of "alcoholism" have not paid attention to withdrawal symptoms, but have concentrated entirely on organic anomalies in the explanation of the "uncontrolled use" of alcoholic beverages without any allusion to possible addictive developments in the pharmacological sense.

The discussion of the withdrawal symptoms comes largely from physicians who are frequently called upon to treat patients with acute alcoholic intoxication and from a few experimental studies. From the times of the Hippocratic writings (Epidemics, III, 110–116) to the present day the symptoms most consistently observed are tremors and convulsion.

One of the largest series of recent observations was reported by Victor and Adams (1953). Their material consisted of 266 unselected patients admitted consecutively to the Boston City Hospital in various states of acute and chronic alcohol intoxication. Seventy per cent of these patients were characterized by tremulous, hallucinatory, convulsive and delirious states. There were 101 instances of delirium tremens. Tremulousness combined with transient hallucinations occurred in 50 per cent of the patients within 24 hours following cessation of drinking. Seizures occurred within 48 hours after the drinking bouts in 60 per cent of the patients. Psychomotor and autonomic overactivity, tremulousness, hallucinations and confusion had the highest incidence 3 or 4 days after cessation of the bouts. "It is difficult to escape the conclusion that the clinical states under discussion depend for their production not only upon the effects of prolonged exposure to alcohol, but temporarily on abstinence from the drug."

Godfrey, Kissen and Downs (1958) state that

"The acute withdrawal state is so stereotyped as to warrant fully the term syndrome. [It suggests] specific physiological disturbances. . . . First and foremost the patient is frightened, depressed, weak, restless and unable to sleep. . . . Some of these signs and symptoms, along with markedly exaggerated tendon reflexes, sometimes with ankle clonus, nystagmus, and grand mal, epileptiform convulsions, are obviously related to disturbances in the central nervous system of unknown etiology. They are sufficiently clear to the physician and painful to the patient to demand immediate attention. . . . In adequately treated cases there will frequently be an elevation of temperature between 99° and 100° during the first 12 hours."

In the cases treated merely with sedation this may persist much longer.

The statement that the acute withdrawal state is "stereotyped" of course does not imply that all of the withdrawal symptoms will appear in all instances. Pohlisch (1954) as well as many others have pointed out that withdrawal symptoms after an alcoholic bout vary considerably according to the duration of the bout and the quantity of alcohol consumed. This latter point is evident in the data of Isbell, Fraser et al. (1955). Pohlisch (1954) also noted that while withdrawal symptoms in the drug addictions show a certain degree of variability, the variation is greater in alcoholism. But at the same time it must be said that in spite of all variation the nature of the withdrawal symptoms is the same in alcoholism as in the drug addictions. For recent descriptions of the more constant and often minor withdrawal symptoms see Albert, Rea et al. (1954); Burroughs (1957); Cummins and Friend (1954); Fazekas, Shea and Rea (1955); Grandon, Heffley et al. (1956); Greenfield (1956); Greenhouse (1954); Izikowitz, Mårtens and Dahlborn (1952); Kalinowsky (1942); Mitchell (1956); Page (1947). Bensoussan (1956) covers the French literature on this subject. Anorexia, insomnia, dysphoria, psychomotor hyperactivity, tremor and nausea are usually present even after milder bouts.

Frequently dehydration is mentioned as a manifestation of the withdrawal syndrome. This is more correctly formulated by Godfrey, Kissen and Downs (1958) who state that the alcohol withdrawal syndrome is "associated with both dehydration and starvation." "Associated with" is the correct expression as dehydration cannot be regarded as a withdrawal symptom, but does appear after prolonged bouts largely as a result of near starvation caused by the neglect of food intake during a spree.

Withdrawal of alcohol, however, especially after bouts of long duration and extremely high alcohol intake, may produce severe and dangerous symptoms. "It is not generally realized that patients in this condition [acute intoxication], if not treated effectively . . . may develop severe physical and mental complications" (Nason, 1947). The same author also mentions fatal outcomes. Solms (1954b) also reports on withdrawal symptoms with fatal termination. Extreme instances of agitation may present grave dangers. "Psychomotor agitation is one of the most distressing symptoms observed in alcoholic patients during the period of recovery from an acute bout of intoxication" (Kissen, Yaskin et al., 1951). The severest forms of withdrawal symptoms, however, are convulsions and in limited instances delirium tremens.

Convulsions following alcohol withdrawal have received either too much or too little attention. The fairly large—often rather obscure—literature on "alcoholic epilepsy" has built a case on the epileptogenic properties of alcohol but an evaluation has been difficult because of the undoubtedly higher incidence of alcoholism among epileptics than among the general population. There is, however, sufficient evidence that epileptiform convulsions may occur on alcohol withdrawal in persons who have neither epilepsy nor an epileptic family history. As far back as 1849 Magnus Huss found that "chronic alcoholics" may develop convulsions which resemble chorea and he distinguished clearly between the convulsions of alcoholic epileptic patients and those of nonepileptic alcoholics brought about by alcohol withdrawal (Jellinek, 1943).

Out of his great clinical experience one of the foremost students of alcoholism, Rudolf Wlassak (1929), came to the conclusion that convulsions following alcohol withdrawal should not be equated with epilepsy unless in the special case evidence should be obvious. In the past 15 or 20 years the literature on the treatment of acute alcohol intoxication and specifically on withdrawal symptoms tends to deal with alcoholic convulsions rather as withdrawal symptoms than as epilepsy provoked by alcohol. It is recognized that alcohol exacerbates epileptic conditions.

It has been suggested that the appearance of convulsions after severe alcoholic bouts may be related to magnesium deficiency. Klingman, Suter et al. (1955) have shown in 10 patients with delirium, confusion, tremors and convulsions that these symptoms could be stopped within a short time through intravenous administration of 10 to 40 grams of magnesium sulfate. The same investigators, experimenting with rats, found some indications of this relation, although the results were not quite clear cut. Klingman and his associates suggest that seizures involve a derangement in brain cell electrolytes. An electrolyte imbalance could conceivably result from the absence of or an insufficient level of alcohol in nerve tissue that had adapted its metabolism to the presence of that drug. The process is not quite clear but this is true of the mechanism of all withdrawal symptoms, whether from alcohol or other drugs.

Electroencephalographic changes too have been seen after alcohol withdrawal:

"A characteristic electroencephalographic pattern was obtained during chronic intoxication with alcohol and during the withdrawal period. Early during chronic intoxication, the EEG's were generally slowed whenever the patients had high blood alcohol levels and were showing clinical evidence of intoxication. Later during chronic intoxication, the EEG's were not as slow, even though blood alcohol levels were higher than during the early part of the period of intoxication. Following withdrawal of alcohol, the EEG first became normal. Between the sixteenth and thirty-third hours of abstinence, the percentage of alpha activity declined and random spikes and bursts of slow waves were observed" (Isbell, Fraser et al., 1955; see also Wikler, Pescor et al., 1956).

Whether the EEG changes themselves constitute withdrawal symptoms or whether they are merely reflections of the various neurological withdrawal symptoms cannot be said. However, no specific changes have been consistently related to hallucinosis or delirium tremens.

The question of delirium tremens as a withdrawal symptom has been reopened since the famous experiment conducted by Isbell, Fraser et al. (1955). Actually the question was never quite closed. By the end of the nineteenth century, a majority of European authorities had relegated the withdrawal causation of delirium tremens into obsolescence, as can be seen from Rosenfeld's (1901) review of the effects of alcohol. Nevertheless, in Europe a sizable minority of physicians continued to regard delirium tremens as a withdrawal symptom although not to the exclusion of other causation.

In the United States the trend toward the view that delirium tremens was not caused by alcohol withdrawal really began in the 1930's although such opinions had been voiced sporadically since the turn of the century. It may be said that American authorities broke definitely with the withdrawal theory in the 1930's when vitamin deficiencies were postulated as etiological factors in delirium tremens although up to the present day no proof has been given to this effect. There remained a small minority of American authorities who did not give up the withdrawal etiology of delirium tremens and their number was already growing slightly (see, for instance, Victor and Adams, 1953) when the experiments of Isbell and his associates called for a revision of opinions. Isbell, Fraser et al. (1955) decided on an experimental investigation of alcohol withdrawal symptoms in human subjects to whom alcohol was to be administered over periods well exceeding the duration of ordinary bouts and in quantities approaching the theoretical maximum of alcohol intake. They were led to this by the following considerations:

"A large proportion of the alcoholics admitted to general hospitals have been intoxicated only a brief time or have been on a debauch of only a few days' duration; they cannot, therefore, be expected to develop serious manifestations of an abstinence syndrome on abrupt withdrawal of alcohol. Furthermore, as was pointed out by Kalinowsky, even though alcohol is withdrawn, these patients are almost invariably given some type of sedative medication, most frequently paraldehyde, and such medication may be equivalent to continuing to give alcohol. On the other hand, total withdrawal of alcohol may not be necessary for the precipitation of abstinence symptoms—that is, a reduction in alcohol intake may be sufficient to precipitate them. They may be analogous to the situation in barbiturate addiction, in which a sudden reduction of dosage may be followed by convulsions or delirium or both."

All the 10 subjects were former morphine addicts who were serving sentences for violation of the Harrison Narcotics Act, and who volunteered for the experiment. Four of the subjects also had a history of heavy drinking and were at least incipient alcoholics before their morphinism.

Three of the subjects drank only from 7 to 16 days and averaged daily amounts from 266 to 293 cc. of absolute alcohol. The remaining seven subjects drank from 34 to 87 consecutive days. Their daily average amounts ranged from 346 to 489 cc. of absolute alcohol.

"It is noteworthy that all the patients exceeded the amount of alcohol that is usually cited as the average (100 mg. per kg. per hr., or 224 ml. of 95 per cent alcohol daily) that can be metabolized by a man weighing 70 kg., and four patients nearly attained the daily consumption (400 g. or 533 ml. daily) regarded as the maximum intake possible. . . .

"[The three subjects] who drank for only 7 to 16 days, sobered up rapidly after they discontinued alcohol. As the degree of intoxication declined, they became slightly tremulous, perspired excessively, complained of gastric distress, nervousness and weakness. . . . [They] recovered rapidly, and after 1 to 3 days appeared to be completely normal. The over-all picture in these three patients was merely that of a severe 'hangover'. . . . [One who] complained the most . . . requested drinks to relieve his symptoms. . . .

"Six of the patients drank for 48 to 87 days. Following abrupt withdrawal of alcohol, all developed tremors, marked weakness, nausea, vomiting, diarrhea, hyperreflexia, fever and hypertension. Two of these six patients had seizures; three had a frank delirium (one of these three was receiving large amounts of barbiturates at the time delirium occurred);

two had transient visual or auditory hallucinations or both; and one escaped both convulsions and hallucinations. These phenomena occurred despite the ingestion of an adequate diet, with multiple vitamin supplements throughout the periods of intoxication and withdrawal."

While the above experimental results have created great interest and rethinking of the problem among students of alcoholism, words of caution have been expressed on account of the fact that the experimental subjects were all former morphine addicts and that some of them had been at least incipient alcoholics before their morphinism (e.g., Himwich, 1956). I would repeat this caution, but I do not believe that the experimental results are invalidated, particularly since two of the three subjects who developed delirium tremens after withdrawal had no alcoholic history.

Isbell and his associates do not maintain that delirium tremens is necessarily caused by withdrawal, but rather that under certain circumstances it can emerge as a withdrawal symptom; their views are given verbatim below:

"Results obtained in this study indicate that withdrawal of alcohol from chronically intoxicated persons is at least one of the factors which will precipitate convulsions or a delirium or both. Of the 10 patients 3 . . . withdrew so soon after the experiment began that severe abstinence symptoms were hardly to be expected. [One] discontinued after a month, and was probably marginal in this respect. All of the 6 patients who drank for 48 days or more exhibited significant symptoms on withdrawal. All had tremor, weakness, perspiration, nausea, vomiting, diarrhea, hyperreflexia, slight fever, elevated blood pressure, and insomnia. Convulsions occurred in 2. . . . Hallucinations with insight and clear sensorium were observed in 2 patients . . . , and frank delirium occurred in 2. . . .

"While the data strongly support the thesis that withdrawal of alcohol did precipitate a characteristic train of symptoms, including convulsions and delirium, they do not preclude the possibility that factors other than withdrawal of alcohol may precipitate these phenomena under other conditions. Nor do they exclude the possibility that the symptoms would have occurred, without alcohol being withdrawn, had the patients continued to drink for longer periods of time.

"One might ask why convulsions and frank delirium did not occur in all the patients. This is scarcely to be expected, since individual variation following withdrawal of drugs other than alcohol is rather great. Abrupt withdrawal of barbiturates from chronically intoxicated persons results in convulsions in only 75 per cent of the cases and delirium in only 60 per cent. The factors responsible for this variation are unknown but, by analogy, similar variation would be expected after withdrawal of alcohol. Actually, the variations following withdrawal of alcohol may be greater than with barbiturates. . . . Most of the clinical syndromes attributed by Victor and Adams to withdrawal of alcohol were represented in the present experiment. . . .

"From our data, it appears that severe withdrawal symptoms may occur after consumption of 400 to 500 ml. of 95 per cent alcohol (equivalent to 770 to 950 ml. of 100-proof whisky) for 48 days or more. Much more information on the relationship of the amount of alcohol consumed and the length of the debauch to the severity of the symptoms of abstinence is needed" (Isbell, Fraser et al., 1955).

The indications are that, under such extreme conditions as described above, delirium tremens may arise as a consequence of alcohol withdrawal. Apparently this severe form of abstinence symptoms does not occur at decreasing alcohol levels, but rather after disappearance of almost all alcohol in the body tissues, from 2 to 3 days after termination of the drinking bout. On the other hand, the material of Isbell and his associates does not point to alcohol withdrawal as the sole etiological factor of delirium tremens.

In the refutation of delirium tremens as a possible withdrawal phenomenon an argument presented by Bowman, Wortis and Keiser (1939) played a prominent role:

"In the prodromal period of delirium tremens, the patient often experiences a disgust for alcohol sufficient to cause abstinence for several days. The acute gastritis and hepatitis which so many patients have, often makes it impossible for them to retain anything by mouth, including alcohol. It is this type of abstinence which has often been mistaken as a cause rather than a result of delirium tremens."

The above passage was presented in Bowman and Jellinek (1942b) as a potent argument, but it would seem to me now that the inability to ingest any more alcohol on account of gastritis or similar disturbances constitutes a condition of withdrawal although it is not of external origin. Likewise, hospitalization for infectious disease which so often precedes delirium tremens brings about withdrawal, but in this instance lowered resistance due to disease processes presumably also plays a prominent role.

The alcohol withdrawal syndrome is so well documented that its existence can hardly be denied and under exceptional conditions it probably also includes delirium tremens.

There is little doubt that phenomena on the symbolic level enter into the withdrawal syndrome and reinforce some of the symptoms which, however, are basically of a true neurological character, some of them of a neuro-endocrine nature. (The endocrine aspects have been suggested by Gross [1945] among others.)

Some "late withdrawal symptoms" have been suggested which according to Wellman (1954a, 1954b) are most severe during the first 6 months of abstinence, but may occur even after 5 to 10 years. Irritability, depression, fatigue and "sense of aloneness" are mentioned, but these conditions of which members of Alcoholics Anonymous sometimes complain seem to be rather indications of insufficient adaptation on the symbolic level to an alcohol-free life.

III.4.4.4. Craving for or Physical Dependence on Alcohol. Terms such as craving, besoin obsédant, deseo impetuoso and unwiderstehliches Verlangen, are frequently invoked in the explanation of alcoholism but are used in a variety of meanings. The use of the terms physical need and dependence is more stable. The absence of such terms in a paper does not necessarily denote a rejection of certain interpretations of "craving," as frequently the etiological process described is identical with processes that other writers cover with this term. Many psychiatric investigators of alcoholism deliberately do not use the word craving because of the pharmacological connotations that it has acquired through its use in the literature on drug addiction. In some psychiatric papers on alcoholism the term compulsion is substituted for craving; in others, however, compulsion is used strictly in the sense proper to formal psychology and psychiatry.

Most of the papers that use the term craving refer to "craving for alcohol" without stating whether a specific craving for alcohol is meant, though such specificity is sometimes implied. The German psychiatrist Cimbal (1926) was perhaps the first to say expressis verbis that the craving or desire was not directed specifically at alcohol but at intoxication. Similar formulations have been made subsequently, e.g., by Wexberg (1950). Most psychiatric papers that discuss craving do not make explicit statements about specificity. However, the majority seem to imply not a specific craving for alcohol but rather a desire for the effects that alcohol produces, which could be produced by other means. Obviously, the expression "craving for alcohol" is often used carelessly.

The idea of specific craving or desire in connection with alcoholism is based primarily on the assumption that if the alcoholic continues to engage in drinking bouts after many disastrous experiences an uncontrollable desire must be in back of it (an assumption that does not take all the facts into consideration), and secondarily on actual observation of behavior toward the end of the drinking bout.

At this juncture a clear distinction must be made between (a) the mechanism that leads from the completion of one bout to the beginning of another, and (b) the continuation of drinking within a single bout. In many papers distinction has been made only by implication; and the lack of discrimination on this point has been the source of much misunderstanding and conflict, as well as unwarranted therapeutic claims.

In the first stages of alcoholism the drinker regularly arrives at a degree of intoxication sufficient to maintain euphoria for a few hours, but without any gross manifestations of drunkenness and largely without aftereffects. At a later stage (commonly after 10 or 12 years of heavy drinking) this behavior changes. The alcoholic now engages in bouts terminated by such severe intoxication that he cannot continue drinking; he recovers only after several days of care, whether at home or in a hospital. After recovery from the physical effects of the bout a period of a week or two or three goes by before the alcoholic starts another bout, which ends as the preceding one did. This sequence repeats itself over and over again at irregular intervals.

In the actual drinking bout, and more markedly toward the end of it, the alcoholic develops symptoms which clearly constitute a withdrawal syndrome. This disappears for a while when more alcohol is taken. If in the course of the bout the ingestion of alcohol is even slightly delayed, the alcoholic appears to be in great physical distress. The withdrawal symptoms indicate a true physical demand for alcohol in this given situation, but the "craving" may be only an apparent one. It may be that the alcoholic who wants to terminate the distressing symptoms does not see any other remedy than alcohol; and fear of not getting the remedy intensifies the symptoms. This view is held by Jacobsen.[10] In this acute condition it seems justified to speak of an irresistible demand or "craving" for alcohol, but the observations suggest that the "craving" arises to some extent, if not entirely, out of the need for relief of

[10] Jacobsen, E. The Hangover. [Unpublished lecture presented at the "W.H.O. South American Seminar on Alcoholism."] Buenos Aires; 1953.

the distressing symptoms; they definitely do not bear out the idea of an "appetite for alcohol" submitted by proponents of physio-pathological etiologies of alcoholism.

During the period between drinking bouts the situation is entirely different. While there is either overt or covert accumulation of tension, there are none of the symptoms displayed in the interrupted bout, and the alcoholic does not show any signs of "needing" alcohol. After a while, however, he wants to feel "different," and he knows of no other way to achieve this than through alcohol. The previous disastrous experiences with drinking do not deter him because he is convinced that this time he will be able to stop after two or three drinks—just enough to produce the desired euphoria.

If at this point, before starting another bout, he is placed in a situation in which he has no access to alcohol, he will not show any of those behaviors that the absence of alcohol brings forth during the state of intoxication. He may stay in an institution for many months without showing any distress, even if no therapy is being carried out. Here one certainly cannot speak of an irresistible craving or a physical demand for alcohol, even though on leaving the institution he may immediately turn to alcohol.

The absence of manifestations of a physical demand for alcohol between drinking bouts or during a prolonged enforced period of abstinence casts grave doubts on the theory postulated by some proponents of nutritional and endocrine etiologies of alcoholism that craving exists at the onset of the heavy use of alcohol by the prospective alcoholic.

One of the salient points is that while the demand for alcohol can be stopped in the acute episode through the administration of various substances which either cause sedation, or relieve bodily discomfort, or restore vegetative equilibrium, no amount of treatment with such substances prevents the recurrence of later bouts, not even on continued administration.[11]

It is of interest to see that French students of alcoholism when speaking about craving approach this question in terms of thirst, and the idea of craving seems strange to them. This viewpoint is, of course, culturally determined by attitudes toward the use of alcoholic beverages.

Dublineau and Honoré (1955) express surprise that 325 out of

[11] The above discussion of physical need or craving for alcohol reproduces essentially the views expressed by Jellinek (1953, 1955).

491 alcoholics stated that they were "not more thirsty than other persons," 84 were doubtful on this score and only 82 thought they were thirstier than others. The investigators suggested that those answering in the negative might have wished to conceal their thirst, but nevertheless the writers conceded that drinking without thirst may be a "special ability" and that these patients drank for other reasons than thirst.

Duchêne (1955) says that "the need to drink alcohol . . . is not necessarily pathological unless the term 'need' is given the significance of irresistible impulse, which is already a petitio principii." The difference in semantics when the term need in relation to alcohol is used by Frenchmen and Anglo-Saxons is noteworthy.

Duchêne makes a distinction between three types of normal motivation for drinking: (1) Thirst: in a country like France there is nothing but alcoholic beverages to quench thirst. (2) "The desire to achieve slight alcohol intoxication can be considered to a certain extent normal." (3) "The customs peculiar to each country pose very different problems as regards drinking." He then proceeds with the argument that "normal" motivations "are not always sufficient to give rise to alcoholism," and he postulates that psychopathological factors are of primary importance in the initiation of alcoholism, although he found such factors in not more than half of his patients. The absence of such traits in the other half he attributes to a lack of thorough psychoanalytic investigation. The emphasis on psychopathological origins, at least with respect to French alcoholics, is one which only a minority of French students of alcoholism would share with Duchêne.

Duchêne, however, further states that "it is certain that chronic intoxication of some duration leads to profound disturbance of the metabolic system and this can be considered the basis of a need for alcohol. The well-known symptoms of sudden withdrawal of alcohol from a confirmed alcoholic give proof of this. . . ." Thus, after coming out of the semantic underbrush, he approaches the conclusions of Jellinek and also of Isbell (1955). The latter says:

"Two kinds of 'craving' for alcohol are postulated. The first is a 'physical' or nonsymbolic craving which occurs in persons who have been drinking excessive amounts of alcohol for long periods of time, and is manifested by symptoms on withdrawal of alcohol. This type of craving is believed to be due to physiological alterations, the mechanism of which is not yet understood. The chief importance of physical craving is that it tends to make drinking bouts even more protracted and continuous.

"The second kind (or kinds) of craving is thought to account for initial abuse of alcohol, and for relapse after abstinence. It is postulated that this second kind of craving is chiefly psychological in origin."

Lundquist's (1955) discussion which proceeds from a different approach implies a similar differentiation.

Mardones (1955) and MacLeod (1955) discuss mainly the possibilities of physiopathological origins of the onset of heavy drinking, with minor attention to the later stages in which the withdrawal syndrome has become established. Both concede that psychological factors may be among the motivations behind the desire for alcohol in human beings and that an overpowering desire has not been shown in animal experimentation. Nevertheless both of these investigators see promising leads for physiopathological researches on the genesis of heavy drinking and MacLeod would like to see well-planned experimental and clinical research in that direction. Both have given penetrating analyses of past researches and have found them inconclusive. It may be added that Mardones suggests for animal experiment the introduction of strong obstacles in the way of obtaining alcohol in order to test whether one may regard increased voluntary alcohol intake by animals as the manifestation of an "overpowering desire."

The World Health Organization's Committee on Alcohol and Alcoholism, comprising pharmacologists, physiologists and psychiatrists from Britain, Chile, France, Sweden, Switzerland and the United States, in spite of wide differences in cultural backgrounds, was able to arrive at a joint formulation on the question of "craving" or, rather, physical dependence on alcohol:

"The terms 'craving,' 'irresistible desire,' 'need,' and sometimes 'appetite,' have been employed in alcohol literature to explain certain or all forms of abnormal drinking behaviour seen in alcoholics.

"There exists a variety of alcoholic drinking behaviour which specifically suggests 'craving' in the vernacular sense, but closer analysis reveals that different mechanisms are at work and that a term such as 'craving' with its everyday connotations should not be used in the scientific literature to describe them if confusion is to be avoided.

"The onset of the excessive use of alcohol, the drinking pattern displayed within an acute drinking bout, relapse into a new drinking bout after days or weeks of abstinence, continuous daily excessive drinking, and loss of control, are all behaviours which have been claimed as being manifestations of 'craving' of the same order.

" 'Craving' and its alternative terms have been used to explain drinking arising from (a) a psychological need, (b) the physical need to relieve withdrawal symptoms, or (c) a physical need which originates in physio-pathological conditions involving the metabolism, endocrine functions, etc., and existing in the drinker before he starts on his drinking career or developing in the course of it.

"It has been pointed out by some investigators that a physical craving for alcohol, as indicated by withdrawal symptoms . . . is seen immediately following withdrawal of alcohol only after prolonged, continuous and heavy use; such a physical craving cannot be postulated as the cause of the resumption of drinking after a considerable period of abstinence when withdrawal symptoms are no longer present.

"The Committee feels that a sharp distinction should be drawn between (a) the processes operative immediately after withdrawal of alcohol in the situation described above, and (b) those which lead to resumption of drinking after the disappearance of withdrawal symptoms.

"Since, on the interruption of continuous drinking, the distressing withdrawal symptoms provoke the drinker to seek relief from them by the use of more alcohol, the Committee would prefer to refer to this condition as a *physical dependence* on alcohol.

"During a period of abstinence, even in the absence of withdrawal symptoms, one observes clinically the building up of psychological tension which provokes a 'pathological desire' for alcohol as a means of relieving this tension; in this condition the individual may be said to be *psychologically dependent* on alcohol. It must be pointed out, however, that mounting psychological tension is not the only cause of resumption of drinking. It can also be caused by social pressure to drink, or sometimes even by the accidental ingestion of alcohol.

"In addition, a physiopathological condition (other than physical dependence) cannot be excluded as one of the factors which may lead to the resumption of drinking after days or weeks of abstinence.

"In all alcoholics, regardless of whether they have an abnormal disposition or suffer from any acquired personality disorder, one observes a weakening of that part of the higher personality from which the inhibition of primitive tendencies derives. As a result there appears a release of the primitive side of the personality. The pathological desire for alcohol therefore becomes more evident as the inhibiting forces weaken and ultimately fail.

"There is also a relatively small group of drinkers in which the pathological desire for alcohol appears practically at the beginning of their drinking career, instead of after many years, and can thus lead to a rapid development of alcoholism. Among these will be found certain types of psychopaths (e.g., the volitionally weak and the impulsive personalities) and certain cases of somatic or mental disorder (e.g., postconcussion states, epilepsy, certain psychoses, and oligophrenia). There is, however, a minority in this group who show none of these conditions and yet manifest a pathological desire for alcohol from the beginning of their drinking history" (World Health Organization, 1955).

III.4.4.5. Loss of Control and the Phenomenon of Short-Range Accommodation to Alcohol. Loss of control was discussed briefly in section III.1.3. This manifestation of the addictive process or, more exactly, of the development of the gamma alcoholic, is seldom if ever seen by psychiatrists and other therapists, except for the aftermath, when the patient is brought to the hospital displaying withdrawal symptoms and clamoring for a drink.

In the tropics (before I became active in research on alcoholism), it frequently devolved upon me to nurse my alcoholic friends through their frequent "benders." Later, in the U.S.A., I made it a point to observe such drinking whenever an alcoholic who had "slipped" telephoned that he was in a certain tavern or bar and needed "help."

The withdrawal symptoms as they occur within a drinking bout, in the presence of loss of control, are tremors of the fingers and lips, slight twitchings, some motor restlessness, and sometimes delusions (but not hallucinations). These symptoms are promptly relieved by more alcohol, but the relief is of short duration and the symptoms recur after a short interval, whereupon the drinker again takes recourse to more alcohol. This process goes on and on until the drinker either cannot ingest more alcohol, or the drinking is stopped through extraneous circumstances.[12]

The loss of control has been aptly designated by Stewart (1956) as loss of freedom. This loss of freedom follows the first ingestion of alcohol in a new bout. The choice of the expression is felicitous as it reflects the despair that the alcoholic feels. Moreover it perhaps brings home to the nonspecialized physician, psychologist and social worker the idea that he is not dealing with a free agent and that it is futile to suggest to the patient that he "cut down on his drinking."

As the bout in the presence of loss of control progresses, anxiety increases in intensity and is relieved by renewed alcohol intake only

---

[12] A statement made in section III.1.3 may be repeated here, namely, that loss of control does not emerge suddenly but develops gradatum, i.e., it occurs more frequently as time goes by (although such occurrences may be few and far between) but even after it is established it need not necessarily occur 100 per cent of the time.

for very short periods. The anxiety may originate in the failure of the euphoric effect of alcohol, and the heaping of drinks gives the impression of an obsessive behavior. The drinking bout in the presence of loss of control differs greatly from one in which a drinker gets drunk deliberately.

In the latter instance he may display some gaiety, some pseudophilosophy, some maudlin sentiments, and ultimately perhaps some degree of depression. He does not manifest withdrawal symptoms in the course of drinking. Unless he belongs to those drinkers who for years have been spreading their drinking from morning until going to bed, he will not suffer withdrawal symptoms even after termination of the bout, except for the signs of the ordinary hangover, such as headache and some nausea.

In the bout with loss of control the elements of jocularity and philosophizing are absent and only anxiety, some degree of panic, the ebbs and tides of withdrawal symptoms, and the demand for more alcohol are conspicuous. The withdrawal symptoms indicate a true physical demand for alcohol (adaptation of cell metabolism to that substance) in the given situation, and the demand for alcohol gives rise to the idea of "craving;" but the "craving" may be only an apparent one—not for alcohol, which may be ingested only with difficulty and sometimes disgust, but for the expected effect, i.e., relief from the painful withdrawal symptoms, be it of very short duration.

The demand for alcohol seems to be of a twofold nature. One part reflects the necessity to allay the distressing withdrawal symptoms, i.e., a physical demand; the other part reflects the obsessive belief that ultimately a sufficient amount of alcohol will bring about the tension reduction which, before the loss of control, was achieved quite easily.

Parenthetically it may be said that the true or apparent obsessive behavior of the alcohol addict at the stage of loss of control in no way contradicts Lolli's view that the addictive alcoholic is an impulsive but not a compulsive drinker (Lolli, 1955). Up to the full establishment of the loss of control the drinker has been drinking impulsively and even when the stage of loss of control is reached his drinking of the first glass of the bout is an impulsive behavior.

The loss of control which is described by members of Alcoholics Anonymous as well as by students of alcoholism as the inability to stop after one or two glasses, and is sometimes referred to as the insatiability of the alcohol addict (e.g., Vogel, 1953; Straus and McCarthy, 1951), seems to be characterized by minor withdrawal symptoms in the presence of alcohol in the blood stream and the failure to achieve the desired euphoria for more than a few minutes. These symptoms explain superficially the behavior observed in the so-called loss of control and they suggest a combination of short-range accommodation of nervous tissue with long-range acquired increased tolerance.

I am offering here a tentative though incomplete explanation, for what it may be worth.

Short-Range Accommodation of the Nervous System. Acquired increased tolerance to alcohol, as discussed above, develops gradually over long periods of time and is a slow, continuous process. Furthermore, the increase in tolerance, once it has been acquired, carries over from one drinking occasion to the next although it may be lost after abstinence periods of long duration.

A number of investigators have observed, on the other hand, that in the course of a single drinking occasion a given blood alcohol concentration—let us say, 0.7 per mil—has a much greater effect on the central nervous system in the ascending phase than in the descending phase of the blood alcohol concentration. In other words, the effect is greater in what may be roughly called the ascending phase. This effect is observed whether the subject is unaccustomed or accustomed to alcohol. This phenomenon was first discovered by Mellanby (1919), and rediscovered by Eggleton (1941), by Newman and Abramson (1941), and by Mirsky, Piker et al. (1941). It has also been observed and described by MacLeod (1948), Alha (1952), and Rauschke (1954).

The decrease in impairment of a given psychological function at a given blood alcohol concentration takes place within half an hour or one hour. I am referring to it here as short-range accommodation of the central nervous system to alcohol, not only on account of the short time required for the effect, but mainly because it does not carry over to the next drinking occasion. To make this clearer, if in a test carried out today the psychological function X is impaired 25 per cent at a blood alcohol level of 0.7 per mil when the alcohol concentration is rising and only 13 per cent when it is falling, a repetition of the test 2 weeks later will produce the same results, i.e., the impairment at the ascending part of the curve will still be around 25 per cent, and it will still be around 13 per cent at the descending part of the curve, at the same blood alcohol level (0.7 per mil) as in the first test. What the mechanism of this short-range accommodation is remains a moot question. Rauschke (1954) has ascribed the drop to a lag between alcohol in the blood and alcohol in the brain, but unfortunately the lag is the reverse of what Rauschke suggests.

On the other hand, as has been noted above, acquired increased tissue tolerance develops only in the course of years of fairly heavy alcohol intake (sometimes to a mild degree in a few months). Once it is established it carries over from one occasion to the next and may increase for some time, unless a long period of abstinence extinguishes it.

Thus in a drinker with acquired increased tissue tolerance to alcohol the impairment of the psychological function X at the ascending part of the curve may be only 12 per cent (for this there is experimental evidence), and at the descending part of the curve only 5 per cent (for this there is no experimental evidence, as the short-range accommodation has not been tested in alcoholics). As acquired increased tolerance progresses, the effect at the descending part of the alcohol concentration may be nullified, and this may be correlated with a greatly diminished production of euphoria. The latter effects may be coupled with disturbances in the metabolism of the nervous tissues, which in turn bring about the withdrawal symptoms with a need for relief through alcohol from these noxious manifestations.

When this idea occurred to me 4 or 5 years ago I was reluctant to put it on paper, but now I find that the noted British biochemist Leslie MacLeod made a similar suggestion some 12 years ago. MacLeod (1948) carried out experiments on rats in order to achieve controlled blood alcohol levels and so determine thresholds at which some definite clinical signs of intoxication appeared. But he found that results showed that the threshold level depended on the rate of rise of blood alcohol. He states that due to change in thresholds the element that must be studied is adaptation (what I have called short-range accommodation). He believes that whatever the interpretation of the mechanism may be, this could account for "alcohol hunger" as well as for the rapid relapse of the temporarily "cured" alcohol addict, should he once more take alco-

THE DISEASE CONCEPT OF ALCOHOLISM

hol into his system. MacLeod admits that this is conjectural and so do I. But it is a conjecture worthy of experimental testing.

The question of why the gamma alcoholic develops loss of control but is able to abstain after a bout, while the delta alcoholic is unable to abstain entirely but does retain control over the amounts ingested, requires another conjecture.

In the delta alcoholic, who spreads beverages of low alcohol concentration over some 16 hours of the day—and the total of the drug is a large amount— the cell metabolism (of nervous tissue) is continually conditioned to the presence of alcohol; but in the gamma alcoholic who drinks concentrated spirits in a concentrated period of time, the metabolism of nervous tissue cells becomes conditioned by the "signal" of the "first drink."

III.4.4.6. Sketch of the Roots and Development of the Addictive Species of Alcoholism. From the preceding discussions I shall attempt to piece together a picture of the addictive species of alcoholism and add a working hypothesis.

The Domesticated Drug. The World Health Organization's Committee on Alcohol and Alcoholism (1955) designated ethyl alcohol as a drug "intermediate in kind and degree" between "habit-forming drugs" and "addiction-producing drugs." Their reason for assigning alcohol to this intermediate position was, largely, the quantitative differences between alcohol and the addiction producing drugs. The latter produce addiction in 70 to 100 per cent of their users, the amounts required to bring about this effect are minute, and the time required for the addictive process is 2 to 4 weeks. Alcohol consumption on the other hand leads to addiction in a maximum of 10 per cent of the users, requires large amounts (several thousand times larger than morphine, heroin or barbiturates), and the time necessary for the addictive process is 3 to 15 years, in some cases over 20 years.

The drug ethyl alcohol is contained in such "respectable" ancient beverages as beer and wine, as well as in the relative newcomers, brandy, whisky and other distilled spirits. Furthermore, these beverages are socially highly valued and their use has a tremendous social acceptance in quasi-social ritual and as a "dietary supplement." Alcohol has become a domesticated drug.

The great social acceptance of the alcoholic beverage may be attributed first to its symbolic value and second to its effects. The symbolism of the alcoholic beverage has not yet been discussed in the present study and must be mentioned at this juncture.

Strangely enough, students of alcoholism have not paid attention to the symbolism of the alcoholic beverage; not even psychoanalysts have touched on this aspect. On the other hand, classical philologists and students of the comparative history of religion interested in the sacrificial and other ritual use of wine (or other alcoholic beverages) have shown the equation between the alcoholic liquid and blood. They have done this without reference to the social or "dietary" custom of drinking. Recently Goodenough (1956) has pointed out the deep symbolic meaning of the act of drinking—irrespective of whether water, milk or an alcoholic beverage is consumed—namely, the taking in of the "stream of life."

There are many Greek, Roman, medieval and later literary passages that bring out the symbolic character of the alcoholic beverage—particularly the meaning of drinking together as an act of identification—much more clearly than the ritualistic material referred to by the students of comparative history of religion.[13]

Through the equation of alcoholic beverages with blood, some of the properties of the latter are transferred to the former; not only those of strength, power and renewal of life but also those of food and medicine. These transferred symbolic properties endow the alcoholic beverage with that tremendous prestige which has led to the extraordinarily wide acceptance of the custom of drinking in a large variety of cultures. The symbolism of the alcoholic beverage gives it its anchorage in society. The act of identification in drinking together is the root of the offense inherent in the refusal of a drink, and generally of "social pressure" to drink. (This deep symbolic meaning should not be neglected in preventive education.)

That the custom of drinking alcoholic beverages has maintained itself in the face of many changes in social and cultural structure, and in spite of the realization of potential dangers, is due not solely to the deep symbolic value of alcoholic beverages but also to their "utility." Nevertheless, the "utility" alone, without the prestige of the symbolism, could not account for the survival of the custom with its many vexatious problems.

[13] I intend to enlarge upon the symbolic aspects of the social use of alcoholic beverages in one or more papers.

The Function of the Domesticated Drug. The tension-reducing properties of ethyl alcohol are not a matter of surmise. There is experimental evidence (Masserman et al., 1945), and there is the evidence of a cross-cultural survey which shows an association between the degree of drunkenness and the degree of subsistence anxiety and anxiety related to institutionalized witchcraft in preliterate societies (Horton, 1943). Furthermore, the tension-reducing properties of alcohol are recognized in the assertion so often heard in a variety of situations: "What you need is a drink."

This utility of alcohol leads to the profanation of the ritual use (Jellinek, 1945a). The useful effects of alcohol are experienced in the course of ritual drinking and through repetition the utilitarian use is "learned." A process in terms of the psychological theory of learning develops.

I do not wish to imply that the profane use of alcoholic beverages emerges a considerable time after purely ritualistic drinking. Perhaps just a few minutes elapse between the symbolic act and the experience of the psychological effects of alcohol. I am, of course, not thinking here of the *token* drinking in the communion, but of ritual drinking in much larger quantities such as in the religions of ancient Greece and Rome and of semibarbaric and primitive societies.

It appears, however, that for long periods ritualistic drinking was the predominant custom and utilitarian drinking was occasional— limited to perhaps three or five occasions in the course of the year and extending to the whole tribe or clan. In the course of time, however, utilitarian drinking became the predominant usage, and purely ritualistic drinking became limited to certain religious occasions. Nevertheless, the symbolic element remains present—even if covertly—in what may be called social ritual, particularly in the act of drinking together.

The development of the utilitarian use of alcohol on a large scale and the change from communal to individual drinking is made possible only through advances in the techniques of brewing of beers and fermentation of wines, preservation and storage of the beverages, distribution facilities (the tavern, transportation, etc.), and through lower cost of the commodity. The profane, i.e., utilitarian use is ultimately reinforced by the rise of the vested interests, their marketing methods and advertising.

The individual use of the tension-reducing properties of alcoholic beverages—in contrast to the original tribal or communal use—becomes more motivated as sources of anxieties, frustrations and tensions in general become more individualized in the higher civilizations than the predominantly communal tensions were in the preliterate societies.

The Development of Alcohol Addiction.[14] Of course persons with great psychological vulnerability may be much more motivated to use the tension-reducing properties of alcohol more frequently and in greater quantities than others.

It was stated above that alcohol addiction in the strict pharmacological sense develops in not more than 10 per cent (actually from ½ of 1 per cent to 10 per cent) of the users of alcoholic beverages. It was also pointed out that large quantities of alcohol and their use over many years are required to produce addiction. The fact that the percentage of persons who become addicted to alcohol is relatively small (that is, compared to morphine, heroin, etc.) may be attributed to the relatively small incidence in the population of those who have an urgent motivation to take alcohol in the large quantities and with the frequency that is required to bring about physical dependence on alcohol through conditioning of the metabolism of nervous tissue. (This in no way precludes a true addictive process in persons with low alcohol tolerance, i.e., persons who become intoxicated after drinking small quantities of alcohol. In spite of their "alcohol intolerance" these persons may consume prodigious quantities.)

It is by no means implied that the utilitarian use of alcohol, i.e., for its effects, necessarily leads to excess and some species of alcoholism. Persons with minor tensions and ample resources to manage those tensions engage in utilitarian drinking in small amounts only and, according to the culture to which they belong, in connection with meals (either just before or in the course of eating) or on certain social occasions.

Nor should it be thought that excessive drinking necessarily produces physical dependence, i.e., addiction. There may be heavy, frequent drinking which does not go beyond psychological dependence, but still may cause social damage and damage to the user's

---

[14] I am limiting this "sketch" to gamma alcoholism, and to some extent also to delta alcoholism; thus no inferences should be made as to my opinions relating to other species of alcoholism.

THE DISEASE CONCEPT OF ALCOHOLISM

health, and thus may be seen as a species of alcoholism (alpha alcoholism as described in section III.1.2).

In sections III.3 through III.3.3 the psychological and psychiatric etiologies of alcoholism and the most frequently invoked underlying psychological difficulties were discussed fairly extensively. It is not necessary to summarize that discussion here. It will suffice to recall that in spite of a great diversity of personality structures among alcoholics there appears in a large proportion of them a low tolerance for tension coupled with an inability to cope with psychological stresses. For such persons alcohol may represent a "great value" which may induce them to use this substance in such quantities and with such frequency that the pharmacological process of addiction (physical dependence) is facilitated. The addictive process may develop without initial psychological dependence, but in a large proportion of alcoholics—the predominant species of alcoholism on the North American continent—pre-alcoholic, high psychological vulnerability is essential (see the description of gamma alcoholism, section III.1.2).

The prerequisite frequent large alcohol intake is not always the result of high psychological vulnerability, but may stem from such socioeconomic constellations as were described in sections II.2 and II.3. The socioeconomic factors are predominant in France and other viticultural countries; on the other hand, high psychological vulnerability is predominant in the etiology of alcoholism on the North American continent and in Anglo-Saxon countries generally. A tentative explanation of these differences is given on pages 28–29. It may be pointed out here again that the predominant species of alcoholism of the Latin countries (delta alcoholism) is represented in America and generally in Anglo-Saxon countries too, but as a minority species, and that France and other viticultural countries have a minority incidence of the predominant Anglo-Saxon species of alcoholism (gamma alcoholism).

Given a large and frequent intake of alcoholic beverages, whether for individual psychological reasons or on account of socioeconomic factors, the exposure to the risk of addiction (in the pharmacological sense) becomes great.

In gamma alcoholics one finds the sequence of acquired increased tissue tolerance, an increase in the need for alcoholic beverages, and withdrawal symptoms with physical need for alcohol (craving), and consequent loss of control. It is the gradual, slow development of the loss of control which generates the dramatic behavior changes in this species of alcoholics. The loss of control, even in its earlier less obtrusive forms, brings about a feeling of insecurity on account of the gradual narrowing of choice for the individual concerned. When the addictive process is on its way, the role of the person diminishes and alcohol takes the upper hand as the nervous tissue becomes gradually conditioned by that substance. Progressively alcohol "takes over" until it becomes the decisive factor in what the addict may or may not do. Thus the slogan that "alcoholism is not in the bottle but in the man" may be a dangerous one.

A Working Hypothesis. The various psychological and psychiatric etiologies of alcoholism may fully explain the heavy drinking which paves the way for addiction, but they do not explain the great changes, the progressions, and the loss of control as they occur in gamma alcoholism. The same is true of sociocultural etiologies, although some drinking patterns inherent in certain sociocultural constellations play a role in the conditioning of the cell metabolism (particularly in the genesis of delta acoholism).

As far as America is concerned, where the therapist is predominantly concerned with the gamma alcoholic, I would suggest that the main structure around which research should center is the pharmacological process of addiction.

I do not wish to imply that the process of addiction is a full explanation of gamma and delta alcoholisms (not to speak of other species of alcoholism). It seems to me, however, a convenient axis of research. To this view I am led by the following considerations.

First I should like to dwell on one feature which constitutes a challenging question, and that is that the time necessary for the development of addiction may vary from 3 years to 15 years and even longer periods in persons who are equally heavy users of alcoholic beverages. In sections III.4.2, III.4.3 and III.4.3.1 I have said that although I could not see a rationale for a "need for alcohol" in the findings of Mardones, or Williams, or Sirnes, or J. J. Smith and his followers, I thought that their findings were of great relevance to alcoholism, at least to the addictive species of the genus.

I should like to suggest that enzyme and vitamin anomalies, liver injuries, adrenal factors, and many biochemical lesions, known at this time, may according to their various degrees weaken the resistance of nervous tissue to the integration of a noxious substance into its metabolism and to becoming dependent upon it. If any physiological or biochemical anomaly—which in itself may not seem grave—can strip the nervous tissue of its resistance to adaptation of its metabolism to a noxious substance, then that adaptation with all its concomitant behavioral changes may be designated as a disease.

Such anomalies and injuries could be products of heredity or they could be brought about through the stresses which prolonged heavy alcohol intake may exert on them. In view of the fact that the establishment of the addictive process may occur in some after 3 years or even less, and in others only after 7, 12 or 18 years, I am inclined to think that heredity may play a role in the time necessary for alcohol to exert serious stresses on the system to which the anomaly attaches.

Moreover, the absence of such anomalies could account for the phenomenon of alpha alcoholism in which very heavy alcohol intake, in spite of marked drunkenness, does not produce any progression, particularly no transition from psychological to physical dependence.

I repeat that I regard the above merely as a working hypothesis, but one which can be tested by means of the newer techniques in pharmacology, physiopathology and biochemistry. It seems to me that some of the profitable targets of research are given in the process of acquired increased tissue tolerance and in the mechanisms of the various withdrawal symptoms.

IV

Attitudes toward the Idea of Alcoholism as an Illness

IV.1. Introductory Remarks

WLASSAK (1929) said that it is an idle pastime to ask whether alcoholism is an illness or not; the main thing is that something should be done for the rehabilitation of the alcoholic.

The above is the kind of epigrammatic utterance that, at first glance, meets with the great approval of the reader. On reflection, however, this dictum might not prove to be cogent. It may not be of any particular importance whether certain species of alcoholism are labeled as illnesses or whether they are designated as medical problems. On the other hand, the acceptance of either of the two labels, or the rejection of both, has a very definite bearing on many aspects of the problems of alcoholism. The consequences of such acceptance or rejection are reflected in such matters as whether ideas on the rehabilitation of alcoholics will be oriented toward therapeutic, social welfare or penal measures. Ullman (1952) extends this idea to the controversy on alcoholism as a disease or a symptom: "Concern over the confusion with regard to alcoholism as a symptom or a disease may appear to be a product of the academic mind, but the position taken on this matter determines the orientation of therapeutic efforts. If . . . alcoholism is regarded as a symptom, then the treatment program is designed to cure the underlying disease." He contrasts this with the approach of Alcoholics Anonymous which regards addictive drinking itself as an illness and whose efforts are directed toward "the break-up of the sequence of activities involved in addictive drinking."

The rejection or acceptance of alcoholism as an illness or medical problem may have repercussions not only in rehabilitation methods but also in the extent of clinical activities and other medi-

157

cal facilities for alcoholics. Furthermore, the degree of acceptance
may affect the research in various aspects of alcoholism. Lape,
Phillips and Edgar (1955) remarked: "A more fundamental reason
why research on alcoholism has not achieved the degree of biological perspective available for research on tuberculosis, cancer,
poliomyelitis, is the slow development of the concept that alcoholism is a disease."

A low degree of acceptance of the disease conception may handicap subsidization of biological research on alcoholism; but, on the
other hand, the vagueness of the conception is a stimulus to the
development of clearer formulations and more stringent experimental research.

Research, treatment and prevention of the various species of
alcoholism are affected not only by the acceptance or rejection
of the disease conception, but also by the formulation of the nature
of such an illness. If the formulation rigidly claims that alcohol
addiction or any other species of alcoholism is purely a medical
problem, any preventive attempt may be seriously impaired. The
usefulness of the idea that alcoholism is a medical and public health
problem depends, to a large extent, upon the recognition of social
and economic factors in the etiology of all species of alcoholism.
By recognition of these factors I do not mean mere assent that
such factors exist but exploration and understanding of them.

In speaking about attitudes toward the idea of alcoholism as
an illness in terms of acceptance or rejection, primarily American
conditions are envisaged and Sections 2 through 6 of the present
chapter are to be understood as pertaining only to the United
States of America; however, since attitudes in the societies of
foreign countries are relevant to this country too, they will be
sketchily reviewed in Section 7.

The attitudes must be reviewed according to various components
of the entity of public opinion. Not all of the constituent parts
can be considered, mainly on account of lack of information concerning some of the sections of our society. First consideration
here will be given to the official attitude of the medical profession
which is, of course, important for the acceptance by other sections
of our society. This will be followed by the attitudes reflected
in state legislation on alcoholism programs. The outlook of law
courts and law-enforcement agencies has been discussed in Chapter III.2.1 and need not be repeated. Section 4 of the present

chapter is devoted to the attitudes of the church and temperance societies. This is followed by the stands of labor and management. And lastly, an attempt to gauge the degree of acceptance or rejection by what might be called the public at large will be made. It would be of interest to consider the attitudes of the civil service and the armed services on these matters, but unfortunately there is little information, if any, available.

Many factors play a role in the degree of acceptance or rejection, among them, the clarity and definiteness of the formulations. It must be admitted that clarity is not an outstanding characteristic of any but a very few of the formulations. And definiteness is, of course, lacking when vehement controversies concerning etiological theories are rampant. The lack of clarity is, at present, not too great a deterrent for public acceptance of the disease idea, but in the course of time it may become a very serious handicap.

Some elements influencing the matter of acceptance or rejection lie in deeply rooted traditions about the custom of drinking which cannot be divorced from the phenomenon of alcoholism. Much depends upon the extent and quality of propaganda which attaches to the idea of "alcoholism" as an illness or, if one prefers the term, education on alcoholism. The way in which these conceptions fit into the sociopolitical ideas of some interest groups is, of course, also of relevance. Some of these and other factors will be considered in the description of attitudes taken by various groups which compose the entity of public opinion.

The question of what formulation of the illness conception is accepted by and large by one or the other section of public opinion cannot be determined on the basis of existing information. The indications for the great majority are that the accepted version is merely that "alcoholism *is* a disease." For the time being this may suffice, but not indefinitely.

In the introductory parts of this study it was said that acceptance of certain formulations on the nature of alcoholism does not necessarily equal validity. I am repeating these words at this juncture lest there should be some misunderstanding on this score.

IV.2. *The Medical Profession*

In Chapter I, it was pointed out that as long as the propagation of the disease conception of "alcoholism" was limited to a small specialized professional group, the idea did not penetrate public opinion and was noticed only by the temperance movement, which rejected it.

Propaganda through the channels of voluntary citizens groups was required, and still is, in the instances of tuberculosis, cancer, heart disease, mental health, etc., in order to bring the teachings of the medical profession closer to the public at large.

All this does not mean that the attitude of the medical profession is not important in this matter. Quite to the contrary, if the medical profession were not to accept the idea of alcoholism as an illness, the movement for its propagation could not maintain itself in the long run, and would sooner or later collapse.

An essential requirement is that the first proponents of the idea be members of the medical profession. In the beginning, it is not necessary that the medical profession as a whole should adopt the suggestion, although later an official stand of the profession as such becomes necessary. In the case of alcoholism, the idea that it constitutes an illness was suggested to Alcoholics Anonymous by a physician, the late Dr. W. D. Silkworth, early in the 1930's. Behind this physician were the opinions of a fair number of American and European specialists as expressed in the course of some 60 or 70 years, although their views did not coincide with the particular conception of Silkworth, namely that alcoholism is an allergy. It cannot be said that at that time the medical profession as a whole was in agreement with the medical proponents of the disease idea, yet the number of physicians of the latter conviction was not negligible. The spread of the disease conception of "alcoholism" to much wider circles of physicians was due not only to the somewhat greater precision of the formulation of the idea, to experimental findings and to new therapeutic methods such as administration of disulfiram (Antabuse), but also to the efforts and ideology of Alcoholics Anonymous who, of course, were propagating, with the greatest vigor, what they thought was a new conception.

The official acceptance by the medical profession of the disease conception of "alcoholism" is required not only for the continued life of its propagation through citizens' groups but also to encourage a much larger number of physicians to acquire experience in the treatment of acute intoxication, alcohol addiction itself and the various organic and mental complications. Medical acceptance is also essential in order to induce hospitals to accept alcoholics for treatment, as hospitals in general had developed admission policies that excluded the alcoholic and such policies were often upheld by the boards of trustees.

Furthermore, medical acceptance is fundamental to a policy of subsidies for clinical activities and research work in the field of alcoholism by the large foundations. Such foundations have quite understandably hesitated to make grants to applicants for research and clinical work and educational activities relating to alcoholism. The aloofness of the foundations (with some exceptions) may be ascribed to the feeling that there was still a strong emotional tone inherent in such activities and that the whole movement might be a passing fad. Now that the American Medical Association has officially gone on record in its acceptance of the conception of alcoholism as an illness and the World Health Organization (1951) has made statements to the same effect and has developed a program of activities in that field, the foundations may feel reassured and may make significant grants, particularly for alcoholism research and education.

The acceptance by hospitals of alcoholics as legitimate patients has made great strides in the past 20 years. A survey by Corwin and Cunningham (1944) showed that at that time admission of alcoholics to general hospitals was much more the exception than the rule. "Most of our hospitals have failed thus to dignify alcohol addiction as a disease worthy of study and intensive care" (Bluestone, 1944).

From the reports of state and voluntary agencies, it appears that the attitudes of the hospitals in this matter have undergone considerable change. Nevertheless, in 1956, it was still necessary to call the matter of admission of alcoholics to the attention of hospital administrators. This matter will not be discussed in any further detail in the present study, as it will form a large chapter of a separate publication on private and public alcoholism programs (in preparation).

In Chapters I–III of the present study, much material has been presented on formulations of the disease conception of "alcoholism" and that material itself showed the growing trend of acceptance among American as well as foreign physicians. It is not necessary therefore, to summarize here again the gist of those chapters. On the other hand, it will be in order to present here some statistical material on the prevalence of the disease conception among physicians and to give documentation of the formal expression of acceptance of that conception by the medical profession as a whole.

Riley and Marden (1946) made a survey on the attitudes of New Jersey physicians toward alcoholism and alcoholics. Of course, the results of the New Jersey survey cannot be extended to the United States as a whole, but they are, nevertheless, indicative of attitudes in the medical profession. Furthermore, the creation of alcoholism committees in a large number of state medical societies and the participation of a great number of physicians on the boards of voluntary agencies is evidence of a wide acceptance of the conception of alcoholism as an illness throughout the country.

Some of the findings of Riley and Marden's survey are given below. Toward the end of each interview the doctors were asked this question: "Just to sum up, do you think alcoholism should be regarded as an illness and be treated by the physician?" This question was asked to elicit a summary statement and the interviewers were instructed to probe for attitudinal details that supported each doctor's answer. The percentages of physicians who subscribed to various attitudes are shown in the following tabulation:

ATTITUDE	PER CENT
Basically a medical problem	40
Basically a psychiatric problem	25
A job for specialists (M.D.'s) in alcoholism	10
Both a physical and mental disease	9
Lay therapists (including Alcoholics Anonymous) are needed	5
A medical problem because there are always complicating conditions	3
Alcoholics are just weak-willed individuals	2
Doctors can do nothing for alcoholics	2
Miscellaneous	3
No opinion	1
Total	*100*

The main finding is that the physicians overwhelmingly placed the alcoholic squarely in the "sick man" category. Fewer than 15 per cent saw no medical aspects of the problem. Doctors felt strongly that medical science has a part to play in it and were articulate in assigning a central role to their own profession. While they believed that most alcoholics need physical rehabilitation first, many were insistent upon psychiatric attention and follow-up service. The following excerpts are illustrative.

"Yes. Alcoholism is an illness involving medical, psychiatric and social-service treatment."

"Alcoholism is an illness in the same sense as drug addiction. It needs medical treatment more in the acute stage."

"Yes. Alcoholism is a mental disease which should be treated by a physician, preferably a psychiatrist who has enough interest in and experience to treat an alcoholic."

"Yes. Fundamentally, alcoholism is a disease; but it is a mental disease needing psychiatric treatment and other big brother aids like Alcoholics Anonymous."

"Alcoholism is a symptom of a mental illness rather than an illness itself."

It is seen that in 1946, at least as far as a representative state in the eastern United States is concerned, physicians were highly receptive to the idea that alcoholism is a medical problem. It is, however, not quite clear from the document whether the recognition of "medical problem" involves the disease conception. Three per cent of the interviewees said that alcoholism was a medical problem because there are always complicating conditions. It is quite possible that a number of those who answered: "Basically a medical problem" were also motivated by the presence of complicating conditions, but even so there were at least 49 per cent whose answers implied the acceptance of alcoholism as an illness as shown by answers under the headings, "Basically a psychiatric problem;" "A job for specialists in alcoholism;" "Both a physical and mental disease;" and "Lay therapists are needed." Of special importance is the fact that only 2 per cent stated that alcoholics are just weak-willed persons. Evidently, the physicians conceived alcoholics to be true addicts and perhaps "problem drinkers."

In a few states physicians have been asked questions on whether or not they treated alcoholics, but their attitudes toward the idea of alcoholism as an illness was not touched upon. Some of the questions asked could be construed as implying the illness conception, but the implication is too uncertain to be considered here.

Progress toward the consolidation of medical attitudes toward alcoholism took a sharp upswing when the American Medical Association in 1951 created the Subcommittee on Alcoholism, under its Committee on Chronic Diseases, which was later formed into the Committee on Alcoholism of the Council on Mental Health of the A.M.A. (Block, 1957). The American Psychiatric Association and the Industrial Medical Association each have committees on alcoholism. Due to the great efforts of the A.M.A. Committee on Alcoholism and its chairman, numerous state medical societies formed committees, commissions or boards on alcoholism. This, of course, contributed significantly toward the extension of the acceptance of the illness conception of "alcoholism" by the profession. These were the preparatory steps for an official declaration by the American Medical Association on the matter of alcoholism. The text of that resolution, headed "Hospitalization of Patients with Alcoholism," is given below (Journal of the American Medical Association, 20 Oct. 1956):

"The problem of the hospitalization of patients with the diagnosis of alcoholism has been considered carefully by the Council on Mental Health and its Committee on Alcoholism. A report and resolution on this subject was submitted to the Board and approved for presentation to the House of Delegates for its action. The statement follows:

"Among the numerous personality disorders encountered in the general population, it has long been recognized that a vast number of such disorders are characterized by the outstanding sign of excessive use of alcohol. All excessive users of alcohol are not diagnosed as alcoholics, but all alcoholics are excessive users. When, in addition to this excessive use, there are certain signs and symptoms of behavioral, personality and physical disorder or of their development, the syndrome of alcoholism is achieved. The intoxication and some of the other possible complications manifested in this syndrome often make treatment difficult. However, alcoholism must be regarded as within the purview of medical practice. The Council on Mental Health, its Committee on Alcoholism, and *the profession in general recognizes this syndrome of alcoholism as illness* [italics mine] which justifiably should have the attention of physicians.

"One of the most consistent complaints of physicians who wish to care for these patients is that many hospitals will not admit such patients with a diagnosis of alcoholism. Many feel that these people are intractable, uncooperative, and difficult to handle. Because of their untoward behavior, hospital authorities feel that they are not equipped to take care of the medical treatment of such overactive patients. Where such patients are unruly and uncooperative, this attitude is understandable. However, for many of these sick people who express a wish to be treated in a general hospital, it has been generally found that cooperation is forthcoming and that no special attention or equipment is necessary for treating these patients. Hospitals should be urged to consider admission of such patients with a diagnosis of alcoholism based upon the condition of the individual patient, rather than a general objection to all such patients. Such objections have been very frustrating for physicians who wish to treat those patients and often discourages them from taking a greater interest in alcoholics."

This statement was accepted and approved by the House of Delegates of the American Medical Association at the 1956 meeting in Seattle, Washington.

The official statement quoted above constitutes, of course, the formal acceptance of the disease conception of "alcoholism" by the American medical profession as a whole. This does not mean that acceptance among physicians is unanimous; but the majority of American physicians are either in agreement with the dictum of the professional body or are willing to accept this viewpoint on the authority of their specialized professional colleagues. It may be assumed that quite a proportion of physicians will be inclined to think of alcoholism rather as a symptom of an illness than as an illness per se. Perhaps the majority of those who accept the illness conception have rather vague ideas about its nature, particularly as many of its medical proponents have themselves indulged in vagueness. The attitude of physicians who are actually concerned with the treatment of "alcoholics" is well summarized by D. Myerson (1957): ". . . acceptance but not condonation; protection but with encouragement toward as much independence as possible. . . ."

The physicians who do not view alcoholism as an illness are perhaps a minority but a rather sizable minority. The close relation of alcoholism to a valued social custom and the fact that, relatively speaking, only a small proportion of users show frank alcoholism, are barriers to the recognition of alcoholism as a particular medical disorder. The words spoken in 1804 by Dr. Thomas Trotter still hold good to a certain extent: "Mankind, ever in pursuit of pleasure, have reluctantly admitted into the catalogue of their diseases, those evils which were the immediate offspring of their luxuries. Such a reserve is indeed natural to the human mind; for of all deviations from the paths of duty, there are none that so forcibly impeach their pretentions to the character of rational beings as the inordinate use of spirituous liquors."

Another barrier to the development of the widest acceptance of alcoholism as an illness has been pointed out by a number of students of the question: that the complexities of "alcoholism" are so great that it does not fit readily into the rigid frame of medicine.

It is much easier to get physicians to agree that alcoholism belongs to the realm of medicine than that it constitutes an illness. As a matter of fact, the former conception meets with very little difficulty, if any. While the first committee report of the World Health Organization (1951) made a statement to the effect that alcoholism is an illness, in subsequent committee meetings the secretariat pointed out that it was not necessary to raise the question of illness but rather to determine whether it constituted a condition belonging in the sphere of medicine. After all, there are many conditions that the medical man legitimately claims as his own although they do not constitute diseases. I entirely agree with this point of view.

While the United States Public Health Service has not made any formal statement on the conception of alcoholism as an illness, their increasing interest in the problems of alcohol and the announcement by the National Institute of Mental Health of funds for large research grants in the field of alcoholism give evidence of the recognition of alcoholism as a public health problem by the competent Federal agencies. It may be noted that prominent members of the United States Public Health Service, in addresses of an unofficial nature, have spoken of alcoholism as one of the largest public health problems. This has led public and voluntary agencies to speak of alcoholism as the number four and even the number one public health problem in the United States of America. A word of caution is in order here, as it is neither desirable nor feasible to determine rank orders for health problems. It suffices to recognize them as large or small problems or middle sized problems as the case may be.

IV.3. Acceptance as Expressed in State Legislation

Public acceptance of the illness conception of "alcoholism" is reflected also in state legislation covering the creation of state alcoholism programs.

Distinction must be made between legislative acts which expressis verbis state that alcoholism is an illness and those which make no reference to illness but designate alcoholism as a public health problem. There are, furthermore, state legislative acts that do not use the term, public health problem, but imply the public health nature of the problem through the assignment of the administration of the alcoholism program to the state public health department or the public health section of some other department.

One or two states, however, seem to imply in their legislation that they do not regard alcoholism either as an illness or as a public health problem but purely as a social problem.

Thirty-seven states and the District of Columbia have legislation on "alcoholism;" or to be more exact, 36 states, because Montana has no specific legislation on this matter but does, on the other hand, have a Narcotics and Alcoholism Commission operated as a unit of the Department of Health. Apparently no legislation was required to create the above-named commission. The 11 states that have no legislation at the time of this writing are: Arizona, Idaho, Iowa, Mississippi, Missouri, Nebraska, Nevada, Ohio, Oklahoma, South Dakota and Wyoming.

Six states, namely, Alabama, Arkansas, Georgia, Michigan, Tennessee and Texas, designate alcoholism as a disease in their laws pertaining to alcoholism programs. In addition, New Mexico says that the alcoholic is a sick person without, however, calling alcoholism a disease, and Vermont defines the "compulsive drinker" or the "alcoholic addict" in terms which imply an abnormal medical condition.

Following are the relevant passages from acts of the states mentioned above. (Italics are mine.)

ALABAMA
An act (16 June 1945):
"To promote the rehabilitation of Alcoholics and to promote the education of the public with respect to Alcoholism and to make an annual appropriation for this purpose. . . .
"WHEREAS, *Alcoholism is recognized as a disease and the Alcoholic as a sick person, and . . . .*"

ARKANSAS
Act 411 (29 March 1955):
"AN ACT to provide for Education, Study, and Research relating to Problems of Alcoholism, and for Commitment, Treatment, and Rehabilitation of Alcoholics; to repeal Act 473 of the 1949 Acts of Arkansas and all Other Laws and Parts of Laws in conflict herewith. . . .
"Section 1. Purpose. . . . *Alcoholism is hereby recognized as an illness* and a public health problem affecting the general welfare and economy of the State, and as an illness subject to treatment and abatement; and the sufferer of alcoholism is recognized as one worthy of treatment and rehabilitation. . . ."

GEORGIA
An act (21 February 1951):

"To recognize Alcoholism as an illness and a public health problem. . . ."

MICHIGAN
Act 216 (2 May 1952):
"Section 47a, 18.1018 (1). . . . *'alcoholism,'* as used in this section, *is recognized as a chronic and progressive illness,* characterized by an excessive and uncontrolled drinking of alcoholic beverages, and as a public health problem affecting the general welfare and economy of the state, and for the control of which there are insufficient programs and facilities within the state."

TENNESSEE
An act (18 March 1955):
"Chapter 232.   Public Acts 1955.   AN ACT *to define alcoholism* and recognize it *as an illness* and a public health problem. . . .

TEXAS
An act (9 June 1953):
"Section 1. . . . *Alcoholism is hereby recognized as an illness* and a public health problem affecting . . ."

The foregoing are the six states with definite statements, and one may add New Mexico and Vermont which either call the alcoholic definitely a sick person or imply this through definition.

NEW MEXICO
An act (16 March 1949):
"Section 7.   Commitment.   The District Courts, pursuant to the provision of the laws of the State of New Mexico, are hereby authorized to take judicial notice of the fact that *a chronic alcoholic is a sick person* and in need of proper medical, institutional, advisory and rehabilitative treatment."

VERMONT
Permanent No. 239 (18 May 1951):
" 'Compulsive Drinker' or 'Alcoholic Addict' means a person affected by an uncontrollable craving for alcoholic beverages, or a person who . . ."

It is, of course, of great interest, that the legislation of some of our states says in so and so many words that alcoholism is an illness. Nevertheless, the legal repercussions of these statements are rather meager. The formulations quoted here are of no great import when it comes to questions outside the field of public care of alcoholics. Thus, it may be greatly doubted that in Michigan the fact that one of their acts says that " 'alcoholism' as used in this section is recognized as a chronic and progressive illness . . ." would have any influence on a decision as to whether or not an insurance company would have any liability in the case of an alcoholic; nor would it seem to have any influence on questions concerning alcoholics other than public care by the state in question.

Most but not all of these acts contain definitions of the alcoholic or the chronic alcoholic or alcoholism, and in many of these instances the definition contained in the Act of the District of Columbia of 4 August 1947, has been copied word for word.

Section 2 of the above act reads as follows: "The term 'chronic alcoholic' means any person who chronically and habitually uses alcoholic beverages to the extent that he has lost the power of self-control with respect to the use of such beverages, or while under the influence of alcohol endangers the public morals, health, safety, or welfare." Of course, this implies that the loss of control is a result of habitual excessive use of alcoholic beverages. That alcohol causes alcoholism is a point which requires careful analysis in the discussion of the illness conception of "alcoholism." As it stands in these various legislative acts, the formulation could be interpreted to mean that "alcoholism" (if it is a disease) is a self-inflicted disease.

Some states, notably Vermont (Permanent No. 239, 18 May 1951) give differential definitions for "chronic alcoholic," "compulsive drinker," "habitual drunkard," etc., etc. The above Vermont act gives some useful definitions in paragraphs IV through VIII and in paragraph IX the various definitions are all lumped under the term "alcoholism," that is, the act arrives at a broad and vague definition of that term such as has been proposed in Chapter III.1.2 of the present study. Paragraphs IV to IX of the Vermont act read as follows:

IV. "Chronic Alcoholic" means a person who, in consequence of prolonged excessive drinking, has developed a diagnosable bodily disease or mental disorder;

V. "Compulsive Drinker" or "Alcoholic Addict" means a person affected by an uncontrollable craving for alcoholic beverages, or a person who chronically and habitually uses alcoholic beverages to the extent that he has lost the power of self-control with respect to the use of such beverages, or while chronically or habitually under the influence of alcoholic beverages endangers public morals, health, safety or welfare;

VI. "Habitual Drunkard" means a person who is frequently or regularly intoxicated from the use of alcoholic beverages and has been three times convicted for a violation of section 6206 of the Vermont Statutes, Revision of 1949, as amended;

VII. "Excessive Drinker" means a person who drinks to an extent which exposes him to the risk of becoming a compulsive drinker or a chronic alcoholic;

VIII. "Inebriate" means a person who may be an uncomplicated excessive drinker, a compulsive drinker, an alcoholic addict, an habitual drunkard or a chronic alcoholic;

IX. "Alcoholic" means a person suffering from a condition defined in paragraph IV, V, VI, VII and VIII;

As most of the states that have an alcoholism program make provisions for the creation of clinics, "medical facilities," hospital treatment, etc., it may be said that nearly all of the state laws reflect the recognition of "alcoholism" as belonging to the sphere of medicine, even though the expressions illness and public health may not be mentioned in the legislative acts.

The states of New Jersey and North Carolina designate "alcoholism" directly as a public health problem. The recognition of the public health nature of the problem of alcoholism is implied by legislative acts of Colorado, Florida, Illinois, Indiana, Louisiana, Maine, Massachusetts, Minnesota, New Hampshire, New York, Pennsylvania and the District of Columbia. This is in addition to the eight states listed above which speak either of alcoholism as an illness or of the alcoholic as a sick person.

There is one deviation from the general trend toward recognizing alcoholism as a medical or public health problem and that is Rhode Island, whose legislation on an alcoholism program is incorporated in an amendment to an act covering "Offences against Chastity, Morality and Decency."

Much of this legislation was stimulated by the Yale research group which was consulted by many states before the drafting of their legislative acts on this matter. Much has been due to the intervention of politically prominent members of local alcoholism committees affiliated with The National Council on Alcoholism, whose staff has also been consulted in various instances, and undoubtedly some of the legislative acts were fathered by Alcoholics Anonymous members active in local parties. At the same time, such legislative action has also served as "a favorable response" to the insistence of temperance societies that state governments should take some action in the field of alcoholism, although such response may not be what the temperance movement was aiming at.

There is no Federal legislation on alcoholism programs, but the program of the District of Columbia (4 August 1947) was, of course, enacted by the Senate and House of Representatives of the United States in Congress assembled.

IV.4. Attitudes of the Churches and the Temperance Societies

Basic attitudes of the Protestant and Roman Catholic Churches have been discussed under the heading, "The Question of Self-Inflicted Disease and the Ethical Involvements," in Chapter III.2, to which reference is made here. In addition, some of the denominations have made official or semiofficial statements on this question which show that certain concessions have been made in response to the scientific progress of knowledge on "alcoholism." While some of the large denominations have recognized their responsibilities toward alcoholics and their families and are ready to foster the rehabilitation efforts of public and private agencies, they, of course, have certain reservations about the conception of alcoholism as an illness. By and large, the modification of denominational outlooks on alcoholism may be attributed to the influence of the Yale Summer School of Alcohol Studies and the large volume of medical literature that deals with the illness conception of alcoholism. The contacts of clergymen with Alcoholics Anonymous groups, and their acquaintance with the spiritual outlook and the striking success of that fellowship, have contributed to the changes in denominational attitudes. Furthermore, it must be taken into account that many alcoholics who recovered in Alcoholics Anonymous have returned to their churches and become active church members, and thus have been able to exert some influence from inside rather than outside.

The Methodist Board of Temperance has not made any declaration on the disease idea of alcoholism but has ceased to express rejection of that idea. In a private interview, I was given to understand that the Methodist Board of Temperance may regard alcoholism as an illness when loss of control develops, but not before that. (This standpoint is highly justified.) Furthermore, the recent publications of the Methodist Board of Temperance show consid-

erable adaptation to modern principles in the approach to "alcoholism." The Baptist Church, too, has issued publications which
show some changes in attitude toward this question, but to a
much lesser degree.

The Mormon Church, which is, of course, strictly opposed to any
use of alcoholic beverages, has made no statement implying any
change in its views on alcoholism, but has nevertheless given evidence of some flexibility through the support of the public and
private agencies in charge of alcoholism programs in the state of
Utah, where political and social life is strongly influenced by the
Mormon Church.

At the 1946 General Assembly of the Presbyterian Church in
the U.S.A., a resolution was passed that concerned the attitudes
of this body toward alcoholics. The pertinent passages are quoted
below:

"There are four reasons why alcoholic beverages merit new concern.
First, the strength of the social pressures toward drinking is increasing.
Second, scientific studies have made available new tools for understanding the problem. Third, only an approach which does not over-
simplify the nature of the problem can have a chance of success.
Fourth, the accelerated tempo of the machine age exacts an increasing
toll of deaths and injuries through the use of alcoholic beverages.

"We begin with pastoral and social concern for alcoholics and excessive drinkers and for their families. Alcoholics, as well as their families, need the full ministry of the church. We recognize that, once
drinking has passed a certain point, alcoholism is a disease; that is,
the drinking cannot be stopped by mere resolution on the part of the
drinker. He needs treatment, not punishment; understanding, not condemnation.

"Under no conditions will pastors permit drinking behavior to produce a withdrawal of pastoral concern for drinkers. We shall encourage
the establishment of clinics and other facilities, when competently conducted, for the diagnosis, referral and treatment of alcoholics. We shall
give all possible aid to those organizations which work on a religious
basis for the cure and rehabilitation of alcoholics.

"While recognizing the dual origin of alcoholism and excessive drinking in both personal instability and social pressures, and accepting alcoholism as a disease which requires treatment, we reassert our conviction
that the ethical aspects of the use of alcoholic beverages are underlined
by our concern on behalf of the victims of alcohol."

The Congregational Church with its quasi-autonomous member
churches is less prone to make general statements, yet through its
Board of Social Action two issues of its official magazine have

been devoted to the question of alcoholism, and those publications give expression to the disease conception of alcoholism. (See Jellinek, 1945b, and McPeek, 1950.)

As mentioned in another section of this study, the Protestant Episcopal Church does not regard the use of alcoholic beverages as a sin, but only the abuse. It is, therefore, much easier for that denomination as a whole to accept the medical verdict on the nature of alcoholism. The Episcopal Church held a national conference on the subject of alcoholism and social drinking and the proceedings were published in a special report. Particular consideration was given to the question of pastoral counseling of alcoholics and their families as well as to the question of preventive education. The report does not contain any direct expression of the illness conception of alcoholism, but the acceptance of that idea is implicit in the trend of thought that pervades the entire report.

Most important among declarations on alcoholism made by religious bodies is the stand taken by the National Council of the Churches of Christ in the U.S.A. Some paragraphs of the statement by the Council are given verbatim below:[1]

"The National Council of the Churches of Christ in the U.S.A. believes that the use of alcoholic beverages is a serious threat to the health, happiness and welfare of many people and to the stability of families and communities. Although differences of conscientious conviction in relation to certain aspects of the alcohol problem exist among the churches of the National Council, the area of agreement is sufficiently large and significant and the problems so urgent as to demand the attention of the Council.

"The churches share a pastoral concern for alcoholics, problem drinkers and their families. We recognize that once drinking has passed a certain point, it becomes alcoholism, an affliction which cannot be met effectively by the victims. Alcoholics are persons in need of diagnosis, understanding, guidance and treatment. They are especially in need of pastoral care and the divine love which the church can bring them. There need be no condoning of their behavior, but neither should a church permit its antagonism to alcohol to prevent its offering an effective ministry to alcoholics and their families. Ministers and churches should not be content merely to direct alcoholics to treatment centers."

The modification of attitudes toward alcoholism through the leadership of large Protestant denominations has facilitated the

---

[1] Adopted by the General Board of the National Council of Churches at New York, 26 February 1958.

acceptance of the disease conception of alcoholism in certain sections of public opinion. Nevertheless, the largest proportion of rejection of that idea comes from the active membership of the pietist churches.

The temperance movement was originally closely related to religious bodies. At present its members are still drawn almost entirely from church membership, particularly of the Methodist and Baptist Churches, but its relation to the organized churches has become rather tenuous and there is sometimes even conflict between temperance societies and the official religious bodies. These conflicts arise more out of methods than principles.

Initially, the temperance movement, which was a late manifestation of the humanitarian movement, was greatly concerned with the rehabilitation of the alcoholic, or to be exact, with the "reformation of the drunkard." Some very vague ideas about the possibility that inebriety might be an illness were, at first, quite acceptable to the American temperance movement, which was greatly influenced by Dr. Benjamin Rush and by the great preacher Lyman Beecher. The concern with the alcoholic is still alive in the European temperance societies which have taken an active part in rehabilitation work, but in the American temperance movement this aspect of temperance activities has vanished to give way to entire concentration on education and legislative controls.

In the view of most American temperance societies, the idea that alcoholism is an illness is a threat to their educational efforts, which aim at total abstinence and the disappearance of alcoholic beverages. Such an interference is by no means a necessary development; but it must be admitted that in America, the scientific literature and the public and private agencies concerned with "alcoholism" have concentrated to such a degree on the true alcohol addict and the problem drinker that other important problems arising from the use of alcoholic beverages have been neglected. The reluctance of the temperance societies to accept alcoholism as an illness stems also from their fear that such a conception might serve as an excuse for the "alcoholic." (This aspect has been touched upon in another section of this study and does not require further comment at this point.)

Another consideration of the temperance societies is that the propagation of the illness conception of alcoholism may favor the interests of the alcoholic-beverage industry and, as a matter of fact, it has been intimated that the disease conception was triggered and has been fostered by those vested interests. No doubt, "alcoholism as an illness" is pleasing to the beverage industry, to which the most acceptable development would be, of course, a definite proof that alcoholism is a physiopathological illness (so long as it does not involve the process of drug addiction), since that would exculpate alcohol to a high degree. But no matter what jaundiced view one may have of the vested interests, their pleasure concerning the illness conception of "alcoholism" cannot form a basis for its rejection, if that conception should turn out to be valid.

The temperance workers are among the few in America who still remember the old Medical Association for the Study of Inebriety, and when they have to refer to alcoholism as an illness, they may say that of course it is so, but that it is an "old story" which does not alter their objections in any way.

The American Business Men's Research Foundation makes the following statement:[2]

"To anyone who has ever cared for an acutely drunk person there can be no denial that a drunk is a sick person. The 'new concept' of alcoholism as a disease is merely what has been known for thousands of years extended to formulate the hypothesis that for some unknown reason or reasons, a diseased condition exists in some persons either mental or physical, which, when alcohol is ingested, results in 'alcoholism,' and does not exist in other persons.

"I mention this to emphasize that to disagree with the ridiculous concept that alcoholism concerns only man (and not environment and alcohol) and is limited as a disease concept only to compulsive drinkers, is not confined to the religious and the drys. Most, by far, objective scientists agree that all three fields, and all degrees of ingestion must be considered."

The first paragraph refers to acute intoxication, but the admission that the individual so afflicted is sick has little relation to the illness conception of alcoholism itself. The second paragraph is directed against the slogan that "Alcoholism is in the man, not in the bottle." The objection is well taken, but the formulation is not particularly felicitous. Substituting the expression "alcohol addiction" for the word "alcoholism" and taking the former term in its strict pharmacological connotation, one must agree that scientists who hold this latter view rightly see that, apart from individual

[2] The disease concept of alcoholism. Foundation Says 16 (No. 1): 65–68, 1958.

psychological factors, a decisive part in the genesis of alcohol addiction as an illness is played by social customs and attitudes and, last but not least, by alcohol itself in its capacity as a drug.

The man versus bottle idea is the weakest link in the armor of the alcoholism programs and it is little consolation that many of the concepts in the propaganda of the temperance movement are even more spurious.

The true attitude of the American Business Men's Research Foundation, which typifies the stand of a large section of the temperance movement, is contained in a sarcastic article entitled "Tie-In Sales."[3]

"Some twenty years ago a group of scientists decided to sell the American people on an old scientific truth—namely that there is a disease which could be called alcoholism. . . .

"And here is where the 'tie-in sales' began.

"These are among the 'tie-ins' which those purchasing the 'disease concept' were apparently asked to buy:

Tie-In No. 1
"That the alcoholism disease concept is restricted only to compulsive excessive drinkers.

Tie-In No. 2
"That the moderate use of alcohol is not harmful and may be beneficial, therefore the moderate use is automatically excluded from the disease concept.

Tie-In No. 3
"That the idea of a beverage alcohol free society is futile and possibly undesirable.

Tie-In No. 4
"That in 'alcoholism' only the host (man) is of great interest and the environment of the disease (availability, sales promotion, attitude towards, etc.) and the causation factors (alcohol in particular) are of little importance.

Tie-In No. 5
"That scientific study could be made objectively only by moderate drinkers, not by total abstainers or working alcoholics (who were defined as compulsive excessive drinkers).

Tie-In No. 6
"That the advantage (or disadvantage) of total abstinence need not be explored.

Tie-In No. 7
"That alcoholism which involves (surely at its original inception as well as during its development, and possibly even after its develop-

* Foundation Says 16 (No. 1): 17–19, 1958.

ment) a decision as to whether to drink or not (and hence involves morality) is not a moral problem, but is exclusively a medical one. This position is maintained at the same time that a moral system—Alcoholics Anonymous—is acknowledged to be one of the most effective arresters of the disease.

Tie-In No. 8

"That all drys are suspect, only advocates of moderation are of intellect above suspicion, and purveyors and distributors of alcoholic beverages need not be considered.

Tie-In No. 9

"That the advertising of intoxicants does not increase their use, only switches from brand to brand. This concept denies entirely the principles of advertising and the picture advertising creates of alcohol as a pleasant, helpful luxury, and with no connotation or implication of possible bad results from use, and thus appeals to non-drinkers."

Evidently, the authors of the "Tie-In" article wish to imply that moderate drinking is as much a disease as "alcoholism," but as they do not take the disease concept truly seriously, the implication is that "moderate drinking" is as dangerous as any form of excess. The philosophy of total abstinence, of course, implies such a viewpoint.

"Tie-In No. 5" shows misconceptions about the requirements of scientific objectivity. Objectivity is not arrogated to moderate drinkers only and not denied to total abstainers, but is linked rather with scientific training.

There have been and are students of alcoholism who are total abstainers without temperance learnings and who have produced highly objective studies and it must be said that some scientists with strong temperance convictions, led by their scientific training, have been able to present the facts on alcoholism with the highest degree of objectivity, e.g., Baer, Wlassak, Staehelin, Levy and Emerson.

By "the group of scientists" who "started some twenty years ago" obviously the Yale University Center of Alcohol Studies is meant, and thus it must be said that "Tie-In No. 7" is an unjustified statement. In recognition of the ethical aspects of "alcoholism," the Yale Summer School of Alcohol Studies has been offering for several years lectures on the moral aspects of alcoholism by Roman Catholic and Protestant clergymen, as it was felt that those lecturers are much more competent in these matters than any member of the Yale Center. (The present study includes a section on ethical aspects, Chapter III.2.)

The idea of "Tie-In No. 4" has been treated above (in Chapter II). Some of the lacks of scientific investigations on alcoholism, as pointed out in some of the "Tie-In" items, are valid, though formulated with obvious rancor.

The efforts to "convert" the temperance societies to a frank acceptance of alcoholism as an illness is, in my opinion, an entirely unnecessary one. The temperance movement has a very definite function in American society, even if the movement does not embrace the rehabilitation of alcoholics. Its function is as wholesome as opposition parties are in the political life of a nation.

IV.5. Labor and Management

Labor and management form very large and influential sections of the American public and thus their attitudes toward the various species of alcoholism represent an important part of public opinion; furthermore, the opinions of these groups may influence quite considerably the attitudes of other sections of the general public.

Whether union attitudes have greatly influenced the stand that management is taking, or whether the converse is the case, or whether the attitudes of both toward the disease conception of "alcoholism" have sprung up independently, would be difficult to assess.

To both groups the idea of "alcoholism" as a disease was rather welcome and this is one of the questions on which labor and management could easily meet.

If there was any initial inclination among labor unions to accept the disease conception of "alcoholism," it was no doubt greatly reinforced by the action of some large industrial and business enterprises in setting up programs for the rehabilitation of those in their employ, who were "suffering from the disease of alcoholism."

According to The Wall Street Journal[4] "few unions will argue if a company fires a man when his drinking interferes with his job. But most unions argue that alcoholism should be considered as an illness, subject to the same benefits and considerations as more commonly recognized illness."

This attitude of labor unions facilitates the attack of management

---

[4] 28 April 1958.

on alcoholism. *The Wall Street Journal*[5] quotes James F. Oates, Jr., chairman and president of the Equitable Life Assurance Society, as saying: "Whether management likes it or not—and there is much to tempt us to shun the subject—we must take a position on alcoholism [and] combat its increasing menace."

Of course, industry wished to avoid the question of alcoholism, as any action could have created the question of interference with private conduct. But the disease conception of "alcoholism" formed an acceptable basis for preventive and curative action in this field.

The interest of management and labor has been awakened and is kept alive through the systematic efforts of the Yale Center of Alcohol Studies, the *Quarterly Journal on Studies of Alcohol,* The National Council on Alcoholism and its numerous local affiliates all over the country, and lately the activities of the state alcoholism programs. The growing number of Alcoholics Anonymous members among the staff and labor force of industrial and business enterprises is no doubt a decisive factor in these trends.

Initially, the contacts with management were disappointing, as there seemed to be considerable suspicion of political motivation. Persistent activity, however, in the form of industrial seminars on alcoholism, and the infiltration of explanatory papers on the disease nature of "alcoholism" into such magazines as *Business Week, The Office, Industrial Relations News,* and other industrial and business periodicals, has overcome the initial resistance.

Furthermore, papers published by staff members of alcoholism programs of large industrial enterprises have greatly encouraged other industrial and business enterprises to join the ranks of those organizations which attack the question of alcoholism on the basis of the disease conception.

Presumably pamphlets issued by the Metropolitan Life Insurance Company under the title "The Alcoholic" have made considerable impression on business and industrial management.

Recent lengthy articles in *Time* magazine[6] and *The Wall Street Journal,*[7] which emphasize the disease conception of "alcoholism," may be expected to foster further interest of the business world in this question.

[5] Loc. cit.
[6] 23 December 1957.
[7] Loc. cit.

Consolidated Edison Company of New York, Allis-Chalmers, Eastman Kodak Company, and du Pont, were the pioneer industrial organizations in this field. They have been joined by such large organizations as Standard Oil of New Jersey, International Harvester, New England Telephone and Telegraph Company, Western Electric Company, California General Petroleum Company, Boeing Airplane, Norton Company and some other industrial and business concerns. Their ranks are growing and the American Association of Industrial Physicians and Surgeons has formed a Committee on Alcoholism which embraces the disease conception.

As mentioned before, most labor unions would like to see alcoholism considered as a disease. While the AFL–CIO has no resolution on the disease conception of "alcoholism," the Community Services Committee of that organization issued in 1957 a pamphlet entitled "What Every Worker Should Know about Alcoholism." In this pamphlet the Committee says of the alcoholic:

"He is a sick person. He can no more control his compulsion to drink than a diabetic can control his reaction to sugar. When he sobers up, the alcoholic intends to stay sober. But a single drink can start him on the same downward spiral. . . .

"The alcoholic is not necessarily a weak-willed person. In most cases he is a compulsive drinker; once he takes his first drink he can't stop drinking, no matter what the consequences to himself, his family, his friends or his job.

"The majority of alcoholics are not 'skid-row' types. They are not found in the Monday morning court line-up, or wandering dazed and shocked through back streets, or discovered in the emergency ward of the city hospital. Quite the contrary.

"Over 85 per cent of them on the surface lead normal lives, have homes and families, are employable and usually working. They often have exceptional skills.

"Alcoholics do not represent any single group in our population. They are professional people, government officials, tradesmen, executives, skilled craftsmen, and workers. Like all disease, alcoholism cuts across all lines, reaches all segments of society."

The above quotation is not on the level of a resolution on the part of the National AFL–CIO. It does appear, however, in an official publication which suffices to identify the AFL–CIO with the above statement, and the New Mexico AFL–CIO found it justified to state that, "The National AFL–CIO has recognized the seriousness of this illness. . . ."

Although labor unions are in general favoring the disease conception of "alcoholism," to date only one AFL–CIO state organization has passed a resolution to that effect, namely, the New Mexico AFL–CIO. Their resolution is given in part below:

RESOLUTION: Education on Alcoholism and Cooperation with the New Mexico Commission on Alcoholism

WHEREAS Alcoholism is increasing in America and is affecting the welfare of the nation in terms of health, family distress and absenteeism; and

WHEREAS Health authorities now recognize the fact that alcoholics are sick people suffering from a disease for which there is no cure since the allergy to alcohol is beyond their control; and

WHEREAS The compulsion to drink can be controlled through constructive help, thereby arresting the progress of the disease through total abstinence and a measure of stability and harmony can be gained for the alcoholic and his family; and. . . .

The State of New Mexico is fortunate in having a tax-supported Commission on Alcoholism maintaining two rehabilitation centers staffed by trained people who also conduct an educational program on the causes of alcoholism for all segments of the general public;

THEREFORE BE IT RESOLVED: That the New Mexico State AFL–CIO go on record as recognizing the problems of alcoholics and their families, and that this Convention commit itself to aiding the program of the New Mexico Commission on Alcoholism in every possible way; and

BE IT FURTHER RESOLVED: That a Committee on Education and Rehabilitation of Alcoholics be formed. . . .

BE IT FURTHER RESOLVED: That copies of this resolution be forwarded to George Meany, President of the AFL–CIO and to Leo Purlis, Director of AFL–CIO Community Service Activities.

Whether there is any outright rejection of the disease idea by some small section of the American labor force cannot be determined at this time. Possibly the socialist wing of labor would be influenced by Vandervelde's view of alcoholism, namely, that it is an entirely capitalistic phenomenon which would disappear in a socialistic world, although the experience of Communist countries has not borne out that assumption.

A mimeographed document under the letterhead of the "Labor Research Council" has seen some very limited circulation in the United States. That circular vigorously protests the disease conception of "alcoholism," which it attributes entirely to the propaganda of the alcoholic-beverage industry. As the "Labor Research Council" (of Bridgeport, Connecticut) appears to be a one-man outfit, it would not seem to reflect the views of any established labor group and does not require any further comment.

As far as management is concerned, it is a reasonable assumption that the disease idea of "alcoholism" is for them probably not more than a convenience for tackling the vexatious problem of alcohol and the belief in the disease conception does not go very deeply with the majority. The degree of sincerity notwithstanding, the net effect is a significant contribution to the acceptance of the disease conception of "alcoholism."

Although the acceptance of the disease conception of "alcoholism" by labor and management is still in its beginnings, it is undoubtedly an important element in the over-all acceptance of this idea by the public in general.

IV.6. The Public at Large

The attitude of the public at large toward the disease conception of "alcoholism" is of paramount importance for various aspects of the problems of alcoholism. The acceptance or rejection of the idea determines to a large extent whether or not the general public will have hope and therefore also the incentive for the rehabilitation of alcoholics. Furthermore, the continuation of public and voluntary agencies concerned with alcoholism depends upon the moral and, to some extent, the financial support of the aggregate of citizens and this support, in turn, depends upon the attitude of the public toward conceptions about the nature of alcoholism.

While the public at large is more susceptible to movements coming from within the community than from either government or professional groups, nevertheless the attitudes of the latter reinforce the opinions of the voluntary agencies and lend them increased prestige. There is thus a continuous chain of interactions between the attitudes of government bodies, professional groups, voluntary agencies and the public in general.

Of the attitudes of the general public, not much is known, but there is some information that gives an indication of the present status of the acceptance of the disease idea as well as the progress made in this respect in the last 10 years.

In 1948, J. W. Riley, of Rutgers University, conducted a nation-wide survey in which a representative sample of men and women were questioned on their opinions about alcoholism. Twenty per cent of those questioned regarded an alcoholic as a sick person, while 58 per cent saw no difference between an alcoholic and a person who gets drunk frequently. Furthermore, 50 per cent of those interviewed thought that alcoholics did not require treatment, but that they could stop drinking if they wanted to (Riley, 1949).

Approximately 10 years later, Elmo Roper and Associates conducted a nationwide survey whose results were reported in a newspaper release of January 1958.[8] For some reason or other, this release hardly became known and found its way into only a few newspapers in spite of general readiness of the press to publish material on "alcoholism."

The Roper interviewers asked the following question: "If you knew someone who habitually drank so much that it affected his job and his relations with people, would you say that he is morally weak or would you say that he is sick?" The percentage distribution of answers to this question is given below:

Morally weak	35 per cent
Sick	58 per cent
Express no opinion	7 per cent

This represents, of course, a tremendous increase in acceptance of the conception of alcoholism as an illness in the short span of 10 years. As a matter of fact, the increase from 20 per cent to 58 per cent is so great that it is somewhat astonishing. I believe, however, that it is quite understandable in view of the fact that there are approximately 600,000 propagandists, namely, 200,000 members of Alcoholics Anonymous and their wives and children, who vigorously spread the idea that alcoholism is an illness, not through public speeches, nor through their numerous pamphlets, but rather by word of mouth in conversation with their many friends and business acquaintances.

A breakdown of the survey by towns and cities according to size is given in Table 4.

Roper makes the following comment:

"But old ways of looking at things die hard. In groups with less education, the idea that alcoholism is a moral lapse still persists—among grammar school educated people, 47 per cent call compulsive drinkers

[8] Elmo Roper and Associates. Public sees alcoholism as an illness. (The Public Pulse; news release of 4 January 1958.) Chicago; National Newspaper Syndicate; 1958.

morally weak' as opposed to only 26 per cent of those with a college background who pronounce that severe a judgment. Forty-four per cent of people living in rural areas looked at the problem from this moralistic point of view, while the figure for the average city was more than 10 per cent lower."

The factor of education does play a significant role in the acceptance of the disease conception of "alcoholism," but I believe that another factor is present too. I should like to point out that the percentage of answers that alcoholism is a sickness is higher in cities of 100,000 to 1 million than in cities of over 1 million, and even higher in cities from 2,500 to 100,000 inhabitants. This is the opposite of the expected trend. I would suggest that this trend may be ascribed to the fact that in smaller cities the population is much closer to and much more aware of A.A. groups than in the large metropolitan agglomerations. On the other hand, in towns under 2,000 inhabitants and in rural areas, Alcoholics Anonymous groups are, of course, practically nonexistent and the population of such areas has much less personal acquaintance with "alcoholics."

The percentage of acceptance of the disease idea of "alcoholism" is 5 to 15 times greater in the United States than in any other country, perhaps with the exception of Canada for which I have seen no estimate.

In spite of the high degree of acceptance by the public at large, it may be surmised that the belief is not deeply rooted as yet. Much of it may be lip service, repeating what has been heard on the radio or at a lecture given by someone who attended the Yale Summer School of Alcohol Studies, or read in a pamphlet, or heard from Alcoholics Anonymous friends. That the belief is of no particular depth may be attributed to the vagueness of the formulations of the disease conception that reach the general public.

TABLE 4.—*Opinions on whether Alcoholics are Morally Weak or Sick, by Population Density of Respondents' Area of Residence (in Per Cent)*

Population	Morally Weak	Sick	Express No Opinion
Over 1,000,000	37	59	4
100,000–1,000,000	33	63	4
2,500–100,000	27	64	9
Under 2,000	40	53	7
Rural	44	49	7

The picture of alcoholism, behind the "acceptance," is perhaps that it is "something mental" and perhaps that an allergy to alcohol is involved, although in medical and scientific circles the latter is the least accepted etiological theory. What has been said in this paragraph does not amount to more than guesswork, but could be made the object of a field survey.

Generally, it may be said not only of the public at large but of the medical profession, industry and labor and all the other sections of public opinion, that their feeling is that the idea that "alcoholism" is an illness "is true, but not really true." This feeling will persist until the disease conception of alcoholism attains to clarity and definitiveness.

IV.7. Attitudes of Some Foreign Nations

The attitudes of some foreign countries toward the illness conception of alcoholism can be discussed here only cursorily. An adequate presentation of the subject would require not only the mention of attitudes but also the relation of those attitudes to official or semiofficial programs in the various countries. A more thorough description of the latter aspects is reserved for a separate publication at a later date.

The great propaganda effort for the acceptance of "alcoholism" as an illness, as practiced in the United States, is largely absent in Europe and South America. In those countries, voluntary agencies concerned with alcoholism, except temperance associations, are few, if any.

On the other hand, such activities have been initiated more recently in Australia, New Zealand and the Union of South Africa, where voluntary agencies have been organized on the pattern of the National Council on Alcoholism.

Generally speaking, European nations have less need for the acceptance of these ideas by the public at large, especially those countries that have compulsory treatment of alcoholics. The decisive factor in such countries is the acceptance by the medical profession and by government welfare agencies. Nevertheless, where the basis of public care of alcoholics rests on the illness conception of alcoholism, the propagandization of that idea might result in greater effectiveness of public care, particularly through the voluntary acceptance of treatment by the early "alcoholics."

IV.7.1 Europe

In countries such as Norway, where very strong groups of Alcoholics Anonymous have developed, the idea of the illness conception of alcoholism is spreading beyond the professional segments of the population and finding some reflection in the public at large. Perhaps this circumstance has played some role in the legislation of Norway, which in 1953 declared alcoholism an illness for which the National Health Insurance must provide the cost of treatment and rehabilitation.

In European countries the official acceptance of alcoholism as an illness is more often a matter of social than of medical consideration. The designation of illness may be incorporated in compulsory health insurance laws in order to compel the agencies to cover the cost of the rehabilitation of alcoholics. The conceptions underlying this idea are not clearer than in America.

A sociological element too may enter into the acceptance of the illness conception, not so much as far as government authorities are concerned but rather in relation to the medical profession and the general public. In countries where alcoholism is practically limited to the lower educational and economic strata, the tendency is to see alcoholism as mere drunkenness and largely of economic origin. On the other hand, where all strata of society are more or less proportionally represented in the alcoholic population, the economic factor is less plausible and the idea of alcoholism as an illness presents itself for the consideration of the medical profession as well as of the public at large.

SWEDEN, NORWAY, DENMARK

In the Nordic nations, except Denmark, the supervision and rehabilitation of alcoholics is compulsory and thus education and propaganda for the treatment of alcoholism is not an essential feature. There remains, however, the importance of the acceptance of the idea by the medical profession. On their acceptance or rejection depends largely whether rehabilitation will follow therapeutic rather than authoritarian methods. In Sweden, outstanding psychiatrists and public health officers (e.g., Lundquist, 1951; Aamark, 1951; Höjer, 1952; Izikowitz, 1946) have made great contributions to the understanding of alcoholism and have embraced the illness conception. Yet until recently these workers have made little impression within the ranks of the medical profession and even less on the governmental welfare agencies which are largely responsible for the supervision and rehabilitation of alcoholics. In the past few years, some reorientation toward therapeutic outlooks has taken place due, to some extent, to the efforts of the alcoholism committee of the Royal Swedish Medical Board and, perhaps to a greater degree, to the impression that the introduction of disulfiram (Antabuse) has created within the medical profession as well as among the welfare personnel. As one Swedish physician said: "Antabuse did more good for the doctors than for the alcoholics." The use of a medicament in the treatment of alcoholics has brought home to the profession and to the welfare people concerned with the rehabilitation of alcoholics that "alcoholism" belongs in the realm of medicine. According to Wiklund (1948), the diagnosis concerning alcoholism, as made by the so-called "temperance boards" which decide upon the compulsory treatment of alcoholics, was not a medical but a social diagnosis. The local temperance boards, at present, are shifting to a more medically oriented approach. An explicit recognition of the illness conception of alcoholism is, however, still lacking in Sweden and the lack of such recognition is hampering the rehabilitation of alcoholics financially, as can be seen from the letter of a foreign correspondent of the Journal of the American Medical Association (1956):

"The national health insurance scheme, which came into force at the beginning of 1956, failed to place alcoholism on the same footing as other better understood diseases. The situation in this respect is clearer in Norway, where a law that came into force in October 1953, provides medical care of alcoholics who are beneficiaries of national health insurance. An appeal is now being made to the Swedish Parliament to bring the provisions of national health insurance in Sweden into line with the modern conception of alcoholism as a disease."[9]

The incidence of pre-alcoholic marked psychological vulnerability is rather high in the alcoholic population of Sweden, as can be seen from the work of Aamark (1951). Nevertheless, the traditional outlook has been that the etiology of alcoholism is to be sought in social pressure and habits. This viewpoint is still strongly represented, although the recognition of individual psychological factors and possible biological elements is on the increase. The fellowship of Alcoholics Anonymous does not represent an influential strong group in that country, at least its influence is much smaller than

* According to private communications, this end has now been achieved.

in Norway, and it has not made much of an impact on public awareness. The Swedish Temperance Movement has no unified view of the illness conception of "alcoholism" and opinions range from rigid rejection of that idea up to qualified acceptance.

Denmark is the only Nordic country which has neither an alcoholic-beverage monopoly nor a public care system for alcoholics. Consequently, there is no need there for an official recognition of alcoholism as an illness by government authorities. Nevertheless, that country has adequate facilities for the treatment and rehabilitation of alcoholics. The "Ring i Ring," which is the Danish version of Alcoholics Anonymous, forms a strong group which has caught the attention of the medical profession. There is a surprisingly large group of Danish physicians who are interested in the treatment of alcoholism and who have formed an association. (This is one of the very few voluntary agencies in Europe which embraces the propagation of the illness conception of alcoholism.) This association works in close cooperation with Ring i Ring. The recognition of alcoholism as an illness is widely spread among the medical profession and has reached wider circles too. This may be due to the fact that Denmark is the country where the Antabuse treatment originated and where it has received the widest publicity. Denmark is proud of this contribution to the problem of "alcoholism" and Dr. Erik Jacobsen, its discoverer, has received one of the major and coveted medical awards of that country. The above-mentioned facts seem to account for a wider recognition of the illness conception—although nonofficial—in Denmark than in other Nordic countries.

FINLAND

Finland belongs to the countries which have compulsory treatment of alcoholics. It cannot be said that the illness conception of alcoholism is widely spread. As a matter of fact, its acceptance is limited to specialists. On the other hand, the idea that alcoholism is, among other things, a medical and public health problem, is recognized by a large professional group. The lack of wider recognition is reflected in the predominating authoritarian approach toward the "alcoholic." This approach may be ascribed to the fact that the problem of true alcohol addiction is overshadowed by the violent manifestations of explosive occasional drinking.

The Finnish temperance movement is, by and large, more orthodox than in other Nordic countries. The conception of alcoholism as a disease is not a palatable one to the majority of Finnish temperance workers, yet they accept the viewpoint of their late outstanding exponent, Verkko, according to whom the explosive drinking involves a biological factor. The acceptance of this latter idea would logically involve the acceptance of the' illness conception, yet this inference is not made by the Finnish temperance workers, except for a small section.

The interest of the excellent Finnish research on alcohol and alcoholism also reflects the absence of an established acceptance of the illness conception of alcoholism. Their research is most developed in the field of sociology, where it contributes significantly toward preventive measures, but in physiology and pharmacology the emphasis is on the exploration of effects of alcohol on various functions and does not embrace possible physiopathological elements in the etiology of alcoholism.

HOLLAND

With the exception of Switzerland, where the compulsory treatment of alcoholics is established in practically all cantons, the countries of Western and Central Europe have either no compulsory rehabilitation of alcoholics or an action limited to special instances. Thus in Holland, referral to a clinic (Consultation Bureau) can be ordered for alcoholics convicted of minor crimes in which drinking was involved, and in France the "dangerous alcoholic" can be compelled to undergo treatment.

Holland has had, since 1912, a service of privately founded "consultatiebureaux" for alcoholics which have developed into ambulatory clinics and which have been supported for a number of years nearly entirely by federal and local governments. Thus one may speak of a "public care system" for alcoholics in the Netherlands. The number of such bureaus has grown to 14, well scattered over the small country, and sufficient to take care of the entire alcoholic population. These clinics are well known by the general public, as many of them are located in small population centers, so the public knows where an alcoholic can find help. The existence of a larger number of clinics in a compact population has resulted, of course, in the public awareness that "alcoholism" is a medical concern, although the term illness is applied to it by a rather limited section of the population. The closeness of the clinics to the population at large has made intensive propaganda on the disease conception of alcoholism dispensable. The medical profession of Holland may be largely inclined to accept the illness idea. No official pronouncement of the profession has been made, nor is it particularly needed at this time.

As for the Netherlands temperance movement, some of the early societies were responsible for the introduction of the illness conception of alcoholism, but later placed no emphasis on this matter. There are too great denominational differences among the temperance groups of Holland to permit a unified stand on the question of illness, but it may be said that there is no militant opposition to the idea.

BELGIUM

Belgium has a National Committee on Alcoholism that originated in the temperance movement. As this organization is now entirely government supported, it has a semiofficial status. The committee has two main program points: (a) the rehabilitation of alcoholics; (b) the problem of alcohol and traffic accidents. This committee, which has been greatly influenced by the seminars and publications of the World Health Organization, propagates the idea that alcoholism is an illness. The committee had a significant role in bringing about the creation of an Alcoholics Anonymous group in Brussels.

While the committee's stand on the illness conception of alcoholism may be regarded as a semiofficial one, it cannot be said that this view has penetrated either the medical profession or the public at large of that country. A survey that I organized which has not yet been published indicated that perhaps one-tenth of one per cent of the intellectual classes holds such an opinion. In the other strata of Belgian society this conception is practically unknown. Nevertheless, the viewpoint taken by the National Committee suffices to place the rehabilitation of alcoholics in Belgium on a medical level.

FRANCE

In France the recrudescence of alcoholism after the second World War to, or even above, the pre-war level has caused grave concern in wide circles. Certain groups in the French medical profession have taken a stronger stand than ever before. The French National Institute of Demographic Studies has also taken a great interest in this question and has produced fundamental surveys and statistical investigations in this field. The medical papers of Dérobert (1952, 1953,) May (1954), Perrin (1949, 1950), and the demographic work of Ledermann (1952a, 1952b, 1953, 1956) and Bastide (1954), have induced various French governing bodies to tackle the problem of alcoholism. The government has created a Council on Alcoholism attached to the Prime Minister's office. This council is principally concerned with preventive education and the collection of data for consolidation and dissemination. The rehabilitation of alcoholics is not prominent in the council's activities, but has received more attention from local governments as well as some legislation from the national government. As mentioned before, most recent French legislation requires the compulsory treatment of "dangerous alcoholics." This is, of course, a rather limited measure and in no way implies the conception of alcoholism as an illness. As has been seen in Chapter III, the younger generation of French psychiatrists inclines toward the illness conception, but this viewpoint is not particularly popular with the French medical profession and is hardly known at all among the population at large. It may be noted, however, that French physicians were the first (in the 19th century) to regard alcoholism as a public health problem.

There are those who recognize that a campaign for the control of alcoholism should include the illness conception of alcoholism. Fouquet and Paumelle (1956) advocate that the physician and the social worker should educate the public on the disease nature of alcoholism.

Interestingly enough, the illness conception of alcoholism is making much greater strides among French social workers and the Catholic clergy than in the medical profession. No one in that country has made such definite statements on this matter as one of the leading social workers, Mlle. Forey (1957), in whose work the influence of the World Health Organization is acknowledged. Addressing herself to the social workers, Mlle. Forey says: "Alcoholism is a disease which we must think of scientifically and objectively. We shall not engage in antialcohol propaganda, but shall be professional workers in the social service and shall act as such. Therein lies our strength and our opportunity." This motion is ably seconded by Mme. Galluet (1958), another prominent social worker.

In his preface to the treatise on alcoholism and the pastorate by Canon Gallez (1958), the Archbishop of Paris states: "At a certain stage, alcoholism is a true illness. An illness from which one cannot recover without the aid of others. The freedom to react adequately is impaired or abolished, and the energetic but understanding intervention of society becomes indispensable." This archdiocesan utterance may accomplish much more in bringing the illness conception to a large segment of the French population than educational efforts from any other source.

The acceptance of the illness conception of alcoholism by the clergy and by social workers may influence public opinion in France to a perceptible degree in the course of time. Generally, however, the traditional outlook on alcoholism as primarily an economic problem (which, in the case of France, does not lack some justification) is a strong barrier against the spread of the illness conception.

It is noteworthy that France has voluntary agencies (e.g., Comité National de Défense Contre l'Alcoolisme) which are moderation societies rather than temperance societies in the American sense and which propagate the illness conception of alcoholism (as in the journal, *Alcool ou Santé*).

The various municipal and departmental clinical facilities that have developed in the past 10 years in France have a definitely medical as well as psychotherapeutic outlook. (Among specialized therapists for alcoholics, interest has been shown in the creation of Alcoholics Anonymous groups. It is recognized, however, that such groups are nearer to the temperance groups of "former alcoholics" than to the American idea of A.A.)

ENGLAND

It is not easy to do justice to the status of affairs in the British Isles as far as alcoholism is concerned. That country had a large problem which was commonly spoken of as the problem of drunkenness. The problem has undoubtedly diminished greatly since the first World War and at present, on a worldwide comparative scale, it may be said to be at the lower range end of the middle range. The public at large is much less interested in the problem than it was 50 years ago. On the other hand, the English medical profession shows a growing interest.

Since 1892 the *British Journal of Inebriety*, now known as the *British Journal of Addiction*, has been published by a group of eminent medical men and scientists. From its very beginings that *Jour-*

nal has kept up a high scientific level. The *British Journal* has been propagating the idea of alcoholism as an illness for the past 66 years, but in spite of many contributors of high prestige no great impression has been made on either the medical profession of the British Isles or the public at large. That the public has not been influenced is perhaps due to the fact that the membership of the Society for the Study of Addiction, which publishes the *Journal*, is constituted entirely of physicians, there being only some associate members from the non-medical side. Furthermore, the Society has not taken any recourse to propaganda measures.

That the great majority of physicians did not take to the illness conception of alcoholism may be explained by the old British traditional view that alcoholism is nothing but drunkenness and that it is "a bad behavior," which just does not occur among decent people. It must be added to this that while alcohol addiction does occur in the higher educational and economic levels of the British Isles, it is, relatively speaking, sporadic in those classes, and by and large is limited at present to the lower economic and educational classes. As has been pointed out before, the recognition of the illness conception of alcoholism is to some extent related to the proportionate occurrence of species of alcoholism in the upper social classes.

Nevertheless, England had an Inebriety Act dating back to 1878, which provided special institutions for "inebriates." There is some recognition inherent in that act that inebriety has some aspects which distinguish it from other misdemeanors. These special institutions were very little used and the Inebriety Act soon fell into obsolescence.

At present, theoretically at least, the National Health Act should offer every "alcoholic" in that country the opportunity to receive gratuitous treatment of his condition. Actually, an alcoholic who applies to a physician for the treatment of any of the consequences of his "alcoholism" will receive such treatment, but if his request relates to the treatment of his habit, the matter will not be regarded as a medical one except by a few highly specialized psychiatrists and internists. It comes back to the conception that the habit is just "bad behavior" and the remedy is to behave better.

In view of this situation, some physicians have urged special legislation for the creation of facilities for the medical treatment and rehabilitation of "alcoholics." Such proposals, however, are met with the argument that the National Health Act makes such specific legislation unnecessary. Theoretically, of course, this argument is correct.

The managements of some of the mental hospitals have felt the need for special services for "alcoholics" and have created such services on a highly efficient level although of very limited extent. Among those hospitals are, notably, the Warlingham Park Hospital and the Maudsley Hospital. Of course, in these institutions, the basis of treatment is the acceptance of "alcoholism" as an illness. Some publicity has developed around these few treatment facilities and that has brought the idea of alcoholism as an illness somewhat nearer to the general public. The BBC too has contributed in a limited way to such publicity and the few groups of Alcoholics Anonymous in England add somewhat to the spread of the idea among the public. The English Alcoholics Anonymous, however, are extremely cautious in their propaganda as the anonymity principle is much more jealously guarded by them than by their American brethren.

Besides temperance societies and the scientific Society for the Study of Addiction, there is only one voluntary agency in the British Isles which is concerned with alcoholism and that is the British Council on Alcoholism. The latter, however, has a nominal existence only and may be entirely unknown in England.

Thus, one cannot speak of any degree of acceptance of the illness conception of alcoholism in the British Isles, but there are some indications that the traditional view of "bad behavior" may be modified sometime in the future.

GERMANY

With the exception of Switzerland, interest in the treatment of "alcoholics" has greatly diminished in Central Europe. The once vast alcohol literature of Germany has practically vanished and is restricted more or less to the problem of alcohol and traffic accidents, the determination of alcohol in body tissues and, to a small extent, some of the organic complications of various forms of alcoholism. Some of the great contributions toward the knowledge of alcoholism and its conception as an illness came in the first 30 years of the present century from such outstanding German physicians as Bonhoeffer, Bumke, Schrödinger, Rüdiger and others. Such significant contributions from the German side have ceased, but there are signs now of a rebirth of the German alcohol literature.

For the purposes of health insurance alcoholism has been defined as a disease in Germany since 1915. According to Konsten (1955) this definition is applied only to extreme instances of alcoholism. Furthermore, there is no acceptance of alcoholism as a disease in employment or penal law.

The rehabilitation of alcoholics in the West German republic rests in the hands of a government-subsidized group basically akin to the temperance movement. This group is devoted to the care of persons "exposed to the risks of addiction." The group is largely constituted of volunteer social workers or, to be more exact, welfare workers. They adopt the idea of alcoholism as an illness, but in an even vaguer form than is prevalent in America and without regard to the treatment requirements involved in that conception. Nevertheless, their rehabilitation efforts should command respect.

The German medical profession is not adverse to the acceptance of the illness conception of alcoholism but, on the other hand, they make no effort toward the general recognition of the idea. The public in general does not take much notice of the problem of alcohol and is indifferent to the medical conceptions concerning alcoholism.

Austria

In Austria, too, interest in the problems of alcohol diminished greatly between 1935 and 1950. In the past 4 or 5 years a small group of specialists at the Vienna University Psychiatric Clinic and in the Austrian Mental Health Society have initiated some activities. A few outpatient clinics for alcoholics have been established as well as some groups of recovered "alcoholics." The latter are not of the nature of Alcoholics Anonymous but have a strong temperance orientation which is perhaps much more suitable to the recovered alcoholic of Central Europe than the true Alcoholics Anonymous ideas of America. It may be noted that the formation of groups of discharged alcoholic patients for the practice and propagation of the temperance idea had been practiced in Austria before and is now merely revived.

Alcoholism finds official recognition as an illness in the national health insurance fund which covers the costs of the treatment of alcoholics.

SWITZERLAND

Of all countries—and this refers not only to Europe but also to America—Switzerland has given the most thorough consideration to the question of the illness nature of "alcoholism." The illness conception, in that country, was proposed in a rather vague form by the various temperance societies although some opposition to the idea was also expressed within their ranks. Switzerland is the home of the Blue Cross which set up dispensaries for "alcoholics" and manned them with volunteer welfare workers. A number of Swiss physicians were attracted by the efforts of the Blue Cross and gave thoughtful consideration to the illness conception. Independently from temperance societies to which they may have belonged, volunteer welfare workers grouped themselves into an association known as the Fürsorger. These dedicated men and women have created consultation bureaus for "alcoholics" all over the country. As Switzerland is burdened with a rather widespread problem of alcoholism, the cantonal governments took a hand in the care and rehabilitation of "alcoholics" and have largely availed themselves of the consultation bureaus founded and operated by the Fürsorger. These consultation bureaus are subsidized by the cantonal governments and thus indirectly by the federal government, which assigns funds from the alcohol monopoly to the cantons, 10 per cent of which must be used for the prevention and treatment of "alcoholism." It may be said that the treatment and rehabilitation of alcoholics in nearly all the Swiss cantons is compulsory and thus considerable expenditure devolves on the cantons. Even with these expenditures, the medical aspects of rehabilitation of alcoholics are rather defective. (Some of the cantonal activities date back 60 or 65 years, e.g., in St. Gallen.)

The question of care and treatment of alcoholics is a cantonal matter in Switzerland but the national government maintains a Federal Commission against Alcoholism which is of a purely advisory capacity and has no executive powers. On the other hand, the Federal Commission may undertake studies in order to furnish a basis for action on the cantonal level.

The Federal Commission has seen that the costs of adequate medical treatment can be supplied only if the Health Insurance Agencies (Krankenkassen) can be obliged to cover not only the cost of the medical treatment of organic complications of alcoholism but the treatment of alcoholism itself. Compulsory health insurance is obliged to contribute toward the cost of treatments of any disease, but as alcoholism is not so classified they are not under obligation to cover the costs of its treatment. Parenthetically, it may be remarked that some of the larger health insurance agencies have voluntarily contributed to the costs of rehabilitation as they recognized that this policy was in their own interests.

In order to make such contributions obligatory for the health insurance agencies, "alcoholism" would have to be declared a disease within the frame of some legislation. This, however, is not a cantonal but a Federal matter and such a declaration cannot be made through some highhanded gesture. Consequently, the Federal Commission against Alcoholism has undertaken a survey among psychiatrists, other physicians, and the heads of hospitals and clinics, in order to determine whether or not alcoholism, or rather certain species of it, could be regarded as a disease or diseases from a medical point of view. As this survey constitutes the only official government attempt to clarify this matter, the result is of considerable importance and the report of the Federal Commission is given nearly in its entirety in Appendix B. In the present section it will suffice to mention that the outcome of the survey was a practically unanimous acceptance of the illness conception of alcoholism by the interviewees. It must be mentioned that the interviews were limited to those psychiatrists and physicians and hospital heads who had had direct contact with alcoholics, and this procedure seems to be justified, as the relevant opinion must be that of specialists and not of physicians who have no direct knowledge of alcoholism. On the other hand, the unanimous acceptance by the experts assures an acceptance by the majority of the non-specialists. The results of this survey are to form the basis for a legislative act which would declare alcoholism a disease. A draft of such an act was recently still under consideration.

The intensive work of temperance societies and the propaganda of the Fürsorger, although not systematic, have brought the illness conception of alcoholism nearer to the Swiss general public opinion, and while this has not brought about a true intellectual acceptance of the idea, it has at least resulted in an absence of opposition.

SPAIN, PORTUGAL, ITALY

Southern European countries such as Italy, Spain and Portugal, have taken little interest in the problems of alcoholism. Generally, in those countries, the existence of alcoholism is denied, save by a small group of specialists who have experience with alcoholics. In Spain the incidence of alcohol addiction is relatively small but not negligible. For Portugal, the determination of the incidence is difficult but it is apparently of no great magnitude.

The Italian problem, while many times greater than the Italians would believe, is still, on a comparative scale, at the lower range end of the middle range. Italy has an alcohol literature which deals predominantly with the metabolism of alcohol and its effects on the liver and other body organs, as well as the frank psychotic manifestations of alcoholism. In the last 10 years, however, literature on alcoholism without psychosis has been growing in volume. The younger psychiatrists, e.g., G. Bonfiglio, are quite aware of a fair sized problem of alcoholism and while they do not talk about it in terms of illness, or as a symptom, their admission of strong psychological factors in the etiology does imply a view that alcohol addiction is at least the symptom of an underlying psychological disorder. Such a view has not found an echo in the Italian medical profession and has surely not reached nonprofessional circles. Nevertheless, the public safety laws of Italy make it mandatory for physicians and others who may know of alcohol addicts ("chronic alcoholics") to report them to the provincial prefects or police authorities. One may say that, by law, alcohol addiction is a reportable disease. These "chronic alcoholics" are differentiated from the "habitual drunkards," who are liable to penal measures, while the former may be compelled to undergo treatment. This differentiation implies that "chronic alcoholism" is regarded as not merely a moral question. The regulations concerning the "chronic alcoholics" are, however, rather on the books than in practice.

The Spanish alcoholism literature is entirely negligible. Not more than one or two medical papers are published in Spain each year. Lately, the disulfiram treatment has added to some extent to the published reports. It was only in 1957 that Spain produced its first book meriting the designation of scientific treatise. Dr. José Viñes, Chief of the Public Health Service of the Province of Navarra, has taken up the subject and has stated that "alcoholism," far from being non-existent in Spain, is a public health problem of some importance. The theoretical part of his book is based, to a large extent, on committee reports of the World Health Organization. Viñes is at least doubtful about the illness conception of alcoholism, but says that many public health men of Spain will accept the idea that alcoholism belongs in the realm of public health and that that service must shoulder the responsibility for tackling the problem. He points out, however, that because of pressures from the extensive vested interests, any action concerning the control of alcoholism may be expected to meet with great resistance.

RUSSIA

Eastern Europe, with Russia, Poland and Czechoslovakia, arouses particular interest in America. The question whether the problems of alcohol have decreased or increased is frequently posed. In the frame of the present study, an evaluation of the magnitude of the problem in these countries would be out of place, as the subject is limited to the conception of alcoholism in its various species.

Russia's claim that "alcoholism" has greatly decreased since the Communist regime has come to power may be accepted, as all the world over the aggregate of all species of alcoholism has decreased when compared with pre-World War I days. Of course, the decrease is not a continuous downward trend. In various periods since World War I ups and downs may be noted, but even the peak years remain below the levels of the first 15 years of this century. Whether in Russia the decrease is proportionately greater than in other countries, cannot be determined on the basis of accessible material. It may be stated with assurance, however, that the concern over alcoholism shown by Russian medical authorities indicates that the problem still exists and that treatment measures are being carried out by health authorities of the U.S.S.R. The illness conception of alcoholism does not fit into the Communist outlook on these matters. Gubar' (1955) says:

"In a capitalist country where there is unemployment, immorality and severe exploitation, social diseases such as alcoholism, prostitution, narcomania and others are organic consequences of the regime; in a socialist state where the material welfare of the workers increases from year to year there can be no question of exhaustion and social diseases. Alcoholism under the conditions of our system is a vestige of capitalism with which we must wage unending war."

Nevertheless there is some indication that the disease conception is being utilized in Russia to some extent. Thus, the Metropolitan of the Russian Orthodox Church says that while to him the idea of alcoholism as an illness seems somewhat strange, he is ready to accept it on the insistence of others.[10]

Treatment for "alcoholism" is carried out in a large number of dispensaries where the patient may be given (1) medicines, (2) oxygen, (3) hypnosis, (4) counseling (a form of psychotherapy), (5) physiotherapy. If the dispensary treatment fails, the patient goes to a hospital where he receives conditioning treatment.[11] Thus, while the illness conception of "alcoholism" may not have any standing officially, the matter is treated definitely as a medical problem.

CZECHOSLOVAKIA

In Czechoslovakia the basic attitude toward the various species of alcoholism is similar to the one in Russia, but there is recognition that the communist tenet concerning alcoholic behavior is not borne out by the developments. Skála (1957), in his informative book about alcoholism in Czechoslovakia, says:

"Even though in Czechoslovakia many of the economic causes (fear of unemployment, destitute old age) which lead to alcoholism in capitalist countries have been eliminated, it cannot be said that the problem of alcoholism has thereby been solved. If alcoholism is a blot on any period, or on any social system, it particularly blots a socialist society where one counts on the productive contribution of individuals and where a lower work performance or loss of work of any citizen involved in the productive process must be made up by others."

In that country, the control of "alcoholism" is officially a matter for the public health administration which has created numerous facilities for the treatment of alcohol addicts and other alcoholics. Skála refrains from acceptance of the illness conception, but his adoption of Jellinek's phases of alcohol addiction would indicate an approach to a psychosomatic view of addictive behavior. The activities of the Public Health Administration of Czechoslovakia definitely point to the acceptance of the problem as belonging, in part, to the realm of medicine. The same may be said of the activities and viewpoints prevalent in Poland.

YUGOSLAVIA

While Yugoslavia is geographically a Southern European country, it belongs ideologically to the above mentioned Eastern nations.

[10] Carter, C. and Carter, D. Cancer, Smoking, Heart-Disease, Drinking in our Two World Systems Today. Toronto; Northern Book House; 1957.

[11] Scope Weekly, 9 January 1957.

The problem of alcoholism in Yugoslavia is acknowledged as one of considerable magnitude. The army is much concerned with the problem and is working hand in hand with the Ministry of the Interior and with health authorities toward control of alcoholism.

The predominant species of alcoholism is similar to the prevalent one in France, that is, it is more rooted in excessive social custom than in gross psychological vulnerability. The majority type represents a development of addiction in the true pharmacological sense, and this constitutes a physiopathological process which may legitimately be classed as a disease. It is understandable, however, that where socioeconomic elements in the etiology overshadow the individual psychological elements, the idea of alcoholism as an illness is less appealing to the medical profession and the public in general. Furthermore, the incidence of "alcoholism" in Yugoslavia is greatest in the lower educational levels while it is rather sporadic in the higher educational strata. As a matter of fact, in the latter group there is quite a tendency toward total abstinence, at least in comparison to total abstention in the higher educational levels of other nations.

In the Serbian and Slovenian parts of Yugoslavia the control of "alcoholism" is in the hands of the Red Cross, which has proceeded from fumbling beginnings to a fairly efficient handling of the problem. In Croatia, on the other hand, the control of alcoholism, which is largely concerned with rehabilitation, is carried out by the mental health authorities.

Generally, it may be said of European countries that while some show a high degree of acceptance of the illness conception of alcoholism, the predominant view is that the latter constitutes a medical and public health problem with strong reservations on the importance of socioeconomic factors in the etiology of that problem.

IV.7.2. The Americas

The Americas, outside of the United States, have quite extensive activities concerning the problem of alcohol, but only the Canadian activities are fairly well-known in the U.S.A.

CANADA

At present, nearly all Canadian provinces have alcoholism programs which embrace the illness conception of alcoholism. Voluntary agencies, in the United States sense, do not exist in Canada.

Most of the provincial "alcoholism foundations," however, have grown out of citizens' endeavors which through public subsidy have become either semiofficial or fully official agencies, but do not come under public administration. Most of the Canadian alcoholism programs publish magazines or newsletters as well as a large number of pamphlets which strongly emphasize alcoholism as an illness. Although the Canadian alcoholism programs show a great deal of originality, the impress of the Yale University Center of Alcohol Studies is evident. This is quite natural as most, if not all, of the administrators of the provincial alcoholism programs are past students of the Yale Summer School of Alcohol Studies.

From the Canadian medical literature it would appear that the medical profession as a whole has a favorable attitude toward the disease conception. An official recognition such as that given by the American Medical Association has not come forth from the Canadian medical group. Nevertheless the ties with the American Medical Association are so close that the latter's pronouncements carry considerable weight in Canada too.

The repercussions of the provincial alcoholism programs are, in some ways, more marked than those of the state programs in the U.S.A. There is evidence of this in the adoption of the illness conception by the Canadian Civil Service and the Royal Canadian Air Force. Those bodies have made that conception a basis for dealing with alcoholic members of their groups. To what degree the Canadian public at large has accepted these ideas cannot be expressed at present statistically. It may be inferred, however, that the great publicity which the illness conception has received in the press, frequent radio programs, television and educational films all over the country, must have brought about an increasing recognition of the idea. It must be considered, also, that next to the United States, Canada has the largest Alcoholics Anonymous membership and thus a strong contingent of zealous propagandists.

MEXICO

There are some remarkable activities among the Latin countries of North Central and South America. The Mexican public health authorities are carrying out an effective rehabilitation program which is limited to the largest cities. The health authorities work in close cooperation with Alcoholics Anonymous groups, which are not of any great magnitude but have impressed the illness conception upon their collaborators. In the treatment program of Mexico the illness conception is basic, but this has not penetrated into the ranks of the medical profession in general or of the public at large.

GUATEMALA

For its size, the Republic of Guatemala has a remarkable alcoholism program which is administered by a voluntary agency, subsidized almost entirely by government funds. Treatment facilities are good, but insufficient in extent. The treatment is based on the idea that alcoholism is an illness, but such a conception, of course, does not find its way into the large illiterate Indian population which forms the largest part of the alcoholic contingent. As far as the medical profession of that country goes, the interest is limited to a few but highly efficient specialists. All the other Central American republics show a beginning of some service for alcoholics, largely through the endeavors of citizens' groups. The activities, however, are as yet too small to warrant any description.

SOUTH AMERICA

The northern republics of South America, that is, Colombia, Venezuela and Bolivia, have no alcoholism programs, and interest in these matters attaches to a few individuals. In Ecuador, on the other hand, interest is evident in wider medical circles, and recently in Peru the public health service has taken an active role in the control of alcoholics. It cannot be said, however, that either the medical profession or the public at large in those countries shows any awareness of the medical aspects of the problems of alcoholism.

Four of the five southern republics of South America, namely, Brazil, Uruguay, Argentina and Chile, have systematic activities concerning the control of alcoholism and the development of the idea of alcoholism as a medical and public health problem, including the illness conception.

BRAZIL

Brazil has created, within the frame of the Federal Commission on Narcotic Drugs, a subcommission on alcoholism whose brief is patterned largely on the recommendations of World Health Organization committees. The idea of alcoholism as a disease has been propagated by this subcommission perhaps with too much zeal and too little recognition of alcohol problems arising from other sources than true alcohol addiction. (That, of course, is a reproach in which the North American alcoholism programs, too, must share to a considerable degree.) The Brazilian medical profession would not seem to be adverse to the acceptance of the illness conception but, on the other hand, has not taken any steps toward making the idea its own. As to the acceptance of the idea by the wider public, the prospects of propaganda through a Federal agency are not particularly favorable. Such rehabilitation efforts as exist in Brazil, however, are based on the illness conception.

URUGUAY

The small but highly progressive Republic of Uruguay was first among the South American countries that seriously considered the problem of "alcoholism." The disease conception was first proposed in the country by a temperance group, which represents the strongest of its kind in all of South America. The vigorous campaigns of the Uruguayan Temperance Society were much more successful in propagating the illness conception than in infiltrating a temperance ideology. It may be noted that many of the members of that temperance society are medical men. Of all the South American countries, Uruguay shows the widest acceptance of the illness conception in medical as well as nonprofessional circles. This may be related to the fact that in Uruguay the various social classes contribute proportionately to the alcoholic population, while in other republics the problem occurs more frequently in the lower educational and economic levels.

The government of Uruguay, through its Public Health Service, has created a national committee for the consideration of alcohol problems, and this committee is active in drafting legislative acts, at least one of which would incorporate the conception of alcoholism as an illness. The compulsory treatment of "alcoholics" is also under consideration. Furthermore, the Public Health Service is actively engaged in alcohol education. And, although such education is directed more toward preventive aspects (as it should be), the idea of alcoholism as an illness is included in the educational efforts.

ARGENTINA

The Republic of Argentina, as a whole, has a small problem of alcoholism, perhaps the smallest in South America. Nevertheless, in two or three districts of the country one species or another of alcoholism is quite troublesome. The government has created within the Ministry of Health a section on alcoholism, which has the tasks of public education on alcohol and alcoholism, as well as the rehabilitation of alcoholics. The existence of this section is a rather precarious one and the rehabilitation activities are frequently suspended for quite lengthy periods. Such treatment of alcoholics as may be provided in Argentina is based on the illness conception, but that conception reaches a very small segment of the public and even in that small segment does not meet with acceptance. The problem is most frequent in the low economic level with scattered alcoholics at the higher economic and educational levels. The small group of Alcoholics Anonymous—about 30 members— in Buenos Aires is drawn from the higher levels and is neither large enough nor zealous enough to make any impression on public opinion. It may be said that awareness of the illness conception of alcoholism does not exist in Argentina and this includes the medical profession.

CHILE

The Republic of Chile, the next neighbor to Argentina, has the largest alcoholism problem in South America and, with scattered exceptions, the problem is limited to the labor classes. The traditional view in Chile is the same as in France, namely, that alcoholism has a purely socioeconomic origin, largely ascribable to overproduction of alcohol and the resultant sales pressure. The public at large and the majority of physicians have either never heard of the disease conception or are opposed to it. In view of these facts, it is particularly interesting that a relatively small number of physicians have been able to develop intensive rehabilitation activities and outstanding research projects. These activities have perhaps received a great impetus from the realization of public health men that many of their health campaigns are being frustrated by the high incidence of various species of alcoholism.

While the adequate rehabilitation facilities and the highly developed research activities are based on the illness conception of alcoholism, no educational effort has been made, and this may account for the lack of acceptance of alcoholism as a disease outside the specialized clinical and research group. Nevertheless, Chile is the only South American country in which Alcoholics Anonymous have made remarkable beginnings. Alcoholics Anonymous groups exist not only in the metropolis but also in some provincial centers, and they are steadily growing. These groups have received little publicity, but if they become better known, some change in the public outlook may result.

In the southern republics of South America activities in the field of alcoholism are medically oriented and they are in the hands of either government agencies or semiofficial agencies. On the other hand, with the exception of Uruguay, the acceptance of alcoholism as an illness is extremely limited.

IV.7.3. Other Continents

In the past 2 years, educational and rehabilitational activities have developed in Australia, New Zealand and the Union of South Africa. In those countries the committees and councils on alcoholism have been organized on the American pattern of the National Council on Alcoholism. These organizations, which enjoy at least some government subsidy, were initiated by local Alcoholics Anonymous groups and thus, of course, are strongly propagating the illness conception of alcoholism through the press, various publications and the radio. In Australia and New Zealand the idea may be regarded as fairly widespread in view of the short time of the existence of the voluntary agencies. There is, of course, quite some opposition on the part of temperance organizations.

In the Union of South Africa the temperance forces are rather militant on this question. Rea (1956) tells about a meeting in Pretoria called by the South African Minister of Health. Physicians, psychiatrists and members of Alcoholics Anonymous said the way to deal with alcoholism was by treating it as a disease. The temperance workers declared that the road to recovery was repentance. There was a serious clash on this issue. In Rea's opinion, "Alcoholism is in most cases a result of sin, but it represents a phase at which drinking has become a disease; to cure it, therefore, it must be treated first of all as a disease."

The attitudes of 25 foreign countries have been viewed in the briefest space possible and that, of course, can be done only at the price of superficiality. Nevertheless, this brief discussion may give at least some indication of attitudes toward the disease conception of alcoholism, and its acceptance or rejection, outside the United States of America.

Appendix A

A few paragraphs of the following paper are quoted verbatim as an example of the early controversy surrounding the disease conception of alcoholism.

Drunkenness a Vice, Not a Disease[1]

A paper by J. E. Todd

*   *   *

The prevalent opinion at the present day is, that drunkenness is a disease. Medical authorities are divided on the subject. Many physicians, especially specialists who make the treatment of drunkenness a business and source of profit, are positive that it is a disease. The American Association for the Cure of Inebriates, a society composed chiefly of officers of inebriate asylums, at their first meeting adopted this as the fundamental article of their creed; and various papers were subsequently read by Dr. Parrish, the president, and others, in explanation and maintenance of it; and at their fifth meeting they declined to accept a report presented by Dr. Harris, the physician to the Franklin Reformatory for Inebriates, at Philadelphia, in which he treated drunkenness as a habit, sin, or crime, and spoke of cases being reformed, and not cured as in a hospital, on the ground that the truth of intemperance being a disease was the base of their organization, failing which their very name would be a fraud upon the public. . . .

In opposition to the medical authorities just quoted, a very large proportion of the leading physicians deny emphatically that drunkenness is in any sense a disease. Among many other similar testimonies which I have received, an eminent London practitioner writes me, "I have never said that there were no such drunkards as insane drunkards; I have only fought against the mischievous and foolish contention that all drunkenness is a form of disease, especially when it has lasted a certain time, and has attained a certain intensity.". . .

In order to answer the question before us intelligently and correctly, we must first settle what disease is, and what vice is, and how they differ.

Disease may be called an abnormal or morbid condition of the body,

---

[1] Read at the General Association at Middletown, June 21, 1882, and by vote of that body printed and distributed to the churches. Hartford, Conn.; Case, Lockwood & Brainard; 1882.

or some part of it. But this is loose and inaccurate; for a wound may put some part, and even the whole, of the body into an abnormal condition and yet the patient may be free from disease. A more exact medical definition is, "Disease is a condition of some one or more parts of the organism, inherited or acquired, which always involves and implies an abnormal state of the nutrition of those parts, and necessarily tends, if prolonged and increased, to diminish or destroy the vital activities of the organism." Disease is always an affection of the body. There is no such thing as disease of the mind. When we speak of disease of the mind, we either speak figuratively, and use a very improper figure, or we mean disease of the brain, affecting mental operations. . . .

The same author who gives the definition of disease above quoted defines vice as "a habit of the nervous centers of energizing in an emotional direction mischievous to the well-being of the individual and of the community, but consistent with healthy nutrition, and not necessarily tending to destroy the vital activities of the individual." . . . Vice is the habitual choice and practice of evil. . . .

It is the more necessary to distinguish accurately between disease and vice that there are some resemblances between them. Thus the tendency to disease is sometimes hereditary, and so is that to vice. The causes of acquired disease are sometimes small, gradual, and accumulative, and so are those of vice. By continuance and repetition diseased conditions become inveterate, and so do vicious ones, indeed, by far the more so. And disease is cured by removing the cause, and vice is abrogated by the same means; and in both, when the cause returns, the effect is reproduced. Such are the resemblances pointed out by Dr. Bucknill. But on the other hand there are essential differences between vice and disease. Disease consists solely and entirely in some change in the organization, which is often known to and is always thinkable by the physician; but it is not known that vice consists in or is even accompanied by any such change. Certain vices may produce such a change as an effect, but such changes are not known to exist as constituent conditions of vice. The causes of disease are physical, and the last link in the chain of causation, the causal condition, is invariably so; the cause of vice, on the other hand, is always moral, even where the conditions of the vice are grossly material and sensual. . . .

Keeping these distinctions steadily in mind, we are prepared to discuss the question, Is drunkenness, in its last stages, an irresistible propensity caused by a diseased condition of the brain, or is it from first to last the choice of a depraved and wicked will? . . . .

Dr. Bucknill writes: "In a somewhat large experience, I have myself never yet met with an undoubted instance of pure dipsomania; and I observe that very few examples are on record in medical literature, and that these are copied by one author from another in a manner which sufficiently testifies their rarity. The evidence, however, of credible observers is perhaps sufficient to establish the fact of their occasional occurrence." Mr. Bunting writes me: "I do not think that in the five years that I have been in the New York Christian Home for Intemperate Men we have had one case of dipsomania, although in that time we have had nine hundred confirmed drunkards.". . . .

Once more, the question is not whether the drunkard is in a healthy or diseased condition; but it is, whether he has a disease which is the cause of a resistless propensity to drink, and is not merely an effect of drinking. . . .

The mere existence of an abnormal condition of the brain proves nothing. There must be proof that this abnormal condition of the brain is the cause of an irresistible propensity to drink, and not a mere effect of drink; otherwise we might as well reason that because drunkards usually have red noses and ragged breeches, therefore their red noses and ragged breeches are the cause of an irresistible propensity in them to drink. . . .

But it will at once be said, that the difference is, that in the later stages of drunkenness the appetite is irresistible. To this I reply, in the first place, by questioning the fact. . . . I have never heard of a temperance society's refusing a drunkard's pledge, on the ground that it was impossible for him to stop drinking; and therefore it is reasonable to conclude that all temperance societies believe that the drunkard is not subject to an irresistible propensity. . . .

But, it will be asked, may not the will become so weakened and broken-down through indulgence, that the man is unable to resist the craving of appetite? Possibly it may; the question is whether it does. The drunkard's will weak! That is news! Put a drunkard in circumstances in which it is difficult for him to get liquor, and see how weak his will is! . . .

Granting, for the sake of the argument, that in some extreme cases, or even in many or all cases if you choose, the will is helpless. This is not necessarily or probably the effect of disease. For it is in the nature of vice to become inveterate. . . .

It is important to observe that all vices partake of the nature, and exhibit the phenomena of drunkenness, to a greater or less extent; yet it is not pretended in the case of any other of them that there is disease. . . .

But there is a meaning in the universal unconscious testimony of drunkards. When they come out of their spells of debauchery, if they have any moral sense at all left, they are always ashamed, penitent, remorseful. What on earth are they ashamed of, or remorseful about, if they have only had an attack of disease? Men are not ashamed of having had the typhoid fever, or penitent for having had the rheumatism. Ah, the drunkard knows that he is guilty, and not unfortunate.

I hold that there is a great deal of tenderness misplaced on the drunkard in these days, and that he does not, in public opinion, occupy the place to which he is entitled. . . .

In the last annual report of the New York Christian Home for Intemperate Men I find that out of 176 confirmed drunkards who were ad-

mitted to the Home last year, only 28 had intemperate parents. And it
does not follow, even in these cases, that because the parents were
intemperate the children inherited a tendency to intemperance; which
shows, as the Report well says, "the fallacy" of the notion of inherited
appetite. . . .

There is no gain whatever in the establishment of the theory that
drunkenness is a disease. Of course the object is, to relieve the drunkard of responsibility and to shield him from the condemnation of his
fellow men. In the latter respect the attempt is no doubt to a great
extent successful. But there is no real deliverance from responsibility. . . .

Every human soul is worth saving; but what I mean is, that if a choice
is to be made, drunkards are about the last class to be taken hold
of. . . .

Inebriate asylums have proved costly failures. In some places expen-
sive buildings, originally designed for such institutions, have been turned
into asylums for the insane, as in the province of Ontario, in Canada,
avowedly because of the failure of such institutions in this country. . . .

Appendix B

The following report of the Swiss Federal Commission against Alcoholism, which has been mentioned briefly in the present study, is given here nearly in its entirety in a literal translation from the French original.[1] A few passages which are of relevance to Swiss conditions only, or are not of particular interest to the subject matter of this study, have been omitted.

Under What Conditions Should Alcoholism be Considered and Treated as a Disease?

I

This question has been claiming the attention of the Federal Commission against Alcoholism for several years.

Already in their session of 30 January 1947, the subcommission on assistance to alcoholics deemed it of great importance to determine "whether and to what degree alcoholism may be considered as a disease." They suggested that this question should be referred to the committee on scientific research or to the Swiss Psychiatric Society or to a medical school. Lastly, it was proposed to write to the Association of Swiss Health Insurance Agencies "in order that they should consider whether it would not be in their own interests to assume a part of the costs occasioned by the treatment of alcoholics. Such an action would certainly result in savings by the health insurance agencies, as the sufficiently early treatment of alcoholics could obviate greater expense arising from graver conditions incumbent upon alcoholism."

After due consideration the Federal Commission against Alcoholism finally entrusted the subcommittees on scientific research and public assistance to examine the entire question. These two subcommissions were reluctant to pronounce judgments on these matters without consulting competent persons for this purpose. The following questionnaire was devised and distributed to some 70 persons: directors of psychiatric institutions and clinics for internal medicine, heads of institutions for alcoholics, psychotherapists, medicolegal experts, etc.

[1] Commission Fédéral contre l'Alcoolisme. Dans quelles conditions l'alcoolisme doit-il être considéré et traité comme une maladie? Bull. schweiz. GesundhAmt, Suppl. B-4, pp. 85–98, 1951.

QUESTIONNAIRE

Alcoholism and Health Insurance Agencies

A. *Alcoholism considered as a disease*

1. May one speak of a disease in the instance where persons without evident psychiatric anomalies give themselves over long periods habitually to drinking by virtue of their occupations, local customs, social situation?

2. Should one not speak of disease unless the habitual consumption of alcoholic beverages becomes a craving, that is, results from an irresistible urge?

3. May one speak of disease when a person becomes an alcoholic as a result of a mental disease or trouble (disorder of character, feeble-mindedness, neurosis, psychopathy, traumatic encephalopathy, etc.)? Which are the psychiatric troubles or disorders which may be taken into consideration?

4. Are you of the opinion that bodily or psychiatric disorders incumbent upon the abuse of alcohol by themselves favor the abuse of alcoholic beverages, that is, that a primary alcoholism may turn into a secondary alcoholism?

5. What are in your opinion the forms of alcoholism which should be considered without question as a disease and treated as such: intolerance to alcohol, acute alcoholic intoxication, etc.?

6. Are there in your opinion forms of alcoholism which should not be considered as a disease? If so, which?

B. *Therapy*

1. Should all habitual drinkers who are in need of assistance be subjected to a physical or mental examination in order to determine the necessary therapeutic measures?

2. Which cases of alcoholism may be treated ambulatorily?

   (a) By a physician.
   (b) By an anti-alcoholic dispensary.

3. In which cases should internment be considered?

   (a) In a psychiatric institution.
   (b) In an institution for alcoholics.
   (c) In a workhouse.

4. To what extent does medical treatment (provided under B-1) seem to be indicated for patients handled in institutions for alcoholics or handled in dispensaries?

C. *Coverage of cost of treatment by health insurance agencies*

1. Should the health insurance agencies be obligated to cover the costs of treatment in all instances where alcoholism is to be considered as a disease according to Section A of the present questionnaire? If so, for what type of treatment?

2. Are there instances where the alcoholic should be considered as responsible for his condition and where the health insurance agencies should be entitled to refuse or to decrease their contribution?

   (a) In which instances may they refuse?
   (b) In which instances may they decrease their contribution?

3. What costs of treatment should be covered by the health insurance agencies?

   (a) Medical treatment and medicines;

(b) Treatment and supervision by dispensaries;
(c) Treatment in a psychiatric institution;
(d) In an institution for alcoholics;
(e) In other institutions (workhouse or institutions for reeducation);
(f) Daily compensation;
(g) Other costs.

4. What conditions may the health insurance agencies exact from the institutions for alcoholics?

(a) Medical certificate of admission;
(b) Regular medical supervision in the course of treatment;
(c) Medical care in case of diseases and other complications;
(d) Medical control and report on discharges;
(e) In your opinion which of the above medical interventions should be carried out by a psychiatrist?

The replies to the questionnaires were scanned with the greatest care. Dr. Bersot, vice president of the commission, submitted a report in plenary session, a résumé of which is presented in the second part of the present exposition. This session was attended also by representatives of the Swiss Federation of Physicians, of the health insurance agencies and of the Federal office of social insurance.

II

DR. H. BERSOT's REPORT

Approximately three-quarters of the questionnaires were returned to the committee and the largest part of the 53 responses was conscientiously completed. This great proportion of responses shows that all respondents recognized the importance of the question and the need for careful consideration.

We shall give here only the essentials of this inquiry.

To question A-2 asking whether one may speak of a disease "when the habitual consumption of alcoholic beverages becomes a craving, that is, results from an irresistible urge," 52 respondents answered *yes*. Some of them remarked that the recognition of the craving is not always an easy task. One of the respondents deems that it is the physician's duty to determine whether or not a disease exists and to define in this case the determining organic lesions. To question A-3, "May one speak of a disease when people become alcoholics as a result of a mental disease or disorder (character disorders, mental deficiency, neurosis, psychopathy, traumatic encephalopathy, etc.)" all answers were in the affirmative.

To question C-1, "Should the health insurance agencies be obligated to cover the costs of treatment in all instances where alcoholism must be regarded as a disease in the sense of Chapter A of the present questionnaire?" we received 51 affirmative answers. Two physicians abstained as they felt that the question was not within their competence.

The results of the inquiry are thus perfectly clear: all the persons questioned (except one) *agree on the conditions under which alcoholism may be considered as a disease, and for which patients should receive aid from the health insurance agencies for treatment, including hospitalization.*

Conditions which Justify the Consideration of Alcoholism as a Disease

We were able to formulate these conditions with great precision due to the completeness of the responses received.

A. As to effects:

The question is to establish at which moment, in the course of its noxious process alcoholism becomes a disease.

A professor of internal medicine:
"Alcoholism is a disease when somatic symptoms appear or when troubles arise in the behavior of the alcoholic in relation to other persons. . . . We do not consider as disease even the greatest consumption of alcohol if no noxious effect is manifested. . . . The craving for alcohol constitutes a disease. . . . Acute occasional alcoholism without pathological symptoms should not be considered as a disease inasmuch as it does not exert a noxious effect on health or social relations."

A professor of psychiatry:
"As long as a person does not present evident physical and/or psychological symptoms he cannot be considered as a sick person. Disease is constituted by symptoms and one cannot speak of disease when a person commits certain abuses which do not cause any signs of poisoning except the transitory symptoms of acute intoxication; but when symptoms of long duration on the affective or intellectual level appear, the persons in question should be considered as sick and should be submitted to appropriate measures."

A professor of psychiatry:
There is no disease "as long as the person is capable of renouncing this bad habit without treatment. A disease obtains when the diagnosis 'alcoholism' is made after the establishment of bodily and/or psychological troubles. In the absence of these, one should speak only of abuse of alcohol."

The medical director of a mental hospital:
"Medically speaking," alcoholism is a disease, "when the consumption through habit, effect of the environment, etc. . . . even in a predisposed person, permits the diagnosis of chronic alcoholism, through the determination of visceral changes, or functional troubles evidenced in the mental faculties."

A specialist in internal medicine:
"Alcoholism is a disease. Actually, with the exception of simple intoxication without underlying alcoholism and all the other forms of alcoholism through habit where the person does not present either character troubles or organic disorders or psychological disorders, all forms of chronic alcoholism arise out of a diseased state.
"(a) Primary alcoholism, without preexistent psychological or physical terrain, becomes a disease as soon as characteristic troubles (decreased blood urea, lowered alkaline reserve, increased cholesterol, etc., even in the absence of any organic pathology), organic troubles (cirrhosis, gastritis, polyneuritis,

etc.) or psychological troubles (character disorder, memory disorder, anomalies of sleep, sexuality, 'craving' or 'need for alcohol' etc.) arise;

"(b) Secondary alcoholism is based on a physical terrain (bodily pains, insomnia) or on psychological troubles (constitutional psychopathy, character disorder preceding alcoholism, mental deficiency, obsessive timidity, anxiety, phobias);

"(c) Intolerance to alcohol is due to the constitution of the alcoholic, or acquired through cranial trauma;

"Furthermore, biochemical and humoral disorders which are practically constant in chronic alcoholism as well as psychological troubles are equally characteristic. In all drug addicts or alcoholics craving inhibits the volition of the patient, so that he is incapable of struggling against the craving, exactly as in the case of the morphinist."

A psychiatrist:
"For practical reasons, we esteem it opportune to speak of a disease when there is a habitual consumption of such quantities of alcohol that it causes bodily and psychological harm or in other words that it causes trouble to the drinker or his fellow men.

"We consider as disease all alcoholic intoxication which leads to perceptible modifications, and all forms of habitual abuse which cause bodily or psychological damage or character troubles."

The director of a mental hospital:
"From the instant that an individual is incapable of resisting the the temptation to drink, he must be considered as a sick person.

"When the habitual consumption of alcoholic beverages becomes a craving one is confronted with the presence of a drug addict; drinking is for him a physiological necessity created by his intoxication. The patient thus lives in a vicious circle, on the one hand an organism poisoned by alcohol, on the other hand an irresistible need to feed the intoxication."

The physicians agree in stating that the distinction between "habitual alcoholism" and the craving to drink (addiction) cannot be treated with much precision. The following is an opinion of a professor:

"The answer to this question depends upon philosophical and religious conceptions. The term disease cannot be defined absolutely; it is understood differently according to social, professional and religious environment as well as by each individual. I wish to add merely that it isn't possible to establish a strict line of demarcation between 'habitual alcoholism' and the craving for alcohol."

In either case one must speak of disease, affirms another professor: "A veritable craving always presents something of the nature of a disease." This opinion is confirmed by the experiences in neurological clinics where often a preventive treatment must be applied in order that repeated abuse should not degenerate into craving, that is, into chronic alcoholism.

From these responses we conclude that alcoholism must be considered as a disease when it provokes durable symptoms of a mental, affective or bodily nature. We are not dealing here with the transitory symptoms of acute intoxication, but with the gravest consequences which arise in

the organism through alcoholization. These consequences may be of a
mental order (depression, anxiety, auto-accusations, inferiority feelings,
character troubles, memory disturbances) or of a nervous order (neuri-
tis, tremors, disorders of equilibrium, etc.) or of a bodily order (lesions
of liver, kidneys, heart, arteries) or of a mixed order, the mental troubles
and nervous troubles aggregating themselves to the somatic troubles.

B. *As to the causes* (replies to question A-3):

Alcoholism is considered as a disease not only according to its effects,
but also according to its causes.

The chief medical officer of a clinic:
"Chronic alcoholism as a consequence of a mental disorder must also be
considered as a disease. The essential psychopathological cause is constituted
by a psychopathic disposition which is manifested in the form of lack of
volition and self-control."

A professor of psychiatry:
"One must distinguish here the primary disease which may be considered
itself as warranting aid by the health insurance agency. The alcoholism which
attaches itself to such a disease aggravates the latter and thus the whole
picture must be considered as relevant to the health insurance agency.

The medical director of a hospital:
"The psychological troubles which are involved in secondary alcoholism
cannot all be enumerated; this is a matter of individual diagnostics, but in
practice there should be mentioned all cerebral changes, functional, organic,
hereditary or acquired."

A psychiatrist:
"The mental diseases and disorders enumerated all can account for habitual
abuses of alcohol, but not one of those conditions is indispensable to the
development of the grave disease called alcoholism."

A professor of neurology:
"In such an instance alcoholism constitutes a particular symptom resulting
from influencing factors, whether endogenous or exogenous." According to
this professor, the following psychological troubles may be considered: "Schiz-
ophrenic psychopathy, emotional instability, depressive and reactive neurosis
and onset of schizophrenia."

The physicians are unanimous in their opinions that alcoholism consequent to psychological or bodily disorders must be considered as a
disease. The medical treatment will have to be directed toward these
causes either on psychological or somatic levels.

[Note: A brief recapitulation by Dr. Bersot as well as various remarks on medical diagnosis and medical supervision during treatment
and also a statement on the involvements of these questions in relation
to compulsory health insurance are omitted in this translation.]

After the discussion of Dr. Bersot's report the Commission formulated
the matter as follows:

III

1a. Mental and bodily disorders incumbent upon the excessive consumption of alcoholic beverages and which require medical treatment must be regarded as a disease and should be treated with all the resources of somatic and psychiatric medicine.

1b. In a large number of instances alcoholism is secondary to nervous and character disorders (neuroses, onsets of mental disorders, psychopathies of various natures, diabetes, post-traumatic encephalopathies, etc.) which cloud the insight of the individual, impairing the volition as well as the resistance to alcohol intoxication. These primary troubles must be treated at the same time as alcoholism itself with all the resources of medical therapy.

2. The treatment of alcoholics requires a medical diagnosis based on a careful examination of the patient as well as an inquiry into the social environment. . . . It should devolve on the physician to determine the course of treatment. . . .

3. It should devolve upon the physician to determine whether the treatment should be carried out in a hospital, in an institution for alcoholics, by an alcoholic dispensary, in a medical establishment or a neurological or psychiatric polyclinic, etc. . . . It also devolves upon the physician to supervise the patient and to decide the moment for discharge.

4a. The health insurance agencies should grant their assistance for the treatment of alcoholics exactly as in the case of the treatment of mental and nervous disorders or other drug addictions from the time that a course of treatment has been prescribed by a physician. The physician should sign a declaration of disease requiring treatment.

4b. The health insurance agencies should grant their assistance as early as possible in order to avoid serious organic troubles provoked by alcoholism such as cardiac disorders, hepatic diseases, renal disorders, disorders of the nervous system, etc.

5. All institutions for the rehabilitation of alcoholics including the alcoholic dispensaries should have a medical consultant, preferably a physician specialized in neurology or psychiatry, in order to direct and supervise the necessary treatment. Where this is not feasible recourse should be taken to the services of a physician on the staff of the nearest polyclinic or other medical establishment, neurological or psychiatric clinic.

Appendix C

List of 19th-Century Papers on the Disease Nature of Alcoholism

Only papers not referred to either in the text or in the Bibliography are cited in this appendix.

AMERICAN ASSOCIATION FOR THE STUDY AND CURE OF INEBRIETY. Disease of Inebriety from Alcohol, Opium and other Narcotics; its Etiology, Pathology, Treatment, and Medico-legal Relations. New York; 1893.

BARELLA, H. De l'Abus des Spiritueux, Maladies des Buveurs. Bruxelles; H. Manceaux; 1878.

BROWNSON, W. G. The disease theory of intemperance. Proc. Conn. med. Soc. 4 (No. 3): 60–72, 1890.

CHAPPLE. Public health aspect of alcohol. Brit. med. J. 1: 1101, 1896.

CRONIN, P. H. The alcoholic question medically considered. Proc. Conn. med. Soc. 3: 73–77, 1887.

CROTHERS, T. D. The disease of inebriety and its treatment. Int. Congr. Med. 1: 188–193, 1887. Abst. in: Lancet 2: 21, 1887; and Med. Rec., N.Y. 32: 347, 1887.

DELAUNOIS, G. Etude sur les Maladies du Buveur. Mons, Belgium; 1880.

EDWARDS, O. C. The treatment of inebriety as a disease. Montreal med. J. 24: 736–737, 1896.

FOOTE, G. F. Inebriety and Opium Eating: in Both Cases a Disease. Method of Treatment and Conditions of Success. Portland, Maine; 1877.

FRENCH, J. M. Treatment of alcoholism as a disease. Indian med. Rec. 18: 100–101, 1900.

GANSER, S. Die Trunksucht eine heilbare Krankheit. Dresden; 1901.

GABRIEL, M. Essai sur l'Alcoolisme Considéré Principalement au Point de Vue de l'Hygiène Publique. Thèse, Montpellier; 1866.

HARRIS, S. On Inebriety, Continuous and Periodical, Considered as a Result of Physical Disease and Distinct from the Vice of Intemperance, its Causes, Nature, Treatment, and Cure. London; 1872.

HILL, C. G. Inebriety as a disease. Trans. med. chir. Fac. Md, pp. 183–191, 1888.

HILLS, R. On the pathology and medication of intemperance as a disease. Proceedings of the Medical Convention of Ohio, pp. 15–20, 1849.

JACQUET, L. Alcool, maladie, mort. Pr. méd. 7²: 337–343, 1899.

KEELEY, L. E. Drunkenness a curable disease. Amer. J. Politics 1: 27–43, 1892.

KAIN, J. H. On intemperance considered as a disease and susceptible of cure. Amer. J. med. Sci. 2: 291–295, 1828.

KERR, N. Inebriety; a Disease Allied to Insanity. London; 1884.

KERR, N. Inebriety, or Narcomania. Its Etiology, Pathology, Treatment and Jurisprudence. London, Philadelphia; Lewis; 1888. (2d ed., 1891; 3d ed., 1894.)

MANN, E. C. On the treatment of the disease of inebriety and the morphine habit, with clinical cases. Brooklyn med. J. 1: 299–308, 1888.

Intemperance: vice or disease? Med. Temp. Rev. 3: 237–239, 1900.

MOORE, G. The Desire for Intoxicating Liquors, a Disease; its Causes, its Effects and its Cure, with the Danger of a Relapse. Baltimore; 1864.

PARRISH, J. The classification and treatment of inebriety. Proc. Amer. Ass. Cure Inebriates 2: 61–76, 1872.

PIEPER, M. A pathological view of inebriety in Germany, and its therapeutic treatment. MAYER, N., transl. Quart. J. Inebr. 3: 65–77, 1879.

POOLE, G. K. Inebriety: a crime or a disease? (With discussion.) Proc. Soc. Stud. Inebr., Lond., No. 66, pp. 2–13, 1900.

Quarterly Journal of Inebriety (later, Journal of Inebriety). [Approximately 80 papers and editorials dealing specifically with the question of alcoholism as an illness in the last quarter of the 19th century.]

STEPHENS, C. R. Inebriety or Vini Morbus, a Disease and to be Treated as Such, Modes of Treatment, etc. Salem, Mass.; T. J. Hutchinson; 1877.

TAYLOR, C. F. Alcoholism; the treatment and cure of the disease. Ther. Gaz. 10: 238–240, 1894.

WILLETT, J. The Drunkard's Diseased Appetite, What is it? If Curable, How? By Miraculous Agency or Physical Means? Which? Fort Hamilton; 1877.

WILLETT, J. The drunkard's diseased appetite. Is it curable by miraculous or physical means? Quart. J. Inebr. 2: 199–202, 1878.

Bibliography

The following list includes all references used in the preparation of this book. Approximately 80 per cent are referred to directly in the text. Appendix C contains an additional list of references to 19th-century papers on the disease nature of alcoholism.

Unauthored articles in this bibliography are alphabetized by their responsible source, e.g., the name of the journal in which they appear, the publisher, or, in the case of certain common reference works, the title.

English, French, German, Italian and Spanish titles are given in the original language only; titles in all other languages are given in the original and in English translation (in parentheses).

This bibliography was closed in mid-1958; however, a few later references were incorporated in the course of preparing the book for publication.

AAMARK, C. A Study in Alcoholism. Clinical Social-Psychiatric and Genetic Investigations. (Acta psychiat., Kbh., Suppl. 70.) Copenhagen; Munksgaard; 1951.

AAMARK, C. Alkoholismens orsaker. (The causes of alcoholism.) Svenska Läkartidn. 52: 2297–2314, 1955.

ABDERHALDEN, E. Bibliographie der wissenschaftlichen Literatur über den Alkohol und Alkoholismus. Berlin and Vienna; Urban & Schwarzenberg; 1904.

ABELMANN, W. H., KOWALSKI, H. J. and McNEELEY, W. F. The circulation of the blood in alcohol addicts. The cardiac output at rest and during moderate exercise. Quart. J. Stud. Alc. 15: 1–8, 1954.

ACEVEDO CASTILLO and CALVO, M. Alcoholismo y su tratamiento médico. Hosp. Viña del Mar (Bol.), Chile 5 (No. 1): 1–6, 1949.

ADAMS, E. W. What is addiction? Brit. J. Inebr. 33: 1–10, 1935.

ALBERT, S. N., REA, E. L., DUVERNEY, C. A., SHEA, J. and FAZEKAS, J. F. The use of chlorpromazine in the treatment of acute alcoholism. Med. Ann. D.C. 23: 245–247, 1954.

Alcoholics Anonymous. The Story of How More than 100 Men Have Recovered from Alcoholism. New York; Works Publishing Co.; 1939.

Alcoholics Anonymous. The Story of How Many Thousands of Men and Women Have Recovered from Alcoholism. New and rev. ed. New York; Alcoholics Anonymous Publishing; 1955.

ALEXANDER, F. Views on the etiology of alcoholism. *II.* The psychodynamic view. In: KRUSE, H. D., ed., Alcoholism as a Medical Problem; pp. 40–46. New York; Hoeber-Harper; 1956.

ALHA, A. Det tilltagande och det avtagande ruset. (The rising and receding phases of drunkenness.) Alkoholpolitik, Hels., No. 2, pp. 51–55, 1952.

ALLAN, F. D. and SWINYARD, C. A. Evaluation of tissue tolerance to ethyl alcohol by alterations in electroshock seizure threshold in rats. Anat. Rec. 103: 419, 1949.

AMERICAN MEDICAL ASSOCIATION, COMMITTEE ON ALCOHOLISM. Hospitalization of patients with alcoholism. (Reports of Officers.) J. Amer. med. Ass. 162: 750, 1956.

ANDERSON, D. Alcohol and public opinion. Quart. J. Stud. Alc. 3: 376–392, 1942.

ANDERSON, D. The process of recovery from alcoholism. Fed. Probation 8 (No. 4): 14–19, 1944.

222   E. M. JELLINEK

BACON, S. D. Alcoholism and industry. Civitan Mag., pp. 1–8, March 1951.
BACON, S. D. Evolutions dans la conception américaine de l'alcoolisme durant les vingt dernières années. Int. J. Alc. Alcsm 2: 17–32, 1957.
BACON, S. D. Alcoholics do not drink. Ann. Amer. Acad. polit. soc. Sci. 315: 55–64, 1958.
BAER, A. A. Der Alcoholismus, seine Verbreitung, und seine Wirkung auf den individuellen und socialen Organismus sowie die Mittel, ihn zu Bekämpfen. Berlin; Hirschwald; 1878.
BALES, R. F. Cultural differences in rates of alcoholism. Quart. J. Stud. Alc. 6: 480–499, 1946.
BASTIDE, H. Une enquête sur l'opinion publique à l'égard de l'alcoolisme. Population 9: 13–42, 1954.
BEDOS, J. F. A. A Propos du Vin et de l'Alcoolisme en France. Paris; Imprimerie R. Foulon; 1955.
BEERSTECHER, E., JR., SUTTON, H. E., BERRY, H. K., BROWN, W. D., REED, J., RICH, G. B., BERRY, L. J. and WILLIAMS, R. J. Biochemical individuality. V. Explorations with respect to the metabolic patterns of compulsive drinkers. Arch. Biochem., N.Y. 29: 27–40, 1950.
BELL, R. G. Clinical orientation to alcoholism. Industr. Med. 21: 251–260, 1952.
BELL, R. G. Blood alcohol levels and toxic drinking. Univ. Toronto med. J. 30: 133–139, 1953.
BELL, R. G. An after-care and rehabilitation program for alcohol addicts. Acad. Med N.J. Bull., Vol. 1, No. 3, n.p., June 15, 1956.
BENNETT, A. E., DOI, L. T. and MOWERY, G. L. The value of electroencephalography in alcoholism. J. nerv. ment. Dis. 124: 27–32, 1956.
BENSOUSSAN, P. Syndromes de sevrage et états de besoin observés au cours de l'alcoolisme chronique. Sem. Hôp. Paris 32: 3078–3091, 1956.
BERGLER, E. Contributions to the psychogenesis of alcohol addiction. Quart. J. Stud. Alc. 5: 434–449, 1944.
BERLIEN, J. D. Alcohol and the soldier. Quart. J. Stud. Alc. 5: 405–412, 1944.
BERMAN, L. New Creations in Human Beings. [Section: Alcoholism and the interbrain, pp. 276–279.] New York; Doubleday, Doran; 1938.
BERNER, P. and SOLMS, W. Alkoholismus bei Frauen. Wien. Z. Nervenheilk. 6: 235–301, 1953.
BERREMAN, J. V. The escape motive in alcoholic addiction. Res. Stud. St. Coll. Wash. 18: 139–143, 1950.
BERTAGNA, L. La psychologie des alcooliques. Rev. Prat. 3: 2377–2380, 1953.
BEUTNER, K. R. Treatment of alcoholism. Mod. Med., Minneapolis 19 (No. 5): 18, 21, 24, 1951.
BINDER, H. Alkoholiker und ihre fürsorgerische Behandlung. Fürsorger 15: 1–17, 1947.
BINDER, H. Zur Frage der einjährigen Entziehungskur für Alkoholsuchtige. Gesundh. u. Wohlfahrt, Zurich 30: 547–549, 1950.
BIRD, B. One aspect of causation in alcoholism. Quart. J. Stud. Alc. 9: 532–543, 1949.
BJÖRK, S. Psykologiska synpunkter på alkoholismen. (Alcoholism from the psychological viewpoint.) Svenska Läkartidn. 47: 1018–1026, 1950.
BLAKESLEE, A. L. Alcoholism—a Sickness that Can Be Beaten. (Public Affairs Pamphlet No. 118.) New York; Public Affairs Committee; 1952.
BLEULER, M. A comparative study of the constitutions of Swiss and American alcoholic patients. In: DIETHELM, O., ed., Etiology of Chronic Alcoholism; pp. 167–178. Springfield, Ill.; Thomas; 1955.

BLOCK, M. A. Alcoholism is a disease. Today's Hlth 34: 36–39, November 1956.

BLOCK, M. A. The progress of community action against alcoholism in the United States of America. Int. J. Alc. Alcsm 2: 1–16, 1957.

BLUESTONE, E. M. Institutional facilities for the treatment of alcoholism: foreword. Quart. J. Stud. Alc. 5: 5–8, 1944.

BOUDREAU, E. N. The medical and social challenge of alcoholism. N.Y. St. J. Med. 41: 2407–2414, 1941.

BOWMAN, K. M. Alteration of mental processes by chemical and hormonal agents. Res. Publ. Ass. nerv. ment. Dis. 19: 108–111, 1939.

BOWMAN, K. M. and JELLINEK, E. M. Alcohol addiction and its treatment. Quart. J. Stud. Alc. 2: 98–176, 1941. Also in: JELLINEK, E. M., ed., Alcohol Addiction and Chronic Alcoholism; ch. 1, pp. 3–80. New Haven; Yale University Press, 1942 (a).

BOWMAN, K. M. and JELLINEK, E. M. Alcoholic mental disorders. Quart. J. Stud. Alc. 2: 312–390, 1941. Also in: JELLINEK, E. M., ed., Alcohol Addiction and Chronic Alcoholism; ch. 2, pp. 81–169. New Haven; Yale University Press; 1942 (b).

BOWMAN, K. M., WORTIS, H. and KEISER, S. The treatment of delirium tremens. J. Amer. med. Ass. 112: 1217–1219, 1939.

BRADY, R. A. and WESTERFELD, W. W. The effect of B-complex vitamins on the voluntary consumption of alcohol by rats. Quart. J. Stud. Alc. 7: 499–505, 1947.

BREIT, H. Recent concepts on alcoholism. Med. Times, N.Y. 81: 774–782, 1953.

BRESARD, M. Enquête sur la consommation des boissons en France. Paris; Bull. Inst. nat. Hyg. 13: 267–356, 1958.

BROCKLEHURST, T. Alcoholic addiction—its classification and cure. S. Afr. med. J. 23: 771–774, 1949.

BRORSSON, B. Miljö och konstitution såsom betingelser för alkoholism. (Milieu and constitution as conditions for alcoholism.) Tirfing 40: 13–23, 1946.

BROWN, E. A. Sensitivity to grape and grape products, including wine. Case report. Ann. Allergy 11: 590–593, 1953.

BROWN, P. R. The problem drinker and the jail. Quart. J. Stud. Alc. 16: 474–483, 1955.

BRUNNER-ORNE, M. and ORNE, M. T. Directive group-therapy in the treatment of alcoholics: technique and rationale. Int. J. Group Psychother. 4: 293–302, 1954.

BSCHOR, F. Studien über den Ablauf der Alkoholintoxikation unter besonderer Berücksichtigung der pharmakopsychologischen Beziehungen in der Resorptionsphase bei Alkoholgewöhnten. Dtsch. Z. ges. gerichtl. Med. 40: 399–420, 1951.

BUMKE, O. and KANT, F. Rausch- und Genussgifte; Giftsuchten. In: BUMKE, O. and FOERSTER, O., eds., Handbuch der Neurologie 13: 828–915. Berlin; Springer; 1936.

BURKHARDT, H. Das Suchtproblem. Fortschr. Neurol. Psychiat. 22: 473–492, 1954.

BURROUGHS, W. Letter from a master addict to dangerous drugs. Brit. J. Addict. 53: 119–131, 1957.

BUTTON, A. D. The psychodynamics of alcoholism: a survey of 87 cases. Quart. J. Stud. Alc. 17: 443–460, 1956 (a).

BUTTON, A. D. The genesis and development of alcoholism: an empirically based schema. Quart. J. Stud. Alc. 17: 671–675, 1956 (b).

CARLSON, A. J. The conditioned-reflex therapy of alcohol addiction. Quart. J. Stud. Alc. 5: 212–215, 1944.

CARRETTE, P. La baisse de tolérance chez les alcooliques. Rev. Alcsme 4: 381–382, 1958.

CARROLL, R. S. What Price Alcohol? New York; Macmillan; 1941.

CARSTAIRS, G. M. Daru and bhang. Cultural factors in the choice of intoxicant. Quart. J. Stud. Alc. 15: 220–237, 1954.

CARTER, H. R. Conditioned reflex treatment for alcoholic addiction. Rocky Mtn med. J. 40: 318–321, 1943.

CARVER, A. E. Biochemical factors in idiosyncrasy to alcohol. Brit. J. Inebr. 42: 65–83, 1945.

CATHELL, J. L. The occurrence of certain psychosomatic conditions during different phases of the alcoholic's life. N.C. med. J. 15: 503–505, 1954.

CHEYMOL, J. and THUILLIER, J. Peut-on guérir l'âlcoolisme chronique? Ann. pharm. franç. 8: 422–428, 1950.

CIMBAL, W. Trinkerfürsorge als Teil der Verwahrlostenfürsorge. Allg. Z. Psychiat. 84: 52–86, 1926.

CLINEBELL, H. J., JR. Understanding and Counseling the Alcoholic through Religion and Psychology. Nashville; Abingdon Press; 1956.

CONGER, J. J. The effects of alcohol on conflict behavior in the albino rat. Quart. J. Stud. Alc. 12: 1–29, 1951.

CONGER, J. J. Reinforcement theory and the dynamics of alcoholism. Quart. J. Stud. Alc. 17: 296–305, 1956.

Congreso Internacional contra el Alcoholismo. Montevideo; [Liga Nacional contra el Alcoholismo;] 1948.

COREY, S. J. A chaplain looks at drug addiction. Fed. Probation 15 (No. 3): 17–24, 1951.

CORWIN, E. H. L. and CUNNINGHAM, E. V. Institutional facilities for the treatment of alcoholism. Quart. J. Stud. Alc. 5: 10–85, 1944.

COURVILLE, C. B. Effects of Alcohol on the Nervous System of Man. Los Angeles; San Lucas Press; 1955.

COURVILLE, C. B. and MYERS, R. O. Effects of extraneous poisons on the nervous system. II. The alcohols. Bull. Los Angeles neurol. Soc. 19: 66–95, 1954.

COWLES, E. S. Chronic alcoholism. In: Don't Be Afraid; ch. 10, pp. 155–169. New York; Whittlesey House; 1941.

CROTHERS, T. D. A review of the history and literature of inebriety. The first journal and its work up to the present time. J. Inebr. 33: 139–151, 1911.

CUMMINS, J. F. and FRIEND, D. G. Use of chlorpromazine in chronic alcoholics. Amer J. med. Sci. 227: 561–564, 1954.

DAHLBERG, G. Aer alkoholism att betrakta som sjukdom? (Is alcoholism to be considered a sickness?) Tirfing 41: 113–122, 1947.

DALLA VOLTA, A. New aspects of the psychological problem of alcoholism. Sci. med. ital. 5: 510–529, 1957.

DAVIDSON, G. M. The syndrome of acute (alcoholic) hallucinosis. Psychiat. Quart. 13: 466–497, 1939.

DENT, J. Y. Anxiety and its Treatment: with Special Reference to Alcoholism. London; John Murray; 1941.

DENT, J. Y. Anxiety and its Treatment: with Special Reference to Alcoholism. 3d ed. London; Skeffington; 1955.

DÉROBERT, L. In: JELLINEK, E. M., ed., European Seminar and Lecture Course on Alcoholism. Geneva; World Health Organization; [1952].

DÉROBERT, L. L'Economie de l'Alcoolisme. (Monographie de l'Institut National d'Hygiène, No. 2.) Paris; Ministère de la Santé Publique; 1953.

DESHAIES, G. Les conditions psychologiques de l'alcoolisme. Hyg. ment. 36: 1–16, 17–36, 1946–1947.

DESRUELLES, M. and FELLION, G. A propos des traitements actuels de l'alcoolisme (désintoxication, tétraethylthiuram disulfide, apomorphine). Ann. méd.-psychol. 109[1]: 638–644, 1951.

DEWAN, J. G. The treatment of alcoholism. Canad. med. Ass. J. 60: 296, 1949.

DIETHELM, O. Research project on the etiology of alcoholism. Quart. J. Stud. Alc. 9: 72–79, 1948.

DIETHELM, O. Advances in the treatment of chronic alcoholism. Bull. N.Y. Acad. Med. 27: 232–244, 1951.

DOWDEN, C. W. and BRADBURY, J. T. Eosinophil response to epinephrine and corticotropin. Studies in alcoholics and nonalcoholics. J. Amer. med. Ass. 149: 725–728, 1952.

DREYFUSS, A. Peut-on guérir les grands buveurs? Une étape nouvelle dans la lutte anti-alcoolique. Méd. Usine, Paris 13: 380–385, 1951.

DUBLINEAU, J. and HONORÉ, B. Relations statistiques entre le sentiment de soif et la typologie du buveur interné. Ann. méd.-psychol. 113²: 848–850, 1955.

DUCHÊNE, H. Les possibilités actuelles de traitement de l'alcoolisme. Arch. Méd. soc. 5: 225–294, 1949 (a).

DUCHÊNE, H. Les possibilités actuelles de traitement de l'alcoolisme. Bull. Inst. nat. Hyg. 4: 1–66, 1949 (b).

DUCHÊNE, H. The need to drink. Quart. J. Stud. Alc. 16: 47–51, 1955.

DUCHÊNE, H., SCHUTZENBERGER, M. P., BIRO, J. and SCHMITZ, B. Particularités de l'écart d'age des couples dont le mari est alcoolique. Bull. Inst. nat. Hyg. 7: 609–612, 1952. Also in: Sem. Hôp. Paris 28: 1857–1859, 1952.

DUNCAN, R. E. Alcohol as a medical problem. Kans. Cy med. J. 23 (No. 6): 9–12 1947.

DURFEE, C. H. To Drink or Not To Drink. New York; Longmans, Green; 1938.

EGGLETON, M. G. The effect of alcohol on the central nervous system. Brit. J. Psychol. 32: 52–61, 1941.

FAZEKAS, J. F., SHEA, J. and REA, E. Use of chlorpromazine in the management of acute and postalcoholic states. Int. Rec. Med. 168: 333–339, 1955.

FELDMANN, H. Contribution à la Thérapeutique Biologique de l'Alcoolisme Chronique. Le Traitement par l'Apomorphine. Paris; Expansion Scientifique Française; 1951.

FELDMANN, H. The modern treatments of alcoholism, with special reference to apomorphine, biological, psychological and social aspects. Brit. J. Addict. 52: 7–38, 1955.

FELIX, R. H. An appraisal of the personality types of the addict. Amer. J. Psychiat. 100: 462–467, 1944.

FIGUERIDO, C. A. El problema etiológico de las toxicomanías. Rev. Sanid. Hig. publ., Madr. 21: 780–797, 1947.

FLEETWOOD, M. F. and DIETHELM, O. Emotions and biochemical findings in alcoholism. Amer. J. Psychiat. 108: 433–438, 1951.

FLEMING, R. The treatment of chronic alcoholism. New Engl. J. Med. 217: 779–783, 1937.

FLEMING, R. In: JELLINEK, E. M., ed., European Seminar and Lecture Course on Alcoholism. Geneva; World Health Organization; [1952].

FLEMING, R. On certain medical aspects of alcoholism. Acad. Med. N.J. Bull., Vol. 1, No. 3, 1956.

FORBES, J. C. and DUNCAN, G. M. The effect of acute alcohol intoxication on the adrenal glands of rats and guinea pigs. Quart. J. Stud. Alc. 12: 355–359, 1951.

FORD, J. C. Depth Psychology, Morality and Alcoholism. Weston, Mass.; Weston College Press; 1951.

FORD, J. C. The general practitioner's role in alcoholism. Linacre Quart. 23: 95–108, 1956.

FOREY. Service Social et Alcoolisme. Paris; [Caisse Familiere?] 1957.

FORIZS, L. Alcoholic rehabilitation. N.C. med. J. 14: 97–100, 1953.

FORIZS, L. A closer look at the alcoholic. N.C. med. J. 15: 81–84, 1954.

FORSSMAN, H. Psykoanalytikern och alkoholismen. Kommentar till dr. Stig. Björks artikel. (Psychoanalysis and alcoholism. Commentary on Dr. Stig Björk's article.) Svenska Läkartidn. 47: 1129–1134, 1950.

FOUQUET, P. Reflexions cliniques et thérapeutiques sur l'alcoolisme. Evolut. psychiat., Paris, No. 2, pp. 231–262, 1951.

FOUQUET, P. In: JELLINEK, E. M., ed., European Seminar and Lecture Course on Alcoholism. Geneva; World Health Organization; [1952].

FOUQUET, P. and CLAVREUL, J. Une Thérapeutique de l'Alcoolisme. Paris; Presses Universitaires de France; 1956.

FOUQUET, P. and PAUMELLE. Rôle de l'assistante sociale dans une consultation de désintoxication alcoolique. Rev. Hyg. Méd. soc. 4: 762–765, 1956.

FOUQUET, P. and ROPERT, R. Essai sur les critères de guérison de l'alcoolisme. Ann. méd-psychol. 110^1: 236–242, 1952.

FOX, R. and LYON, P. Alcoholism, its Scope, Cause and Treatment. New York; Random House; 1955.

FOX, V. Treatment of withdrawal symptoms in the management of alcoholism. J. med. Ass. Ga 45: 139–142, 1956.

FRANK, L. K. The problem of the alcoholic personality. Quart. J. Stud. Alc. 5: 242–244, 1944.

GABRIEL, E. and KRATZMANN, E. Die Süchtigkeit, eine Seelenkunde; pp. 47–98. Berlin; Neuland Verlag; 1936.

GALLEZ, E. Alcoolisme et Pastorale. Paris; Imprimerie Allain; 1958.

GALLUET. Un aspect du rôle de l'assistante sociale dans la lutte contre la maladie alcoolique. Alc. Santé, No. 29, pp. 34–38, 1958.

GELMA, E., KAMMERER, T., BATZENSCHLAGER, A., WOLF, E. and FORGET, J. Valeur de l'encéphalographie gazeuse dans la maladie de Korsakoff. Cah. psychiat. 9 (No. 2): 21–26, 1952.

GERARD, D. L. Intoxication and addiction. Psychiatric observations on alcoholism and opiate drug addiction. Quart. J. Stud. Alc. 16: 681–699, 1955.

GIBBINS, R. J. Chronic Alcoholism and Alcohol Addiction. A Survey of Current Literature. (Brookside Monograph No. 1.) Toronto; Alcoholism Research Foundation; 1953.

GISCARD, P. and GIRAUDON, C. Le placement et le traitement des alcooliques. J. Sci. Med. Lille 69: 483–487, 1951.

GLATT, M. M. A treatment centre for alcoholics in a public mental hospital: its establishment and its working. Brit. J. Addict. 52: 55–92, 1955.

GODFREY, L., KISSEN, M. D. and DOWNS, T. M. Treatment of the acute alcohol withdrawal syndrome. Quart. J. Stud. Alc. 19: 118–124, 1958.

GOLDBERG, L. Quantitative studies on alcohol tolerance in man. The influence of ethyl alcohol on sensory, motor and psychological functions referred to blood alcohol in normal and habituated individuals. Acta physiol. scand. 5 (Suppl. 16): 1–128, 1943.

GOLDBERG, L. Alcohol research in Sweden 1939–1948. Quart. J. Stud. Alc. 10: 279–288, 1949.

GOLDBERG, L. In: JELLINEK, E. M., ed., European Seminar and Lecture Course on Alcoholism. Geneva; World Health Organization; [1952].

GOLDBERG, L. and STÖRTEBECKER, T. P. Criteria of alcohol intoxication in animals in relation to blood alcohol. Acta physiol. scand. 3: 71–81, 1941.

GOLDFARB, A. I. and BERMAN, S. Alcoholism as a psychosomatic disorder. *I.* Endocrine pathology of animals and man excessively exposed to alcohol; its possible relation to behavioral pathology. Quart. J. Stud. Alc. 10: 415–429, 1949.

GOODENOUGH, E. R. Jewish Symbols in the Greco-Roman Period. (Bollingen Series, XXVII.) [Vol. 5 (in 2 vols.), Fish, Bread and Wine.] New York; Pantheon; 1956.

GORDON, J. E. The epidemiology of alcoholism. In: KRUSE, H. D., ed., Alcoholism as a Medical Problem; pp. 15–31. New York; Hoeber-Harper; 1956.

GOTTESFELD, B. H. and YAGER, H. L. Psychotherapy of the problem drinker. Quart. J. Stud. Alc. 11: 222–229, 1950.

GRANDON, R. C., HEFFLEY, W., HENSEL, T. and BASHORE, S. A new medical adjunct to the treatment of alcoholism. The use of reserpine (Serpasil). Amer. Practit. Dig. Treatm. 7: 231–234, 1956.

GRAY, M. G. and MOORE, M. A comparison of alcoholism and drug addiction with particular reference to the underlying psychopathological factors. J. crim. Psychopath. 4: 151–161, 1942.

GREENFIELD, A. R. A new type of sedation for the acute alcoholic. Amer. Practit. Dig. Treatm. 7: 241–244, 1956.

GREENHOUSE, H. R. Treatment of the postintoxication state in alcoholics with mephenesin and other drugs. Quart. J. Stud. Alc. 15: 43–46, 1954.

GRIFFIN, M. A. Treatment of chronic alcoholism. N.C. med. J. 3: 632–633, 1942.

GROSS, M. The relation of the pituitary gland to some symptoms of alcoholic intoxication and chronic alcoholism. Quart. J. Stud. Alc. 6: 25–35, 1945.

GUBAR', V. L. O vrednom deistvii alkogolya na zheludok. (On the injurious effect of alcohol on the stomach.) Vop. Pitan. 14 (No. 2): 3–8, 1955.

HAGGARD, H. W. Critique of the concept of the allergic nature of alcohol addiction. Quart. J. Stud. Alc. 5: 233–241, 1944.

HAGGARD, H. W. and JELLINEK, E. M. Alcohol Explored. New York; Doubleday; 1942.

HAMPTON, P. J. A descriptive portrait of the drinker. J. soc. Psychol. 25: 69–132, 1947.

HARGREAVES, G. R. In: JELLINEK, E. M., ed., European Seminar and Lecture Course on Alcoholism. Geneva; World Health Organization; [1952].

HARRISON, F. M. The alcohol problem in the Navy. Quart. J. Stud. Alc. 5: 413–425, 1944.

HEATH, R. G. Group psychotherapy of alcohol addiction. Quart. J. Stud. Alc. 5: 555–562, 1945.

HENDERSON, J. P. Alcoholic craving from the subjective point of view. Brit. J. Inebr. 42: 41–51, 1944.

HERNDON, R. F. The treatment of alcoholism. Bull. Sangamon Co. med. Soc. 17: 205–210, 1952.

HIGGINS, J. W. Psychodynamics in the excessive drinking of alcohol. Arch. Neurol. Psychiat., Chicago 69: 713–726, 1953.

HIMWICH, H. E. Views on the etiology of alcoholism. *I.* The organic view. In: KRUSE, H. D., ed., Alcoholism as a Medical Problem. New York; Hoeber-Harper; 1956.

HIRSH, J. Alcoholism and the general practitioner. Postgrad. Med. 8: 5–9, 1950.

HOCH, P. H. In: KRUSE, H. D., ed., Alcoholism as a Medical Problem. New York; Hoeber-Harper; 1956.

228 E. M. JELLINEK

Höjer, J. A. The importance of the cooperation of physicians in the attack on alcoholism. Quart. J. Stud. Alc. 9: 363–371, 1948.

Höjer, J. A. In: Jellinek, E. M., ed., European Seminar and Lecture Course on Alcoholism. Geneva; World Health Organization; [1952].

Holmberg, G. and Mårtens, S. Electroencephalographic changes in man correlated with blood alcohol concentration and some other conditions following standardized ingestion of alcohol. Quart. J. Stud. Alc. 16: 411–424, 1955.

Horton, D. The functions of alcohol in primitive societies: a cross-cultural study. Quart. J. Stud. Alc. 4: 199–320, 1943.

Hurley, T. H. The treatment of alcoholic addiction with "Antabuse": observations on a group of patients with nutritional liver disease. Proc. roy. Aust. Coll. Phys. 6: 71–82, 1951.

Huss, M. Chronische Alkoholskrankheit, oder Alcoholismus chronicus. Ein Beitrag zur Kenntnis der Vergiftungs-Krankheiten nach eigener und anderer Erfahrung. Translated from the Swedish, with revisions by the author, by Gerhard van dem Busch. 2 vol. Stockholm; 1852. (Original: Alcoholismus chronicus eller chronisk alkoholssjukdom. Ett bidrag till dyskrasiernas kännedom; enlight egen och andras erfarenhet. Stockholm; 1849.)

Isbell, H. Craving for alcohol. Quart. J. Stud. Alc. 16: 38–42, 1955.

Isbell, H., Fraser, H. F., Wikler, A., Belleville, R. E. and Eisenman, A. J. An experimental study of the etiology of "rum fits" and delirium tremens. Quart. J. Stud. Alc. 16: 1–33, 1955.

Izikowitz, S. Om alkoholismens medicinska terapi och profylax, några synpunkter och erfarenheter. (On the medical therapy and prophylaxis of alcoholism; some viewpoints and experiences.) Nord. Med. 31: 2039–2048, 1946.

Izikowitz, S. Sur le traitement médical de l'alcoolisme. Brux. méd. 32: 1751–1758, 1952.

Izikowitz, S., Mårtens, S. and Dahlborn, L. On the cortisone treatment of alcoholism. Acta. psychiat., Kbh., Suppl. No. 80, pp. 175–180, [1952].

Jellinek, E. M. An outline of basic policies for a research program on problems of alcohol. Quart. J. Stud. Alc. 3: 103–124, 1942.

Jellinek, E. M. Magnus Huss' Alcoholismus Chronicus. Quart. J. Stud. Alc. 4: 85–92, 1943.

Jellinek, E. M. Symposium on therapy of alcohol addiction: introduction. Quart. J. Stud. Alc. 5: 185–188, 1944.

Jellinek, E. M. The problems of alcohol. In: Alcohol, Science and Society; pp. 13–29. New Haven; Quarterly Journal of Studies on Alcohol; 1945 (a).

Jellinek, E. M. Alcohol problems dissected. Soc. Action 11 (No. 3): 5–34, 1945 (b).

Jellinek, E. M. Phases in the drinking history of alcoholics. Quart. J. Stud. Alc. 7: 1–88, 1946.

Jellinek, E. M., ed., European Seminar and Lecture Course on Alcoholism. Geneva; World Health Organization; [1952] (a).

Jellinek, E. M. Phases of alcohol addiction. Quart. J. Stud. Alc. 13: 673–684, 1952 (b).

Jellinek, E. M. The Nosological Position of Alcoholism in the Light of Psychiatry. Document WHO/APD/ALC/6. Geneva; World Health Organization; 1953.

Jellinek, E. M. International Experience with the Problem of Alcoholism. Document WHO/MENT/58, WHO/APD/ALC/12. Geneva; World Health Organization; 1954.

Jellinek, E. M. The "craving" for alcohol. Quart. J. Stud. Alc. 16: 35–38, 1955.

JELLINEK, E. M. The world and its bottle. World Hlth, Geneva 10 (No. 4): 4–6, 1957.

JELLINEK, E. M. and McFARLAND, R. A. Analysis of psychological experiments on the effects of alcohol. Quart. J. Stud. Alc. 1: 272–371, 1940.

JOHNSTON, M. The treatment of alcoholics in an outpatient clinic with adrenal cortex hormones and vitamin B₁. Quart. J. Stud. Alc. 15: 238–245, 1954.

Is alcoholism a disease? (Foreign Letters. Sweden.) J. Amer. med. Ass. 161: 1178, 1956.

Alcoholism as a medical illness. (Queries and Minor Notes.) J. Amer. med. Ass. 164: 506, 1957 (a).

Allergy to alcohol. (Queries and Minor Notes.) J. Amer. med. Ass. 164: 1040–1041, 1957 (b).

Editorial. J. Inebr. 32: 42–48, 1910.

Editorial. J. Inebr. 33: 31, 1911.

KALINOWSKY, L. B. Convulsions in nonepileptic patients on withdrawal of barbiturates, alcohol and other drugs. Arch. Neurol. Psychiat., Chicago 48: 946–956, 1942.

KANT, F. Further modifications in the technique of conditioned-reflex treatment of alcohol addiction. Quart. J. Stud. Alc. 5: 229–232, 1944.

KANT, F. The use of the conditioned reflex in the treatment of alcohol addicts. Wis. med. J. 44: 217–221, 1945.

KANT, F. The Treatment of the Alcoholic. Springfield, Ill.; Thomas; 1954.

KARK, R. M. Eosinopenic response to epinephrine. J. Amer. med. Ass. 149: 1413, 1952.

KASTLER-MAITRON and BURCKARD, E. Quelques considérations sur l'alcoolisme chronique chez la femme. Cah. Psychiat. 10: 31–44, 1955.

KEISTER, B. C. The social glass, a menace to civilization. J. Inebr. 33: 117–126, 1911.

KELLER, M. Alcoholism: nature and extent of the problem. Ann. Amer. Acad. polit. soc. Sci. 315: 1–11, 1958.

KIEVE, R. Alcoholism and the public. Rocky Mtn med. J. 47: 510–513, 1950.

KIRCHER, J. P. and PIERSON, C.-A. Les atrophies cérébrales dans les toxicomanies. Rôle de la pneumonencéphalographie. Essais thérapeutiques. Maroc méd. 35: 668–670, 1956.

KISSEN, M. D., YASKIN, H. E., ROBERTSON, H. F. and MORGAN, D. R. A new adjuvant in postalcoholic psychomotor agitation. Quart. J. Stud. Alc. 12: 587–591, 1951.

KLINGMAN, W. O., SUTER, C., GREEN, R. and ROBINSON, I. The role of alcoholism and magnesium deficiency in convulsions. Trans. Amer. neurol. Ass. 80: 162–165, 1955.

KOLB, L. Alcoholism and public health. Quart. J. Stud. Alc. 1: 605–621, 1941.

KOLLER, A. Über das Phänomen der Alkoholgewöhnung. Gesundh. u. Wohlfahrt 25: 234–239, 1945.

KONSTEN, P. Alkoholismus als Krankheit. Fürsorger 23: 26–31, 1955.

KRUSE, H. D., ed. Alcoholism as a Medical Problem. New York; Hoeber-Harper; 1956.

KRUSE, H. D., ed. Problem Drinking and Alcoholism. Albany; New York State Interdepartmental Health Resources Board; 1957.

KUUSI, P. Suomen Viinapulma. Gallup-Tutkimuksen Valossa. (The Problem of Alcohol in Finland in the Light of a Gallup Poll.) Helsinki; Kustannusosakeyhtiö Otava; 1948.

LAKE, R. Twelve steps for alcoholics. Today's Hlth 35: 18–19, passim, November 1957.

LANDIS, C. and CUSHMAN, J. F. Case histories of compulsive drinkers. Quart. J. Stud. Alc. 6: 141–182, 1945.

LANGE, E. Why are cocktail parties a menace? Glamour, February 1955.

LAPE, E. E., PHILLIPS, E. M. and EDGAR, M. T. Alcoholism. In: Medical Research: a Midcentury Survey; vol. 2, ch. 9. Boston; Little, Brown; 1955.

LARIMER, R. C. The treatment of alcoholism with Antabuse. J. Amer. med. Ass. 150: 79–83, 1952 (a).

LARIMER, R. C. The treatment of alcoholism with Antabuse. J. Iowa St. med. Soc. 42: 400–402, 1952 (b).

LAURENT, J. La Maladie Alcoolique. Paris; 1958.

LAZARUS, A. A. A psychological approach to alcoholism. S. Afr. med. J. 30: 707–710, 1956.

LECOQ, R. Alcool, alcoolisme et thérapeutique par l'alcool. Bull. Sci. pharm. 49: 50–56, 1942.

LECOQ, R. Modification des perturbations humorales et des chronaxies nerveuses sous l'effet de la cure de désintoxication alcoolique. C.R. Soc. Biol., Paris 142: 893–894, 1948.

LECOQ, R. Les perturbations métaboliques de la "maladie alcoolique" et leurs rapports avec l'excitabilité neuro-musculaire et certaines manifestations d'hypertension artérielle, de glycosurie et d'albuminurie. Rev. Alcsme 4: 131–141, 1957.

LECOQ, R., CHAUCHARD, P. and MAZOUÉ, H. Etude chronaximétrique comparative des effets de la cortisone et de la désoxycorticostérone, et leur retentissement sur le système nerveux. C.R. Acad. Sci., Paris 232: 2045–2047, 1951.

LECOQ, R. and FOUQUET, P. Mise en évidence des troubles de la personalité chez les alcooliques. Gaz. méd. Fr. 56: 580–581, 1949.

LEDERMANN, S. Influence de la consommation de vins et d'alcools sur les cancers, la tuberculeuse pulmonaire et sur d'autres maladies. Sem. médicale 28: 221–235, 1952 (a).

LEDERMANN, S. Une mortalité d'origine économique en France: la mortalité d'origine ou d'appoint alcoolique. Sem. médicale 28: 418–421, 1952 (b).

LEDERMANN, S. L'alcoolisation excessive et la mortalité des français. Concours méd. 75: 1485–1496, 1583–1598, 1675–1682, 1767–1774, 1953.

LEDERMANN, S. Alcool, Alcoolisme, Alcoolisation. Données Scientifiques de Caractère Physiologique, Economique et Social. Paris; Institut National d'Etudes Démographiques; 1956.

LEFCOURT, B. G. and FREEDMAN, W. Alcoholism: self-inflicted injury or disease under disability provisions of insurance policies. Temple Law Quart. 23: 39–62, 1949.

LEMERE, F. The nature and significance of brain damage from alcoholism. Amer. J. Psychiat. 113: 361–362, 1956.

LEMERE, F., VOEGTLIN, W. L., BROZ, W. R., O'HOLLAREN, P. and TUPPER, W. E. Heredity as an etiologic factor in chronic alcoholism. Northw. Med., Seattle 42: 110–111, 1943.

LEMIEUX, L. H. L'alcoolisme chronique et ses traitements. Laval méd. 14: 1304–1318, 1949.

LEMKAU, P. V. Alcoholism, a medical and a social problem. Maryland St. med. J. 1: 467–473, 1952.

LEREBOULLET, J., PLUVINAGE, R. and VIDART, L. Les limites de la désintoxication alcoolique. Bull. Soc. méd. Hôp. Paris 70: 527–528, 1954.

LESTER, D. and GREENBERG, L. Nutrition and the etiology of alcoholism. The effect of sucrose, saccharin and fat on the self-selection of ethyl alcohol by rats. Quart. J. Stud. Alc. 13: 553–560, 1952.

Levine, J. The sexual adjustment of alcoholics. A clinical study of a selected sample. Quart. J. Stud. Alc. 16: 675–680, 1955.

Levy, H. Drink. An Economic and Social Study. London; Routledge & Kegan Paul; 1951.

Lévy, J. Contribution à l'étude de l'accoutumance expérimentale aux poisons. III. Alcoolisme expérimental. L'accoutumance à l'alcool peut-elle être considérée comme une conséquence de l'hyposensibilité cellulaire? Bull. Soc. Chim. biol. Paris 17: 47–59, 1935.

Lewis, J. A. Alcoholism. Amer. J. Nurs. 56: 433–435, 1956.

Lewis, N. D. C. Case histories of compulsive drinkers: foreword. Quart. J. Stud. Alc. 6: 139–140, 1945.

Little, S. C. and McAvoy, M. Electroencephalographic studies in alcoholism. Quart. J. Stud. Alc. 13: 9–15, 1952.

Loder, O. Wer ist alkoholkrank? Fürsorger 19: 36–38, 1951.

Lolli, G. Marchiafava's disease. Quart. J. Stud. Alc. 2: 486–495, 1941. Also in: Jellinek, E. M., ed., Alcohol Addiction and Chronic Alcoholism; ch. 5, pp. 263–272. New Haven; Yale University Press; 1942.

Lolli, G. Alcohol addiction; an outline of the processes leading to this condition, and of its symptomatology and treatment. Amer. J. Nursing 48: 505–507, 1948.

Lolli, G. The addictive drinker. Quart. J. Stud. Alc. 10: 404–414, 1949.

Lolli, G. Alcoholism and obesity, both problems of hunger. Conn. Rev. Alcsm 5: 1, 3–4, 1953.

Lolli, G. Alcoholism as a medical problem. Bull. N.Y. Acad. Med. 31: 876–885, 1955.

Lolli, G. Alcoholism as a disorder of the love disposition. Quart. J. Stud. Alc. 17: 96–107, 1956.

Lolli, G., Serianni, E., Golder, G., Mariani, A. and Toner, M. Relationship between intake of carbohydrate-rich foods and intake of wine and other alcoholic beverages. A study among Italians and Americans of Italian extraction. Quart. J. Stud. Alc. 13: 401–420, 1952.

Lovell, H. W. Hope and Help for the Alcoholic. Garden City, N.Y.; Doubleday; 1951.

Alcoholics are people. Conference on alcoholism sponsored by the welfare council of Metropolitan Los Angeles, Southern California Society for Mental Hygiene and individual members of Alcoholics Anonymous. N.p.; [1947].

Lundquist, G. Alkoholismus als medizinisches und soziales Problem. Nervenarzt 22: 373–375, 1951.

Lundquist, G. The craving for alcohol. Quart. J. Stud. Alc. 16: 42–46, 1955.

Luzzatto-Fegiz, P. Gli Italiani e il Vino. Inchiesta sulle Abitudini e Preferenze degli Adulti, Eseguita per Conto del Ministero dell'Agricoltura e delle Foreste. Milano; Edizione Doxa; 1952.

McCullough, W. E. A two-year survey of alcoholic patients in a California State Hospital. Quart. J. Stud. Alc. 13: 240–253, 1952.

McGoldrick, E. J., Jr. Management of the Mind. Boston; Houghton, Mifflin; 1954.

MacLeod, L. D. The controlled administration of alcohol to experimental animals. Brit. J. Addict. 45: 112–124, 1948.

MacLeod, L. D. Biochemistry and alcoholism. Brit. J. Addict. 47: 21–39, 1950 (a).

MacLeod, L. D. "Monthly Bulletin" research report, 1949. Brit. J. Addict. 47: 48–61, 1950 (b).

MacLeod, L. D. "Monthly Bulletin" research report, 1950. Brit. J. Addict. 49: 60–69, 1952.

MacLeod, L. D. Craving for alcohol as a problem for investigation. Quart. J. Stud. Alc. 16: 54–62, 1955.

McPeek, F. W. Alcoholism and religion. Soc. Action 16 (No. 4): 4–29, 1950.

Mann, M. Primer on Alcoholism. New York; Rinehart; 1950.

Mann, N. M. Hypoadrenalism and the alcoholic. Quart. J. Stud. Alc. 13: 201–203, 1952.

Mardones R., J. On the relationship between deficiency of B vitamins and alcohol intake in rats. Quart. J. Stud. Alc. 12: 563–575, 1951.

Mardones R., J. "Craving" for alcohol. Quart. J. Stud. Alc. 16: 51–53, 1955.

Mardones [R.], J., Hederra [D.], A. and Segovia [M.], N. Fluctuacion individual del consumo del alcohol en ratas carenciadas. Bol. Soc. Biol. Santiago 7: 1–2, 1949.

Mardones R., J. and Onfray B., E. Influencia de una substancia de la levadura (¿elementa del complejo vitamínico B?) sobre el consumo de alcohol en ratas en experimentos de autoselección. Rev. Med. Aliment., Chile 5: 148–149, 1942.

Mardones [R.], J., Segovia [M.], N., Alcaino [G.], F. and Hederra [D.], A. Effect of synthetic thioctic or alpha lipoic acid on the voluntary alcohol intake of rats. Science 119: 735–736, 1954.

Mardones R., J., Segovia [M.], N. and Hederra [D.], A. Sobre la no identidad de factor N₁ con elementos conocidos del complejo vitamínico B. Bol. Soc. Biol. Santiago 7: 59, 1950; in Rev. Med. Aliment., Chile, vol. 9, 1950 (a).

Mardones [R.], J., Segovia [M.], N. and Hederra [D.], A. Accion curativa del factor N₁ en el alcoholismo carencial de la rata. Rev. Med. Aliment., Chile 9: 82–84, 1950 (b).

Mardones [R.], J., Segovia [M.], N. and Hederra [D.], A. Herencia del alcoholismo en ratas. I. Comportamiento de la primera generacion de ratas bebedoras, colocadas en dieta carenciada en factor N₁. Rev. Med. Aliment., Chile 9: 61–62, 1950 (c).

Mardones R., J., Segovia-Riquelme, N., Hederra D., A. and Alcaino G., F. Effect of some self-selection conditions on the voluntary alcohol intake of rats. Quart. J. Stud. Alc. 16: 425–437, 1955.

Martensen-Larsen, O. Traitement de l'alcoolisme. Brux. méd. 31: 2285–2299, 1951.

Mason, L. D. The etiology of alcoholic inebriety, and its treatment from a medical point of view. J. Inebr. 33: 15–30, 1911.

Masserman, J. H., Jacques, M. G. and Nicholson, M. R. Alcohol as a preventive of experimental neuroses. Quart. J. Stud. Alc. 6: 281–299, 1945.

Masserman, J. H. and Yum, K. S. An analysis of the influence of alcohol on experimental neuroses in cats. Psychosom. Med. 8: 36–52, 1946.

Masserman, J. H., Yum, K. S. and Nicholson, M. R. Neurosis and alcohol. Amer. J. Psychiat. 101: 389–395, 1944.

May, E. Le traitement des alcooliques. Proph. sanit. 26: 211–212, 1954 (a).

May, E. Le problème de l'alcoolisme en France. Sem. méd. prof. (Sem. Hôp. Paris) 30: 225–229, 1954 (b).

May, E. Le problème de l'alcoolisme en France. II. Les conséquences de l'alcoolisme. Sem. méd. prof. (Sem. Hôp. Paris) 30: 437–446, 1954 (c).

May, E. Le problème de l'alcoolisme en France. III. Les causes de l'alcoolisme. Sem. méd. prof. (Sem. Hôp. Paris) 30: 469–478, 1954 (d).

May, E. Le problème de l'alcoolisme en France. IV. Les remèdes à l'alcoolisme. Sem. méd. prof. (Sem. Hôp. Paris) 30: 525–534, 1954 (e).

Chronic alcoholism as a self-inflicted injury. (Editorial.) Med. Rec., N.Y. 160: 294, 1947.

MEERLOO, J. A. M. Artificial ecstasy. A study of the psychosomatic aspects of drug addiction. J. nerv. ment. Dis. 115: 246–266, 1952.

MELLANBY, E. Alcohol: its Absorption into and Disappearance from the Blood under Different Conditions. London; H. M. Stationery Office; 1919.

MERI, S.-L. Några psykologiska synpunkter på alkoholmissbruket. (Some psychological viewpoints with respect to alcohol abuse.) Tirfing 42: 114–121, 1948.

MEYER, A. Alcohol as a psychiatric problem. In: EMERSON, H., ed., Alcohol and Man; ch. 2, pp. 273–309. New York; Macmillan; 1932.

MIRSKY, A., PIKER, P., ROSENBAUM, M. and LEDERER, H. "Adaptation" of the central nervous system to varying concentrations of alcohol in the blood. Quart. J. Stud. Alc. 2: 35–45, 1941.

MITCHELL, E. H. Chlorpromazine in the treatment of acute alcoholism. Amer. J. med. Sci. 229: 363–367, 1955.

MITCHELL, E. H. Treatment of acute alcoholism with promazine (Sparine). J. Amer. med. Ass. 161: 44–45, 1956.

MÖLLENHOFF, F. Über den Stand der Suchtenbehandlung. Fortschr. Ther. 11: 275–284, 1935.

MONSOUR, K. J. Management of chronic alcoholism in the Army. Bull. U.S. Army med. Dept. 8: 882–887, 1948.

MOORE, M. The treatment of alcoholism. New Engl. J. Med. 221: 489–493, 1939.

MOORE, M. Alcoholism: some "causes" and treatment. Milit. Surg. 90: 481–496, 1942 (a).

MOORE, M. A note on alcoholism. R.I. med. J. 25: 101–104, 1942 (b).

MORE, W. T., MOORE, B. M., NASH, J. B. and EMERSON, G. A. Effects of maze running and sonic stimulation on voluntary alcohol intake of albino rats. Tex. Rep. Biol. Med. 10: 59–65, 1952.

MORREL, F. and SCHIFFERLI, P. Le traitement de l'alcoolisme par la méthode dite de Bruel et Lecoq. Schweiz. med. Wschr. 79: 161–162, 1949.

MORTENSEN, C. The attitude of industrial management toward alcoholism. Quart. J. Stud. Alc. 6: 205–208, 1945.

MUELLER, E. E. Personality and social implications in the life of the alcoholic veteran. Quart. J. Stud. Alc. 10: 258–267, 1949.

MÜLLER, M. Internationale Richtlinien für die Erfassung und Behandlung des Alkoholismus. Wien. Z. Nervenheilk. 9: 54–60, 1954.

MURPHY, D. G. The revalidation of diagnostic tests for alcohol addiction. J. consult. Psychol. 20: 301–304, 1956.

MYERSON, A. The treatment of alcohol addiction in relation to the prevention of inebriety. Quart. J. Stud. Alc. 5: 189–199, 1944.

MYERSON, D. The study and treatment of alcoholism. A historical perspective. New Engl. J. Med. 257: 820–825, 1957.

NACHIN, C. Investigations Préliminaires a une Etude Scientifique de l'Alcoolisme Psychiatrique. A propos de 700 Observations de Buveurs de la Région Lyonnaise. Lyon; Imprimerie Nouvelle Lyonnaise; 1957.

NASON, Z. M. A safe method of detoxicating the acutely ill alcoholic. Quart. J. Stud. Alc. 8: 43–47, 1947.

NEFF, I. H. Treatment of inebriety. J. Inebr. 32: 133–144, 1910.

NEWMAN, H. W. Acquired tolerance to ethyl alcohol. Quart. J. Stud. Alc. 2: 453–463, 1941.

NEWMAN, H. [W.] and ABRAMSON, M. Relation of alcohol concentration to intoxication. Proc. Soc. exp. Biol., N.Y. 48: 509–512, 1941.

NEWTON, R. D. Alcoholism as a neurotic symptom. Brit. J. Addict. 46: 79–92, 1949.

ØDEGARD, Ø. In: JELLINEK, E. M., ed., European Seminar and Lecture Course on Alcoholism. Geneva; World Health Organization; [1952] (a).

ØDEGARD, Ø. Dryckenskapens etiologi. (The etiology of alcoholism.) Alkoholpolitik, Hels., No. 1, pp. 3–7, 1952. Also as: Juoppouden syyopillista tarkastelua. AlkLiik. Aikakausk., No. 1, pp. 3–7, 1952 (b).

OLTMAN, J. E. and FRIEDMAN, S. A consideration of parental deprivation and other factors in alcohol addicts. Quart. J. Stud. Alc. 14: 49–57, 1953.

O'MALLEY, E., HEGGIE, V., TRULSON, M., FLEMING, R. and STARE, F. J. Nutrition and alcoholism. Fed. Proc. 10 (Pt. 1): 390, 1951.

ORELLI, A. VON. Wesen und Behandlung der Süchtigkeit. Schweiz. Arch. Neurol. Psychiat. 70: 411–422, 1952.

OSBORN, L. A. The clinical approach to alcoholism. J. Amer. med. Ass. 143: 165–169, 1950.

OSBORN, L. A. New attitudes toward alcoholism. Quart. J. Stud. Alc. 12: 58–60, 1951.

OWEN, M. A study of the rationale of the treatment of delirium tremens with adrenocorticotropic hormone. I. The eosinophil response of patients with delirium tremens, after a test with ACTH. Quart. J. Stud. Alc. 15: 384–386, 1954 (a).

OWEN, M. A study of the rationale of the treatment of delirium tremens with adrenocorticotropic hormone. II. Clinical correlations to responsiveness to ACTH in delirium tremens. Quart. J. Stud. Alc. 15: 387–401, 1954 (b).

PAGE, R. C. Alcohol in relation to disease. Med. Bull. Standard Oil, N.J. 7: 1–2, 1947.

PAGE, R. C., THORPE, J. J. and CALDWELL, D. W. The problem drinker in industry. Quart. J. Stud. Alc. 13: 370–396, 1952.

PARIS, J. Liaisons entre les médecins du travail, la direction, les représentations du personnel et les travailleurs sociaux dans la lutte contre "la maladie alcoolique." Alc. Santé, No. 29, pp. 40–43, 1958.

PERRIN, P. Pourquoi devient-on alcoolique? Gaz. med. Fr. 56: 567–571, 1949.

PERRIN, P. L'Alcoolisme; Problèmes Médico-Sociaux; Problèmes Economiques. Paris; l'Expansion Scientifique Française; 1950.

PERRIN, P. Y a-t-il une baisse générale de la consommation alcoolique? Rev. Alcsme 5: 378–380, 1958.

PETERS, G. Color blindness and emotional disorganization. Amer. J. Optom. 32: 367–372, 1955.

PFEFFER, A. Z. The natural history of alcoholism: I. Its onset and course. In: KRUSE, H. D., ed., Alcoholism as a Medical Problem; pp. 68–77. New York; Hoeber-Harper; 1956.

PFEFFER, A. Z. Alcoholism. (Modern Monographs in Industrial Medicine, No. 2.) New York; Grune & Stratton; 1958.

PIERSON, [C. A.] and KIRCHER, [J. P.] La pneumoencéphalographie chez l'alcoolique. Rev. neurol. 90: 673–676, 1954 (a).

PIERSON, C. A. and KIRCHER, J. P. La dilatation atrophique des ventricules cérébraux favorise-t-elle l'apparition de l'alcoolisme récidivant. Maroc méd. 33: 1095–1099, 1954 (b).

PLUNKETT, R. J. and HAYDEN, A. C., eds. Standard Nomenclature of Diseases and Operations; 4th ed. (Published for the American Medical Association.) Philadelphia; Blakiston; 1952.

PLUVINAGE, R. Les atrophies cérébrales des alcooliques. Bull. Soc. méd. Hôp. Paris 70: 524–526, 1954.

POHLISCH, K. Die Klinik des Alkoholismus. Allg. Z. Psychiat. 99: 193–202, 1933.

POHLISCH, K. Tabak. Betrachtungen über Genuss und Rauschsucht. (Arbeit u. Gesundheit, Heft 54.) Stuttgart; Thieme; 1954.

Popham, R. E. A critique of the genetotrophic theory of the etiology of alcoholism. Quart. J. Stud. Alc. 14: 228–237, 1953.

Porot, M. and Duboucher, G. La guérison des alcooliques par l'antabus. Algérie méd. 56: 1–21, 1952.

[Portugal.] Anhuario Estadistico do Portugal. Lisbon; 1956.

Protestant Episcopal Church in the United States of America, Joint Commission on Alcoholism. Alcohol, Alcoholism, and Social Drinking. Greenwich, Conn.; Seabury Press; 1958.

Pruitt, M. Alcohol addiction. Mod. Med. 22 (No. 7): 25–26, 1954.

New statement on alcoholic beverages by the General Assembly of the Presbyterian Church in the U.S.A. (Current Notes.) Quart. J. Stud. Alc. 7: 186–190, 1946.

Querido, A. Alcoholism as a public health problem. Quart. J. Stud. Alc. 15: 469–476, 1954.

Randolph, T. G. The mechanism of chronic alcoholism. J. lab. clin. Med. 36: 978, 1950.

Randolph, T. G. The descriptive features of food addiction. Addictive eating and drinking. Quart. J. Stud. Alc. 17: 198–224, 1956.

Rauschke, J. Leistungsprüfung bei an- und abfallendem Blutalkoholgehalt unter besonderen Bedingungen. Dtsch. Z. ges. gerichtl. Med. 43: 27–37, 1954.

Rea, F. B. Alcoholism: Its Psychology and Cure. London; Epworth Press; 1956.

Reeve, B. The problem of alcoholism in industry. Petroleum Refiner, October 1953.

Reichard, J. D. Addiction: some theoretical considerations as to its nature, cause, prevention and treatment. Amer. J. Psychiat. 103: 721–730, 1947.

Remy, M. Nature et traitement des toxicomanies. Mschr. Psychiat. Neurol. 126: 1–27, 1953.

Réquet, A. La situation du buveur et son traitement. Pr. méd. 58: 320–322, 1950.

Réquet, A. Aspect actuel de la cure de l'alcoolisme psychiatrique masculin dans la région lyonnaise. Pr. méd. 59: 1516–1518, 1951.

Réquet, A. La psychiatrisation de l'alcoolisme. Lien méd. Lyon 4 (No. 7): 1, 4, 1955.

Réquet, A. L'intolérance peut-elle expliquer l'endémie éthylique actuelle? Rev. Alcsme 4: 373–378, 1958.

Rice, O. R. The contribution of the minister to the treatment of the alcoholic. Quart. J. Stud. Alc. 5: 250–256, 1944.

Richter, C. P. A study of the effect of moderate doses of alcohol on the growth and behavior of the rat. J. exp. Zool. 44: 397–418, 1926.

Richter, C. P. and Campbell, K. H. Alcohol taste thresholds and concentration of solution preferred by rats. Science 91: 507–508, 1940.

Riley, J. W., Jr. The social implications of problem drinking. Soc. Forces 27: 301–305, 1949.

Riley, J. W., Jr. and Marden, C. F. The medical profession and the problem of alcoholism. Quart. J. Stud. Alc. 7: 241–270, 1946.

Robinson, M. W. and Voegtlin, W. L. Investigations of an allergic factor in alcohol addiction. Quart. J. Stud. Alc. 13: 196–200, 1952.

Rommelspacher, F. Beobachtungen an Suchtkranken. Psyche, Stuttgart 7: 185–196, 1953.

Rosenfeld, G. Der Einfluss des Alkohols auf den Organismus. Wiesbaden; Bergmann; 1901.

Rosenman, S. Pacts, possessions, and the alcoholic. Amer. Imago 12: 241–274, 1955.

Royer, P. H. Psycho-physiologie de la soif. Hyg. ment. 42: 1–14, 1953.

236   E. M. JELLINEK

SACKLER, R. R., SACKLER, M. O., TUI, C., MARTÍ-IBÁÑEZ, F. and SACKLER, A. M. On tolerance to and craving for alcohol in histamine-treated schizophrenics. A physiodynamic interpretation of observations on histamine–adrenocorticohormonal equilibrations. Psychiat. Quart. **26**: 597–607, 1952.

SCHAEFER, E. S. Personality structure of alcoholics in outpatient psychotherapy. Quart. J. Stud. Alc. **15**: 304–319, 1954.

SCHILDER, P. The psychogenesis of alcoholism. Quart. J. Stud. Alc. **2**: 277–292, 1941.

SCHULTZ, J. H. Grundsätzliches zur Suchtfrage. Z. Psychother., Stuttgart **3**: 97–100, 1953.

SELIGER, R. V. Working with the alcoholic. Med. Rec., N.Y. **149**: 147–150, 1939.

SELIGER, R. V. About alcoholism. Industr. Med. Surg. **18**: 481–482, 1949. Also in: Sth. Med. Surg. **111**: 306–308, 1949.

SELYE, H. General adaptation syndrome and diseases of adaptation. J. clin. Endocrin. **6**: 117–230, 1946.

SESSIONS, P. M. Ego religion and superego religion in alcoholics. Quart. J. Stud. Alc. **18**: 121–125, 1957.

SHERFEY, M. J. Psychopathology and character structure in chronic alcoholism. In: DIETHELM, O. ed., Etiology of Chronic Alcoholism; pp. 16–42. Springfield, Ill.; Thomas; 1955.

SHERFEY, M. J. and DIETHELM, O. Evaluation of drugs in the treatment of alcoholism. Res. Publ. Ass. Res. nerv. ment. Dis. **31**: 287–294, 1953.

SHULMAN, A. J. Alcohol addiction. Univ. Toronto med. J. **28**: 219–229, 1951.

SILKWORTH, W. D. Alcoholism as manifestation of allergy. Med. Rec. **145**: 249–251, 1937.

SILKWORTH, W. D. and TEXON, M. Chloride levels in the blood of alcoholic patients in relation to the phenomenon of craving. Quart. J. Stud. Alc. **11**: 381–384, 1950.

SIMMEL, E. Alcoholism and addiction. Psychoanal. Quart. **17**: 6–31, 1948.

SINGER, E. Personality structure of chronic alcoholics. Amer. Psychol. **5**: 323, 1950.

SIRNES, T. B. Voluntary consumption of alcohol in rats with cirrhosis of the liver. A preliminary report. Quart. J. Stud. Alc. **14**: 3–18, 1953.

SKÁLA, J. Alkoholismus. Terminologie, Diagnostika, Léčba a Prevence. (Alcoholism. Terminology, Diagnosis, Treatment and Prevention.) Prague; Státní Zdravotnické Nakladatelství; 1957.

SKILLICORN, S. A. Presenile cerebellar ataxia in chronic alcoholics. Neurology **5**: 527–534, 1955.

SMITH, J. A. Alcoholism. Causes and methods of treatment. Amer. Practit. Dig. Treatm. **4** (No. 7) Suppl.: 1–21, 1953. Also as: Alcoholismo; sus causas y métodos de tratamiento. Arch. méd. Cuba **5**: 43–65, 1954. Also as: Alcoholism. Philadelphia; Lippincott; 1954.

SMITH, J. A. Psychiatric treatment of the alcoholic. J. Amer. med. Ass. **163**: 734–738, 1957.

SMITH, J. A. and BROWN, W. T. Treatment in alcoholism. Amer. J. Psychiat. **109**: 279–282, 1952.

SMITH, J. A., DARDIN, P. A. and BROWN, W. T. The treatment of alcoholism by nutritional supplement. Quart. J. Stud. Alc. **12**: 381–385, 1951.

SMITH, J. J. A medical approach to problem drinking. Quart. J. Stud. Alc. **10**: 251–257, 1949.

SMITH, J. J. The endocrine basis of hormonal therapy of alcoholism. N.Y. St. J. Med. **50**: 1704–1706, 1711–1715, 1950.

SMITH, J. J. The effect of alcohol on the adrenal ascorbic acid and cholesterol of the rat. J. clin. Endocrin. **11**: 792, 1951 (a).

SMITH, J. J. The blood eosinophil responses of the alcoholic to epinephrine and to ACTH, with a note on the treatment of chronic alcoholism with ACTH. Proc. 2d clin. ACTH Conf., vol. 2, pp. 161–171, 1951 (b).

SMITH, J. J. Modern orientation in alcoholism. Nurs. World 127: 18–19, 35, 1953.

SNYDER, C. R. Alcohol and the Jews. A Cultural Study of Drinking and Sobriety. New Haven, Publications Division: Yale Center of Alcohol Studies; and Glencoe, Ill., Free Press; 1958.

SOLMS, W. Ursachen der Trunksucht. Wien. Z. Nervenheilk. 9: 69–75, 1954 (a).

SOLMS, W. Bemerkungen zu der Arbeit von N. Wölkart. "Ist die Verabreichung von Paraldehyd bei Alkoholikern contraindiziert?" Wien. Arch. Psychol. 4: 148–150, 1954 (b).

SOLMS, W. Zur Frage der Monomanien. II. Dipsomanie, Kleptomanie, Pyromanie. Wien. Z. Nervenheilk. 11: 165–195, 1955.

STAEHELIN, J. E. Die Ursachen der Alkoholschädigungen. Die Ursachen des Alkoholismus in der Schweiz. AlkFrage Schweiz 2: 6–19, 1936.

STECK, H. Quelques remarques sur la prophylaxie et la thérapeutique de l'alcoolisme. Schweiz. med. Wschr. 81: 535–537, 1951.

STEFANACCI, F. L'alcoolismo in neuro-psichiatria. Rass. Studi psichiat. 42: 309–330, 1953.

STEIGER, V. J. Gegenwärtiger Stand der Bekämpfung des Alcoholismus im Ausland und in der Schweiz. Mimeographed. Basel; 1952.

STEWART, D. A. Alcoholism as a psychological problem. Canad. J. Psychol. 4: 75–80, 1950.

STEWART, D. A. Empathy in the group therapy of alcoholics. Quart. J. Stud. Alc. 15: 74–110, 1954.

STEWART, D. A. Preface to Empathy. [Ch. 4, "The dynamics of fellowship—illustrated in Alcoholics Anonymous;" pp. 61–76.] New York; Philosophical Library; 1956.

STRAUS, R. and BACON, S. D. Drinking in College. New Haven; Yale University Press; 1953.

STRAUS, R. and McCARTHY, R. G. Nonaddictive pathological drinking patterns of homeless men. Quart. J. Stud. Alc. 12: 601–611, 1951.

STRECKER, E. A. Chronic alcoholism: a psychological survey. Quart. J. Stud. Alc. 2: 12–17, 1941.

STRECKER, E. A. Psychotherapy in pathological drinking. J. Amer. med. Ass. 147: 813–815, 1951.

STRECKER, E. A. and CHAMBERS, F. T., JR. Alcohol: One Man's Meat. New York; Macmillan; 1938.

[SWEDEN] 1944 ÅRS NYKTERHETSKOMMITÉ [DANIELSON, G. (Chairman); NELKER, G. (Secretary)]. I. Statistiska Undersökningar kring Alkoholfrågan. (Statistical Study Concerning the Alcohol Question.) Uppsala; State Department of Finance; 1952.

[SWITZERLAND] COMMISSION FÉDÉRALE CONTRE L'ALCOOLISME. Dans quelles conditions l'alcoolisme doit-il être considéré et traité comme une maladie. (Etude et conclusions de la commission fédérale contre l'alcoolisme.) Bull. eidg. Gesundh-Amt, No. B–4, 1951.

TÄHKÄ, V. Om dryckenskapens psykodynamiska etiologi. (On the psychodynamic etiology of drunkenness.) Alkoholpolitik, Hels., No. 4, pp. 103–110, 1954.

TEIRICH, H. R. Zum Alkoholproblem im Leben des Mannes. Psychol. Berater 4: 325–329, 1952.

TEXON, M. The alcoholic problem. N.Y. Med. 5 (No. 12): 16–18, 1949.

THIMANN, J. Review of new drug therapies in the treatment of alcoholism. New Engl. J. Med. 244: 939–941, 1951.

TIEBOUT, H. M. The syndrome of alcohol addiction. Quart. J. Stud. Alc. 5: 535–546, 1945.

TIEBOUT, H. M. The role of psychiatry in the field of alcoholism. Quart. J. Stud. Alc. 12: 52–57, 1951.

TIEBOUT, H. M. The ego factors in surrender in alcoholism. Quart. J. Stud. Alc. 15: 610–621, 1954.

TINTERA, J. W. Office rehabilitation of the alcoholic. N.Y. St. J. Med. 56: 3896–3902, 1956.

TINTERA, J. W. and LOVELL, H. W. Endocrine treatment of alcoholism. Geriatrics 4: 274–280, 1949.

TODD, J. E. Drunkenness a Vice, Not a Disease. Hartford, Conn.; Case, Lockwood & Brainard; 1882.

TROTTER, T. An Essay, Medical, Philosophical and Chemical, on Drunkenness and its Effects on the Human Body. London; 1804.

TUCK, R. G. The problem of alcohol addiction. Present-day therapy. J. Mich. med. Soc. 42: 536–541, 1943.

TUMARKIN, B., WILSON, J. D. and SNYDER, G. Cerebral atrophy due to alcoholism in young adults. U.S. arm. Forces med. J. 6: 67–74, 1955.

ULLMAN, A. D. The psychological mechanism of alcohol addiction. Quart. J. Stud. Alc. 13: 602–608, 1952.

ULLMAN, A. D. The first drinking experience of addictive and of "normal" drinkers. Quart. J. Stud. Alc. 14: 181–191, 1953.

ULLMAN, A. D. Sociocultural backgrounds of alcoholism. Ann. Amer. Acad. polit. soc. Sci. 315: 48–54, 1958.

VALLEE, B. L. and HOCH, F. L. Zinc, a component of yeast alcohol dehydrogenase. Proc. nat. Acad. Sci. 41: 327–338, 1955.

VALLEE, B. L., WACKER, W. E. C., BARTHOLOMAY, A. F. and ROBIN, E. D. Zinc metabolism in hepatic dysfunction. I. Serum zinc concentrations in Laënnec's cirrhosis and their validation by sequential analysis. New Engl. J. Med. 255: 403–408, 1956.

VALLEE, B. L., WACKER, W. E. C., BARTHOLOMAY, A. F. and HOCH, F. L. Zinc metabolism in hepatic dysfunction. II. Correlation of metabolic patterns with biochemical findings. New Engl. J. Med. 257: 1055–1065, 1957.

VALLEE, B. L., WACKER, W. E. C. and KAEGI, J. H. R. Zinc metabolism in postalcoholic cirrhosis. J. clin. Invest. 36: 993, 1957.

VAN AMBERG, R. J. A study of 50 women patients hospitalized for alcohol addiction. Dis. nerv. System 4: 246–251, 1943.

VARELA, A., PENNA, A., ALCAINO [G.], F., JOHNSON, E. and MARDONES [R.], J. Sugar, pyruvate and acetaldehyde levels in the blood of alcohol addicts after ingestion of dextrose. Quart. J. Stud. Alc. 14: 174–180, 1953.

VICTOR, M. and ADAMS, R. D. The effect of alcohol on the nervous system. Res. Publ. Ass. nerv. ment. Dis. 32: 526–573, 1953.

VIÑES IBARROLA, J. Alcoholismo—Stress—Cancer. Estudio de la Influencia de la Alcoholización en la Demografía. [Pamplona]; Instituto Provincial de Sanidad de Navarra; 1957.

VOEGTLIN, W. L. The treatment of alcoholism with adrenal steroids and ACTH. Quart. J. Stud. Alc. 14: 28–37, 1953.

VOGEL, S. An interpretation of medical and psychiatric approaches in the treatment of alcoholism. Quart. J. Stud. Alc. 14: 620–631, 1953.

VOGEL, V. H., ISBELL, H. and CHAPMAN, K. W. Present status of narcotic addiction. J. Amer. med. Ass. 138: 1019–1026, 1948.

WAGNER VON JAUREGG, J. Die Giftwirkung des Alkohols bei einigen nervösen und psychischen Erkrankungen. Wien. klin. Wschr. 14: 359–362, 1901.

WALL, J. H. Psychotherapy of alcohol addiction in a private mental hospital. Quart. J. Stud. Alc. 5: 547–554, 1945.

WALL, J. H. Alcoholism: a medical responsibility. Med. Rec., N.Y. 47: 497–500, 1953.

WALLINGA, J. V. Severe alcoholism in career military personnel. U.S. arm. Forces med. J. 7: 551–561, 1956.

WANNER, O. Ursachen der Trunksucht. Fürsorger 22: 33–46, 1954.

WASHBURNE, C. Alcohol, self and the group. Quart. J. Stud. Alc. 17: 108–123, 1956.

WELLMAN, W. M. The late withdrawal symptoms of alcoholic addiction. Canad. med. Ass. J. 70: 526–529, 1954 (a).

WELLMAN, W. M. Management of the late withdrawal symptoms of alcohol. Canad. med. Ass. J. 71: 360–365, 1954 (b).

WELLMAN, W. M. Chronic alcoholism in the services. Canad. Serv. med. J. 11: 127–134, 1955 (a).

WELLMAN, W. M. Towards an etiology of alcoholism: why young men drink too much. Canad. med. Ass. J. 73: 717–725, 1955 (b).

WEXBERG, L. E. Psychodynamics of patients with chronic alcoholism. J. clin. Psychopath. 10: 147–157, 1949.

WEXBERG, L. E. A critique of physiopathological theories of the etiology of alcoholism. Quart. J. Stud. Alc. 11: 113–118, 1950.

WEXBERG, L. E. Alcoholism as a sickness. Quart. J. Stud. Alc. 12: 217–230, 1951 (a).

WEXBERG, L. E. Ursachen und Symptome der Arzneimittelsucht und des Alkoholismus. Z. Psychother., Stuttgart 1: 227–235, 1951 (b).

WIKLER, A., PESCOR, F. T., FRASER, H. F. and ISBELL, H. Electroencephalographic changes associated with chronic alcoholic intoxication and the alcohol abstinence syndrome. Amer. J. Psychiat. 113: 106–114, 1956.

WIKLUND, D. Proposal of the Swedish Government Committee for Reform of the Care of Inebriates. Quart. J. Stud. Alc. 9: 372–387, 1948.

WILKINS, W. L. Alcoholism: theory, problem and challenge. I. The idea of proneness in relation to alcoholism. Quart. J. Stud. Alc. 17: 291–295, 1956.

WILLIAMS, L. Some observations of the recent advances in the treatment of alcoholism. Brit. J. Addict. 47: 62–67, 1950.

WILLIAMS, R. J. The etiology of alcoholism: a working hypothesis involving the interplay of hereditary and environmental factors. Quart. J. Stud. Alc. 7: 567–587, 1947.

WILLIAMS, R. J. Biochemical approach to individuality. Science 107: 459, 1948 (a).

WILLIAMS, R. J. Alcoholics and metabolism. Sci. American 179 (No. 6): 50–53, 1948 (b).

WILLIAMS, R. J. Alcoholism as a nutritional problem. J. clin. Nutrit. 1: 32–36, 1952.

WILLIAMS, R. J. Free and Unequal. The Biological Basis of Individuality. Austin; University of Texas Press; 1953.

WILLIAMS, R. J. The genetotrophic concept—nutritional deficiencies and alcoholism. Ann. N.Y. Acad. Sci. 57: 794–811, 1954.

WILLIAMS, R. J. Biochemical individuality and cellular nutrition: prime factors in alcoholism. Quart. J. Stud. Alc. 20: 452–463, 1959 (a).

240   E. M. JELLINEK

Williams, R. J. Alcoholism. The Nutritional Approach. Austin; University of Texas Press; 1959 (b).

Williams, R. J., Berry, L. J. and Beerstecher, E., Jr. Biochemical individuality. III. Genetotrophic factors in the etiology of alcoholism. Arch. Biochem., N.Y. 23: 275–290, 1949 (a).

Williams, R. J., Berry, L. J. and Beerstecher, E., Jr. Individual metabolic patterns, alcoholism, genetotrophic diseases. Science 109: 441, 1949. Also in: Proc. nat. Acad. Sci., Wash. 35: 265–271, 1949 (b).

Williams, R. J., Pelton, R. B. and Rogers, L. L. Dietary deficiencies in animals in relation to voluntary alcohol and sugar consumption. Quart. J. Stud. Alc. 16: 234–244, 1955.

Williams, T. A. The pathogenesis of alcoholism and narcotism and the treatment of their causes. Interst. med. J. 23: 455–462, 1916.

Wlassak, R. Grundriss der Alkoholfrage. Leipzig; Hirzel; 1929.

World Health Organization. Expert Committee on Mental Health. Report of the First Session of the Alcoholism Subcommittee. (W.H.O. Technical Report Series, No. 42.) Geneva; 1951.

World Health Organization. Expert Committee on Drugs Liable to Produce Addiction. Third Report. (W.H.O. Technical Report Series, No. 57.) Geneva; 1952.

World Health Organization. Expert Committee on Alcohol. First Report. (W.H.O. Technical Report Series, No. 84.) Geneva; 1954.

World Health Organization. Alcohol and Alcoholism. Report of an Expert Committee. (W.H.O. Technical Report Series, No. 94.) Geneva; 1955.

Wyss, R. Nouvelles méthodes de traitement médical de l'alcoolisme. Gaz. méd. Fr. 56: 583, 1949.

Yost, O. R. Alcoholism, a challenging problem of today. J. S.C. med. Ass. 47: 162–167, 1951.

Zarrow, M. X. and Rosenberg, B. Alcoholic drive in rats treated with propyl thiouracil. Amer. J. Physiol. 172: 141–146, 1953.

Zurukzoglu, S. Fürsorge für Alkoholkranke und Alkoholgefährdete. AlkFrage Schweiz. 2: 88–91, 1937.

Zurukzoglu, S. and Nussbaum, P. Die Bedeutung des "Minderwertigkeitsgefühls" für den alkoholismus. Entstehung, Behandlung, Verhütung. Schwarzenburg; Gerber; [1952?]

Index of Subjects

Lightning Source UK Ltd.
Milton Keynes UK
UKHW021849240119
336151UK00005B/174/P